The Armed Forces and American Social Change

The Armed Forces and American Social Change

An Unwritten Truce

Troy Mosley

Hamilton Books
Lanham • Boulder • New York • Toronto • London

Published by Hamilton Books
An imprint of The Rowman & Littlefield Publishing Group, Inc.
4501 Forbes Boulevard, Suite 200, Lanham, Maryland 20706
Hamilton Books Acquisitions Department (301) 459-3366

6 Tinworth Street, London SE11 5AL, United Kingdom

Copyright © 2021 by The Rowman & Littlefield Publishing Group, Inc.

All rights reserved. No part of this book may be produced in any form or by any electronic means, including information storage and retrieval systems,without written permission from the publisher, except by a reviewer who may quote passages in a review.

British Library Cataloguing in Publication Information Available

Library of Congress Cataloging-in-Publication Data Available

Names: Mosley, Troy, 1967– author.
Title: The Armed Forces and American social change : an unwritten truce / Troy Mosley.
Description: Lanham : Hamilton Books, an imprint of Rowman & Littlefield, [2021] | Includes bibliographical references and index. | Summary: "Unwritten Truce is a powerful depiction of Black Americans' struggle for equality told through the lens of uniformed military service. Troy Mosley uses superb story-telling, personal vignettes, and historical examples to show how millions of Americans have lifted themselves from stifling oppression through opportunities gleaned from military service"—Provided by publisher.
Identifiers: LCCN 2021027634 (print) | LCCN 2021027635 (ebook) | ISBN 9780761872511 (paperback) | ISBN 9780761872528 (epub)
Subjects: LCSH: United States—Armed Forces—Minorities—History. | United States—Armed Forces—African Americans—History. | United States—Armed Forces—Women—History. | Gay military personnel—United States—History. | Sociology, Military—United States. | Social change—United States.
Classification: LCC UB417 .M67 2021 (print) | LCC UB417 (ebook) | DDC 355.0089/96073—dc23
LC record available at https://lccn.loc.gov/2021027634
LC ebook record available at https://lccn.loc.gov/2021027635

Contents

Foreword		ix
Preface		xi
Notes		xiii
Acknowledgments		xv
Introduction		1
Notes		8
1	**Why This and Black Lives Matter**	11
	My Awakening Moment	13
	The Ebb and Flow of Racism and Social Change	16
	Notes	19
2	**America in 1946: The Events Leading to the Desegregation of the Armed Forces**	21
	The Beatings Will Continue	23
	Truman's Call and Response	26
	Secure These Rights	27
	With Deliberation and Forethought	29
	Flipping the Script	31
	The Check Is in the Mail	35
	The Aftermath of Executive Order 9981	37
	Notes	42
3	**A Brief History of Diversity in America's Armed Forces**	45
	Blacks in the Revolutionary War—Twisted Irony	46
	Blacks in the Civil War: Turning the Tide	48
	The "Buffalo Soldiers": Rough and Ready Regulars!	49
	West Point Follies: The Silent Treatment	50
	Cadet Henry Ossian Flipper	50
	Cadet John H. Alexander	52
	Cadet Charles Young	54
	Blacks in the Spanish–American War	56
	America's Emergent Global Force and the Delicate Balancing Act	58
	Pre-World War I Years	59
	Pre-Cursors to World War I	60
	Blacks in WWI, but First you Have to Pick the Cotton!	64
	The Black Military Experience in World War I	65

	Rioting in Texas	68
	The 93rd Infantry Division	71
	369th Infantry Regiment (Harlem Hellfighters)	71
	370th Infantry Regiment	72
	371st Infantry Regiment	72
	372nd Infantry Regiment	72
	The 92nd Infantry Division	76
	Reintegration and Disillusionment	77
	The Great Migration	79
	Notes	82
4	Minorities in World War II: Sowing the Seeds for the Civil Rights Movement	87
	The Black and Minority Combat Experience in World War II	92
	The 442nd "Go for Broke" Infantry Regiment (Japanese American)	93
	761st Tank Battalion (Black Panthers)	95
	The 333rd Field Artillery Regiment (Colored)	98
	The Tuskegee Airmen "Black Panthers"	100
	The Beginning of the Tuskegee Experiment	104
	Black Sailors in WW II: Fighting for the Right to Fight	107
	Blacks' Early History in the US Naval Academy: The First Black "Middies"	110
	Wesley A. Brown	111
	The Navy's Golden 13	111
	The USS *Mason*	113
	Racial Tension in the Navy Persists	113
	The First Black Marines, "Montford Point Marines"	115
	Black Marines in Combat During World War II	117
	3rd Marine Ammunition Company, 18th and 20th Depot Companies	117
	Lessons Learned from the Segregated Armed Forces in WWII	118
	Korea, the Armed Forces Moves to Full Integration, Really	123
	The Legacy of Our Early Integrators	125
	Notes	127
5	Women in the Armed Services	133
	The Armed Services "Auxiliary" Services	135
	Pioneers of the Women's Army Corps (WAC)	135
	The Navy Makes WAVES	137
	Women Air Force Service Pilots (WASP)	139
	Ethnic Diversity in the WASP	140
	Assessing the Impact of Women in Support of the US WWII Effort	140

Korea, Vietnam, and the Women's Rights Movement ... 141
The US Military Advances in Women's Rights vs. Corporate America ... 143
Women's Rights Advances at Large ... 144
Women in the US Military Service Academies, a Long Road to Commencement ... 144
Modern Pioneers Reaping the Benefits of Women's Inclusion ... 147
The Intersection Between Women's Advances in the Military and Society at Large ... 148
Modern Milestones for Women in the Military ... 150
Achievements, Challenges, and Opportunities ... 151
Twenty-Six Years Before "Me Too," There was Tailhook ... 152
Notes ... 155

6 Lesbians, Gays, Bisexual, and Transgender Members in the Armed Services ... 159
Challenges of the '70s and '80s ... 161
The Evolution of Don't Ask Don't Tell (DADT) ... 161
The Shift of US Public Opinion ... 166
Don't Ask Don't Tell Revisited as Public Law ... 168
The Transgender Struggle ... 172
Notes ... 175

7 Remaining Challenges and Implications for the US and the Armed Forces ... 181
The Military's Problem Is America's Problem ... 181
A Look at the Numbers ... 182
The Military's UCMJ Disparities ... 190
What the Armed Forces Got Right ... 196
Diversity as a Strategic Imperative ... 196
DoD's Remaining Work ... 199
Better Stratification of Data ... 201
Greater Socioeconomic Diversity ... 201
Renaming Confederate Bases ... 203
Protect the Inclusion of Transgender Persons ... 205
Equitable Sentencing for UCMJ Violations ... 206
America's Remaining Work ... 206
Closing ... 209
Notes ... 210

Bibliography ... 215
Index ... 231
About the Author ... 243

Foreword

I am pleased to re-introduce *The Armed Forces and American Social Change: An Unwritten Truce*. This book was originally self-published in 2018 to celebrate the milestone 70th anniversary of the integration of the US armed forces and examined why that achievement was so important for our fledging republic. The author's insights on the armed forces' influence on social justice proved to be so timely in the wake of the 2020 civil unrest sparked by the murders of George Floyd, Ahmaud Arbery, Breonna Taylor and others, that the publishing house of Rowman & Littlefield decided to republish the book so that it could reach a broader audience. The book honors the sacrifices many Americans have made to pave the way for making our nation truer to its founding principles. Troy illuminates the historical significance of these legacy struggles that confound

LTG (R) Russel L. Honoré. *Photo courtesy of Russel Honoré.*

our society today. I speak to many of these challenges in my book, *Don't Get Stuck on Stupid, Leadership in Action*. Every American needs to understand this rich history. Though resistance to social change did not go easily, today the military can boast that the tenants of diversity and inclusion are central building blocks for our nation's military, a dynamic, global, merit-based force unmatched worldwide. Neither gender, race, religion, national origin, nor sexual orientation are barriers to serving in our nation's armed forces because of the foundation established in 1948. The great military strategist, Sun Tzu said, "See the enemy, see yourself, see the terrain." *The Armed Forces and American Social Change: An Unwritten Truce* provides an opportunity for the nation and the armed forces to do precisely that and have a frank discussion on removing the final barriers to inclusion.

Russel L. Honoré,
Lieutenant General (R)
United States Army

Preface

July 26, 2018, marked the 70th Anniversary of Executive Order 9981, which desegregated the US military. This event profoundly shaped the American socio-political landscape and will forever be a milestone achievement. President Truman signed the controversial executive order partly in response to atrocities committed against black servicemen by racist mobs and bigoted police. Seventy years later, professional athletes protesting the murder of unarmed citizens is still somehow controversial. Despite how far America has come, we still have considerable work ahead. *The Armed Forces and American Social Change: An Unwritten Truce* is an acknowledgement of both the progress made and the work that remains. Many of the social advancements made within the military that have impacted our broader society are being directly challenged. The Trump Administration has reversed policies regarding transgender members serving in the military. The subtext of this reversal casts dispersions on other advances the Department of Defense (DoD) has made in expanding the tent for those who wish to serve in uniform. Will a ban on gays serving in the military be next, a reversal of the combat exclusion to women, or more?

This milestone anniversary presents another opportunity for the nation to engage in a conversation that is both illusive and confounding. An old African proverb maintains that life is like a kindergarten teacher; if you do not learn today's lesson, she will gladly teach you again tomorrow. America's current struggles with racism and inclusion are littered with many legacy issues that grew out of slavery, Jim Crow, unfair policing, unfair housing, a jaundiced criminal justice system, unequal educational opportunities, and a lack of employment opportunities. In writing *The Armed Forces and American Social Change*, I hope to celebrate the achievements of the brave men and women, black, white, and brown who led the armed forces to establish themselves as an institution committed to the values of inclusion, tolerance, and justice. America will continue to progress and regress along this continuum until we are able to have the frank discussion on inclusion that ultimately puts an end to the ideals of racial supremacy, sexism, and homophobia—ideals that are antithetical to military values, and undergird discrimination and intolerance.

This is not to say that America is not a great country, or that America has not evolved considerably regarding race-relations and other areas of inclusion. However, it is to say that America still has a way to go before we are true to the letter and spirit of the values in our Constitution—that all men and women are created equal, and should therefore be treated equally, without regard to race, religion, national origin, gender, or sexual orientation.

My personal experiences growing up as a black man in the 1970s and 80s in an upper middle class, predominately white, Southern community, and as a career army officer have shaped my thoughts on race relations in the United States. I developed a unique perspective on America's struggles with race, class, and gender equity that could have only been forged in the crucible of a minority, within a minority, within a minority. I am part of the seven percent of all living Americans who have ever served the nation in uniform.[1] I am part of the twelve percent of Americans whose foundation here begins with the enslavement of my ancestors, and I am part of an even smaller and ever-shrinking percentage of Americans from upper middle class or higher families that have served in uniform.

I spent most of my professional life, serving in uniform overseas and in command. This experience illuminated how the military has influenced race relations, as well as gender and LGBTQ equality. The culmination of my experiences both in and out of uniform have compelled me to write *Unwritten Truce: The Armed Forces and American Social Justice*. My sincere wish is to provide content and context for a forthright dialogue on race, gender equality, and homophobia, that helps Americans and the American Armed Forces in their continued quest for exceptionalism.

Too often in today's military, minorities are marginalized, assigned to middle and lower tier areas of responsibility, and told by assignment officers and senior officials, don't worry about where you are assigned, "bloom where you are planted." This type of cavalier career advice is partly to blame for the disparity between the number of minorities serving in uniform, and the number of minorities serving in positions of historical significance. Black generals comprise about five percent of all generals on active duty, despite making up approximately nine percent of all officers and seventeen percent of the total force.[2]

It is much easier for a rose to bloom in fertile soil, in a garden that is nourishing and nurtured. Yet many of America's minority servicemen and women, particularly officers, are systemically planted in relative deserts. Over time, this decades-long lack of crop rotation inhibits the individual and depletes the soil. America's wellspring of diversity poses unlimited potential for an ever-changing geo-political environment. The time has come for the armed services to fully cultivate this potential; in turn these institutions will blossom into model organizations for the world.

NOTES

1. US Department of Defense, Office of the Deputy Assistant Secretary of Defense for Military Community and Family Policy, *2015 Demographics: Profile of the Military Community*, (Washington, DC: DoD, 2015), pdf, https://download.militaryonesource.mil/12038/MOS/Reports/2015-Demographics-Report.pdf (2016).

2. US Department of Defense, Military Leadership and Diversity Commission, *From Representation to Inclusion: Diversity Leadership for the 21st Century Military, Final Report*, (Washington, DC: DoD, 2011), pdf, https://diversity.defense.gov/Portals/51/Documents/Special%20Feature/MLDC_Final_Report.pdf (2015), 39-43.

Acknowledgments

I want to thank my family for their unyielding support of this project, which has been my life's passion. I hope to inspire my children—Ali, Nile, and Alyssa—to continue to work as hard as they can, to learn as much as they can, and to do as much as humanly possible to help make this nation and their communities better, while taking time to love and have fun along the way. I am also grateful to Karen Carlton-Mosley for being a superior Army spouse who supported my military career unconditionally, while establishing her own career, raising three kids, and maintaining our home through 7 moves and 9 schools. Our children are where they are because of your love and commitment; thank you! I want to thank my parents, Joshua Mosley Jr. and Terrye J. Mosley, for providing me with a nurturing and loving environment, and for insisting that I prioritize my education. Mom, you rock! Dad, you are the best; thank you for providing an example of what a strong father should be, for your vision and leadership of our family and the Jacksonville, FL, community, and for your service to our country in uniform! To my sister Kortney, I'm very proud of you and your husband Jimmy; continue doing great things. I also owe thanks to many educators, coaches, and ministers who have touched my life along the way. Roger Wood, Harold Jansen, Ruben LeCount, Billy Reynolds, Mike McCahon, LTC (R) Donald Harris, and Father Jocelyn Angus Sr., you all touched my life immeasurably. Dr. Yvonne Bell and Dr. James Baldwin, thank you for laying the foundation for my interest in Black History, and for stoking my interest in the social sciences. LTG (R) Eric Schoomaker, you were my first mentor in the Army; I thank you for taking an interest in me, and for giving me the best advice and opportunities you could. You introduced me to MG (R) Elder Granger who has become like an uncle. I am forever indebted for the trust Elder placed in me as a young captain, and for continuing to nourish me throughout the years. LTC David Bitterman, thank you for the opportunity to serve as your right-hand man in the 212th MASH, the last MASH in the Army. Colonel A. Allen Rasper, thank you for your mentorship. LTG (R) Patricia Horoho, thank you for the leadership you role-modeled in all the assignments we shared, and for having a bold vision; you not only talked-the-talk, but you did everything you asked of your subordinates and then some. You are a naturally gifted leader, and I am proud to have served with you. To 1SG (R) Virgina D. Coleman, you are the best soldier with whom I have ever served. God bless you and thank you for all you did for the Headquarters Company, 14th Field Hospital. To the soldiers of the 14th Field Hospital, thank you for being an exceptional unit. Thank you for the pleasure of commanding. To the Medical Platoon of 2/9th Infantry (Manchus), thank you for your service. I would have put our Medical Platoon against anyone. You were superb, "Docs of the Rock!" To Command Sergeants Major (R) Althea Green, PhD, and Gregory "Catfish" Griffin, thank you for the outstanding leadership and consultation you provided not only for myself, but for so many other of America's sons and daughters! You both are an inspiration. To all my remaining family and friends, thank you for your unyielding support in this journey. Thank you from the bottom of my heart.

Introduction

As a young Army captain in 1995, I was serving as a healthcare administrator and Medical Service Corps Officer while enrolled in a career development course known as the Officer's Advanced Course. The course was designed to provide a year of classroom and field instruction for captains between their fifth to tenth years of service. It not only covered academic and classroom subjects on battlefield tactics, field craft, and administration, but also allowed young families a respite from deployments, while making time for fellowship and social interaction. Our class was a hodgepodge of professionals: physicians, nurses, medical-evacuation pilots, pharmacists, psychologists, optometrists, nutritionists, and audiologists. We were from as diverse of backgrounds as one could imagine, and probably a good cross section of America in general. We had West Point graduates, ROTC commissionees, fourth generation officers, first generation college graduates, and everything in between, from every region of the country and almost every state. In all, we totaled around 200. We were enjoying a typical year of studies, intramural basketball games and planned family outings when something transfixed us: the O. J. Simpson trial.

I recall conducting a quasi-social experiment on how sharply the class was divided along racial lines by the trial. I could predict one's position on whether they thought Simpson was innocent or guilty based solely upon their race. Whether you were a doctor, nurse, dietician, healthcare administrator, or psychologist, if you were black you most likely believed the prosecution failed to meet its burden of proof. If you were not black you probably believed that a grave miscarriage of justice had been committed when the not guilty verdict was rendered. While my deepest sympathies are with the Simpson children and the Brown and Goldman families, if I were a juror, I would have probably rendered the same verdict, not because I believe O. J. Simpson was innocent, but because the prosecution did not meet its burden of proof. The prosecution was caught repeatedly in misconduct, such as putting detectives and police department officials on the witness stand who perjured themselves. Videos exposed the police department appearing to plant evidence, which they were later caught lying about, vials of blood went missing, and so on.

For most black Americans, it was obvious that the prosecution would have done or said anything to convict Simpson irrespective of the evidence. The prosecution's "rush to judge" completely discredited them within the black community. If the prosecution lied about the missing vile of blood and the use of the "N word," what else did they lie about? For white Americans, these anomalies were reasonably explained away, but for black Americans these inconsistencies, lies, missteps, and misconduct were lock-step with a centuries-long narrative of state-sanctioned injustice perpetrated against black citizens.

From the black perspective, the Simpson trial was consistent with a history of corrupt policing in which black victims complained of coerced confessions, planted evidence, and perjured testimony. The significant difference in the Simpson case was that the defendant had the means to acquire talented attorneys and subject-matter experts to point out the legal insufficiency—and in some instances, illegalities—of the prosecution's case. The other major difference was the notoriety of the case. Public exposure heightened the level of transparency and media scrutiny, imposing blind justice where all too often none previously existed. This was not business as usual; this was not "we [the state prosecution] said so therefore it is true;" this was not a case of guilty until proven innocent.

The O. J. Simpson Trial was an iconic portrayal of the difference between black and white realities in America. This reality for blacks has persisted for as long as America has existed and holds true for black Americans regardless of socio-economic status. The social experiment I conducted in my mind as a young Army officer illuminated how black and white realities differ in America. There we had a multidisciplinary group of loyal, patriotic, law-abiding Army officers, from all walks of life and all regions of the country, who had vowed to protect and defend the Constitution and the United States with their lives if necessary. As a group, their integrity was beyond reproach and they were largely free of agenda in that none of them wanted to see a murderer walk free. All the officers had relatively the same military training, level of civilian education, and were taught to think logically and tactically. But consistently, with few exceptions, black officers sided with not guilty, and white officers sided with a guilty verdict. The sharp contrast between black and white realities was the byproduct of differing lived experiences in a society with institutional bias, as explained through Critical Race Theory.

Critical Race Theory (CRT), is a scholarly, legal, and academic framework developed in the late 1970s by civil rights advocates to explain historical disparities in the lived experiences of black and white Americans as those experiences relate to laws, public policies and institutions.[1] CRT has become all the rage in recent public discourse. Those who wish to prevent fundamental changes in society to make it more equitable have mischaracterized CRT and used it as a cudgel to prevent open, honest discourse about social justice. My sincere wish is that the readers of this book will use the content here to engage in this difficult conversation with people who may have differing opinions.

I had never heard of CRT, but it was precisely at that moment when I realized some invisible force was at play, shaping the opinions of the black officers but not those of the white officers. Just like Newton deduced an apple would remain on its limb unless some force was at play, I deduced that our opinions should not be so sharply divided along racial lines unless some invisible force was shaping our perceptions. This invisible, perception-shaping force was exerting itself on the perception of realities for black and white Americans. Until that point in my military experience, race had been a non-factor. In 1995, the Army was as color-blind of an experience as I had had in my twenty-six years of life. This experience demonstrated to me that there were often imperceptible social forces shaping perceptions and opinions that even the Army's superior training, mission-oriented culture, and leadership could not overcome. If the force of centuries of institutionalized racism can challenge the homogeneity of military culture, it undoubtedly ripples through America as a whole.

The officers in my class represented America's most forth-right, promising young minds, and despite our greatest efforts, we lacked the tools to fully escape the gravitational pull of American racial bias. But at our core we were still a group of Americans united behind a singular cause. That commonality held us together even though we all carried with us the perspectives, prejudices, and other baggage we were taught as children. *Unwritten Truce* therefore pivots on the notion that our nation's military may be the best force we have to combat the overwhelming force of the systemic, institutionalized racism that we still face today.

During the O. J. Simpson Trial, *Chicago Tribune* reporter Clarence Page quipped, "Race is the one thing you can't get white Americans to talk about and the one thing you can't get black Americans to stop talking about." Those words still hold true today. Although America has come so far from slavery, we still have not tackled the deep-seated racial challenges that prevent us from making huge leaps forward—leaps that could transform not only how we view ourselves and others, but also how we treat one another. In turn, such transformation could inspire our society to achieve the fullest expression of American democracy.

On July 26, 1948, President Harry Truman ended the practice of de jure segregation (segregation sanction by law) in the United States Armed Forces with the stroke of a pen when he signed Executive Order 9981. This was sixteen years before the Civil Rights Act of 1964 outlawed discrimination based on race, religion, color, sex, or national origin, and six years before the Brown vs. the Topeka, KS Board of Education Supreme Court decision ended school segregation. Truman knew the ripple effects of state-sanctioned racism and discrimination had to be stopped, and he knew the armed forces could lead the way.

Executive Order 9981 was bold, decisive, and unprecedented. It is probably the single most important Executive Order ever issued. Truman signed the order during an election year; it shook entire political parties to their foundations and thrust a divided nation into a moral, political, and legal debate about segregation's devastating effects. The opponents of desegregation delayed and pushed back against dismantling segregation laws such that 27 years after the Civil Rights Act of 1964 passed, differences in how blacks and whites were treated solely based upon race were still obvious in my class of Army officers.

Today, many private and political organizations are leading the charge to remove the remaining barriers to inclusion. Some examples include New Orleans Mayor Mitch Landrieu who removed several Confederate statues from public spaces; Alicia Garza, Opal Toeti, and Patrisse Cullors who founded the Black Lives Matter (BLM) movement; and Terrance Cunningham who has worked as the President of the International Association of Chiefs of Police (IACP) and as the Chief of the Wellesley, Massachusetts Police Department.

In 2016, Cunningham issued a formal apology to the nation's minority population "for the actions of the past and the role that our profession has played in society's historical mistreatment of communities of color." He added, "At its core, policing is a noble profession. . . . At the same time, it is also clear that the history of policing has also had darker periods." Cunningham cited unjust state and federal laws that tied the hands of law enforcement, and "a multigenerational—almost inherited— mistrust between many communities of color and their law enforcement agencies." Cunningham then concluded by sharing his hope that Americans can unite to break this cycle.[2] This is the type of candid, forthright conversation Americans must have to move the nation forward.

The entire fight to preserve segregation was simply about preserving unearned privileges for white Americans—white privilege—while denying black Americans the opportunity to achieve to their utmost potential. *Unwritten Truce* provides insights into how President Truman dealt the first major blow to dismantling the system of oppression that followed the Civil War. Beginning with segregation, the armed services went on to wage war against other challenges to a free and open republic by including women in the armed services and opening the services to LGBTQ citizens.

War is diplomacy by violent means. The aim of diplomacy is to advance a nation's will or interests. George Washington fought the Revolutionary War with an eye towards the peace he wanted at the conclusion of the war. Washington wanted to establish normalized relations with England once America won its independence, and he waged the war in such a fashion to make this end-state feasible.[3] Washington's vision of that peace was codified in the Treaty of Paris that ended the American Revolution. The US and England have been allies for centuries, in part due to the treaties that resolved issues that caused conflict. Conversely, there was no comprehensive peace treaty to end the Civil War. The North did not want to legitimize the Confederacy by recognizing them as an independent nation of equal footing. Their primary concern was to end the war, restore the Union, and end the practice of slavery. In this regard, America was successful on those counts.

Yet, the United States only considered former slaves in so far as the abolishment of slavery, but did little to consider the role of race in America more broadly. The task of addressing racial inequality and the notion of white supremacy was left for future American generations. The warring sides essentially entered an unwritten truce regarding race, which maintained that Southern states must end slavery, but the Federal Government would leave them to more or less treat former slaves and their descendants as the states chose. The 13th, 14th and 15th amendments uplifted black Americans from slavery to technical citizenship, but chattel slavery was replaced with a legal-social framework operating at the state level. This state level framework eventually prevented black Americans from fully engaging in mainstream social, cultural, or political life, or from achieving any form of systemic upward mobility.

The immediate terms of surrender for the Confederate Army of Northern Virginia offered parole to Confederate soldiers in exchange for rations and surrender. Generals Grant and Lee signed this agreement on April 9, 1865, which served as a model for the surrender of Confederate Armies still fighting in the west. Lincoln was assassinated five days after Lee's surrender, and Vice President Andrew Johnson, a states-rights Southerner, assumed the presidency. Johnson issued a declaration on August 20, 1866 announcing the end of the American Civil War.[4]

The four Southern States that had previously made declarations of secession (South Carolina, Georgia, Mississippi, and Texas) and specified a belief in white supremacy as the "natural order," never retracted those declarations. In the years following the immediate surrender of the Civil War, Southern states were forced to endorse the 13th, 14th, and 15th Amendments in order to be readmitted to the Union. These amendments abolished slavery, made former slaves into citizens, and granted them the right to vote. In exchange for these concessions, the Union left the Southern states free to govern themselves and free to subjugate blacks to permanent, second-class citizenry. Minus slavery, this unwritten truce preserved the Southern social caste system, as it had been outlined in the Southern declarations of secession.

The Compromise of 1877 sealed this pact when presidential candidate, Rutherford B. Hayes, conceded Southern rule to white supremacists in exchange for Florida, Louisiana, and South Carolina casting their Electoral College votes for him, thereby ratifying the 1876 Presidential election in his favor. While Grant delayed Reconstruction, Hayes brought it to a complete halt.[5] Hayes pledged protection of the rights of former slaves, but undermined that pledge by advocating for the restoration of "wise, honest, and peaceful local self-government."[6] The Ku Klux Klan and other white supremacists unleashed a wave of violence and terrorism to roll back the political gains blacks achieved during Reconstruction. These un-denounced notions of white superiority are the foundation for much of the racial tension that persists in this country today.

President Truman's Executive Order was the first effort to systematically dismantle segregation as an American institution, and the first government sanctioned rebuke of the notion of white supremacy. Truman, the grandson of a former slave owner, became an unlikely champion of civil rights. Several life experiences positioned him to see segregation precisely for what it was: immoral. These experiences included his upbringing on a Missouri farm, his service in World War I, and his humble political beginnings as a county administrator. If President Lyndon B. Johnson was the father of the American Civil Rights Movement, then President Harry S. Truman was its grandfather. When Truman signed Executive Orders 9980 and 9981, he set into motion one of the most sweeping pieces of executive authority of all time and set the US military on a path to champion two of America's most fundamental tenants: freedom and equality of treatment for all. This action helped establish the foundation for the American Civil Rights movement, which hit its full stride over fifteen years later. These executive orders were a part of a series of events that would forever change the face of our nation. EO 9980 prescribed sweeping reforms in federal government hiring practices. It mandated that all personnel actions taken by federal appointing officers shall be based solely on merit and fitness, and such officers are authorized and directed to take appropriate steps to ensure that in all such actions there shall be no discrimination because of race, color, religion, or national origin. Such a policy was unprecedented in the US. EO 9980 and the mandates Truman imposed opened doors for blacks to be employed as civil servants. It also paved the way for black contractors to participate in government contracting, such as the all-black West Area Computing Section at the National Advisory Committee for Aeronautics (NACA) depicted in the movie *Hidden Figures*.[7]

In reflecting upon Truman's decision to integrate the armed services and federal employment, one cannot help but wonder what Truman knew and saw that compelled him to make this decision when his predecessors would not. "Civil Rights" were referred to as human rights until 1946 when the Truman Administration coined the term to promote his platform. Perhaps it's time to readopt the term "human rights" because it captures what is really at stake: the humanity of not only those our society oppresses, but the humanity of our entire society.[8]

Civil rights in the late 1940s was largely a non-issue in America, except of course for the 12 million black Americans and other minorities who were largely relegated to second-class status by de jure segregation. Black Americans were also plagued by a lack of equal education, a dearth of employment opportunities and unfair employment practices, as well as inadequate housing due to racially biased covenants.

The lack of voting rights due to poll taxes and other Jim Crow laws—remnants of the incomplete Reconstruction—were another indignation on top of the other dehumanizing slights forced down the throats of black citizens. For all intents and purposes, equal protection under the law did not apply to black Americans in 1946. The civil rights platform that Truman adopted and presented to Congress on two occasions was the foundation for the modern American Civil Rights Movement. However, both houses of Congress flatly rejected Truman's civil rights platform each time. An obstructionist Congress, in which Southern Democrats and northern "States Rights" Republicans colluded to filibuster any civil rights legislation brought to the floor, effectively blocked Truman's request for civil rights legislation. Undeterred, Truman reintroduced the idea at the 1947 Democratic National Convention. The issue was so politically divisive that three dozen Southern delegates from Alabama and Mississippi literally walked out of the convention. Just five months before the presidential election of 1948, Truman's civil rights platform, which included desegregation of the armed forces, had splintered the Democratic National Party.[9]

Given that it was such a hot-button issue, why was President Truman insistent on advancing a civil rights platform at what appeared to be precisely the wrong time? A March 1948 Gallop poll revealed that eighty-two percent of adults were opposed to Truman's federal civil rights proposals, yet he was willing to risk his political future over the cause. Numerous factors contributed to Truman's decision to move the nation toward "equal rights for all Americans." Most historians agree that his tipping point was the uptick of well documented, racially motivated atrocities committed against black veterans and their families immediately following World War II.

The similarities between what was occurring in America and what occurred under Nazi Germany's control disgusted Truman. "We have only recently completed a long and bitter war against intolerance and hatred. . . . Yet, in this country today," Truman lamented, "there exists disturbing evidence of intolerance, and prejudice similar in kind, though perhaps not degree, to that against which we fought the war."[10] Truman issued this statement following the beating of a black US service member who was still in uniform. His use of the words "intolerance" and "prejudice" indicate that Truman understood the attack was racially motivated. Truman comparing the event to the atrocities America had recently fought a war to end shows that he viewed the subjugation of black Americans through state-sanctioned violence as immoral. Truman's statement also would have reframed the issue of racism in the US for those Americans who supported the allied war effort against Hitler, but failed to recognize the bigotry of their own actions at home.

Finally, Truman knew that segregation and other Jim Crow laws were more than immoral. They posed a glaring weakness in America's bid to present democracy to the world as the model system of governance for war-torn and developing nations. Truman knew that segregation and Jim Crowism were part of a backward, antiquated way of life that would impede the proliferation of democracy across the world (and consequently promote the spread of communism). It was also clear that such perspectives would persist in the US without federal intervention.

Few have fully appreciated the historical significance of Truman's actions as he embarked upon his first presidential civil rights platform. At the same time, a mere tribute to commemorate the 70th Anniversary of Executive Order 9981 would be an injustice to the men and women whose sacrifices were not only catalytic but essential to Truman's vision and actions. This commemorative tribute must also look forward at other modern challenges to diversity, such as gender equality, and barriers to Lesbian, Gay, Bisexual, and Transgender (LGBTQ) inclusion in the armed forces, as well as in the broader context of American society.

The US military can be proud that gender inequality, racism, discrimination based on sexual orientation, and many transgender issues are less problematic in the armed services than they are in mainstream American circles. Nonetheless, there is still work to be done on all fronts. *Unwritten Truce* examines the legacy of the armed services in leading social change and the lingering challenges the military must address to remove the remaining vestiges of institutionalized racism, sexism, xenophobia, and homophobia. In doing so, the military can continue to lead the greater American struggle to honor the words of its charter: that all men [and women] are created equal and should therefore be treated as equals.

NOTES

1. Lewis R. Gordon, "A Short History of the 'Critical' in Critical Race Theory," *American Philosophy Association Newsletter*, 98, no. 2, accessed July 27, 2021, https://web.archive.org/web/20030502193950/http://www.apa.udel.edu/apa/archive/newsletters/v98n2/lawblack/gordon.asp.

2. Tom Jackman, "U.S. Police Chiefs Group Apologizes for 'Historical Mistreatment' of Minorities," *The Washington Post*, October 17, 2016, https://www.washingtonpost.com/news/true-crime/wp/2016/10/17/head-of-u-s-police-chiefs-apologizes-for-historic-mistreatment-of-minorities/.

3. Rebecca Brooks, "British and American Strategies in the Revolutionary War," *History of Massachusetts Blog*, July 28, 2017, https://historyofmassachusetts.org/revolutionary-war-strategies/.

4. Trevor K. Plant, "Ending the Bloodshed: The Last Surrenders of the Civil War." *Prologue Magazine*, 47, no. 1 (Spring 2015), https://www.archives.gov/publications/prologue/2015/spring/cw-surrenders.html(accessed June 13, 2018).

5. History.com Editors, "Reconstruction," *History.com*, October 29, 2009, https://www.history.com/topics/american-civil-war/reconstruction.

6. "Rutherford B. Hayes," *The White House*, accessed April 7, 2017, https://www.whitehouse.gov/about-the-white-house/presidents/rutherford-b-hayes/.

7. Sarah Loft, "Katherine Johnson Biography," *NASA*, 2017, https://www.nasa.gov/content/katherine-johnson-biography.

8. Jon E. Taylor, *Freedom to Serve: Truman, Civil Rights, and Executive Order 9981* (New York: Routledge, 2012), 90.

9. Many historians point to this rift in the Democratic Party as the beginning of the formerly Democratic "Solid South" evolving into what is now a mainstay for the Republican Party.

10. Taylor, *Freedom to Serve: Truman, Civil Rights, and Executive Order 9981.*

ONE

Why This and Black Lives Matter

Two opposing philosophies on the treatment of blacks in America have waged an on-going battle over law, policies, and practices since the before the Civil War. At times this struggle has been violent; at others these battles have been Cold War-esque or symbolic, such as the erection of statues memorializing Confederate leaders following court ordered school desegregation, or black-balling athletes who spoke out against racial injustice.

Whether violent or symbolic, two constants bind these struggles: a desire to subjugate or silence the voices of black Americans fighting for equality, and a deep-seated belief in preservation of the status quo based on an often coded, unstated belief in white racial supremacy. The subtext of the status quo maintains that America was established by white males and therefore white males are the rightful heirs and sole keepers of the fruits of American democracy. Few outside of radical white supremacists will openly express these views, but millions of Americans embrace this ideology whenever they endorse the thinly coded white power themes engrained in the "Make America Great Again" nationalist ideology. This belief in white entitlement, if not outright white supremacy, is a continued manifestation of the unwritten truce to thwart inclusion.

Very early in the struggle for equal rights, black Americans surmised correctly that one of the strongest arguments they could make against segregation and inequality was to serve their country dutifully, faithfully, and with all the strength, courage, and determination they could muster. They have done so in virtually every armed conflict in which the nation has engaged. For those who opposed racial tolerance and inclusion, even service in armed conflict has sometimes failed to undo their desire to strip black Americans of their constitutional rights. This backdrop has cast the US Armed Services as a pivotal institution in the struggle to determine policy regarding inclusion. On July 26, 1948, President Harry S. Truman signed a highly controversial Executive Order 9981, ending segregation in the military and firmly planting the United States Military on the side of inclusion.

Fifty-five years after the Civil Rights and Voting Rights Acts passed, and only a few years after America's first black president left office, the United States is facing a period of profound backlash against the political, socio-economic, and cultural promise of all three of these historic events. FBI Director Christopher Wray testified before Congress in February 2020 that the threat posed by racially motivated violent domestic extremists is equal to or greater than the threat posed by foreign-born terrorist groups such as ISIS and Al-Qaeda. In 2019, the FBI made 107 domestic terrorism arrests, on pace with the number of arrests it made for international terrorism. Racism and other hateful ideologies were driving forces behind most of the ideologically motivated killings and violence in the US in 2018 and 2019, and race-based ones were the most lethal of all domestic extremism movements over the last 20 years. This backlash is emblematic of America's internal conflict with its original sin: American Chattel Slavery.

Following the Civil War, the former Confederate States enacted "black codes" to deny formerly enslaved African Americans the freedom of emancipation. These black codes were laws modeled after former slave laws, ultimately intended to reproduce the outlawed slave-master relationship.[1] The Union capitulated to the desires of the former Confederate states following the Civil War to achieve an expedited but artificial national civility, which came at the expense of resolving the root causes of the war: slavery and a belief in white supremacy. The defeated Southern states never rescinded their specified belief in white supremacy; they simply transformed their ideology for governance into an ideology of resistance, fueling a domestic insurgency that has lasted over 150 years. This incomplete reconstruction, and the prevailing false narrative of the "Noble Lost Cause" led to an ebb and flow of racial discord, and a disconnect between what is written in our founding documents, and what we have consistently practiced over time.

This rift ultimately resulted in the assent of Donald Trump into the Presidency. Foreign and domestic powers have leveraged this racial hatred to sow division and destruction within the United States. This division now poses an existential threat to the American system of governance. In response to the uptick in racial violence, Marine Corps Commandant, General David Berger, prohibited the display of Confederate memorabilia on all Marine Corps bases, but the Army refused to rename the ten bases that bear the names of Confederate Generals. It took Congress overriding former President Donald Trump's veto of the 2021 National Defense Authorization Act to force the Army to rename them. Renaming these bases, named for men who shared an ideology with racist, domestic terrorists, will be transformational for the service and the nation in facilitating racial healing and atonement. These wounds remain raw because they never healed properly from the beginning. As recently as 2021 the US Army was unable to process that bases named for men who committed treason to preserve slavery was a moral failure of leadership. The Army's judgement was marred by their desire to honor a social contract or unwritten truce. This unwritten truce maintains that although chattel slavery is dead, dominant factions in the country can still unite behind denying rights to the formerly enslaved and subjugate them and their descendants to permanent second-class citizenry. Though the Civil Rights Legislation of the 1960s enforced the rights codified in the 13th, 14th, and 15th Constitutional Amendments 100 years after those rights were granted, no apology has ever been issued by both houses of Congress or the President for the atrocities perpetrated against enslaved Americans and their descendants. Such honesty about America's racist past and contrition is required to break the unwritten truce."

MY AWAKENING MOMENT

My introduction to this complex struggle between inclusion and exclusion came as a seven-year-old boy in the Atlanta International Airport. My father had recently separated from active duty Army following two tours in Vietnam. He was part of a wave of black and minority officers being recruited by corporate America for management training programs in an attempt to meet court ordered mandates to diversify its workforce. My father had been promoted to district manager and my family was shopping for a new home in Atlanta; it was 1975 and I was taking my first plane ride. Filled with the enthusiasm and excitement that comes with moving to a new home, I darted in and out of the concourse and gift shops, riding a broom-stick-inspired toy horse on display. I had also taken the liberty of testing the toy pistol and holster. I was taking full advantage of the novel situation and my tired mother, tactically pushing boundaries, mindful to use my inside voice while galloping half speed indoors.

It wasn't until I donned the gray Confederate patrol cap, complete with the stars and bars emblem emblazoned on the top that my mother brought my exploits to a complete halt. With a speed, agility, and grace that would have made Serena Williams blush, she took the cap off my head, corralled my horse, and holstered my pistol. She gave me a book, looked me in the eyes, and quietly told me that I couldn't wear that hat. I thought to myself, thank God I didn't put on the Stetson with the bright red feather! As I sat quietly and pretended to read, I remained transfixed by what happened. My mother didn't yell or punish me, but her actions were so swift and stern I knew whatever I had done was serious. Back home in Florida I asked my mother why I couldn't wear the grey cap from the airport. She explained that it belonged to a group of Southerners who attempted to break away from the US a long time ago. I asked her why they tried to break away, and she told me because they wanted to keep black people as slaves and the rest of America did not. My jaw dropped; I was stunned. What did she mean, "keep," as in maintain the use of black people as slaves? My only reference to slavery at that time was from the movie, *Moses*, which came on every year around Easter. I couldn't fathom that black Americans were slaves like in the movie *Moses*?

I thought to myself, 'You mean to tell me this country fought a bloody civil war over slavery and we were the slaves?' Why had no one ever told me this; it was unbelievable! These events were the beginning of my fascination with history, the military, and racism in America. That was my "awakening." It was the first of many instances that would remind me that race very much does still matter in America. At the age of seven, I had lost a bit of innocence. Such loss is an off-shot of the insidious nature of racism; it forces the children of the oppressed to grow up a little sooner, be a little savvier, and be a little less childlike.

I am forever indebted to my parents for the wonderful upbringing they provided. They protected my sister's and my innocence as best they could, sheltering us from their own struggles with racism.

There were birthday parties and family vacations, things I know they didn't have growing up. Although my father and mother were doting, they came from humble beginnings, even subsisting off of wild game when other sources of protein were scarce. Yet by 1977, my father had worked his way up in his job at Bell South and we were prospering well enough to move into a gated community with clay tennis courts and a huge community swimming pool. By this time, I was keenly aware I wouldn't have been able to enjoy those amenities just ten years earlier. Even though the Civil Rights Act of 1964 ended segregation, many businesses, especially in the deep South, challenged the legislation and delayed full implementation; others ignored the legislation until someone brought lawsuits against them. Other businesses just closed all together rather than comply.

Despite my family's upward mobility, racial tension remained palpable for us. Prior to leaving the Army, my father was given parting gifts for his "I love me wall" as is military tradition. He proudly displayed his trinkets in his work office, except for a bronze paratrooper figurine that he brought home from his office when I was about nine years old. I loved playing with that bronze G.I. Joe! My dad could always tell I had been playing with it because the head would come off if you didn't put it back just so. What he didn't share with me was that he brought the figurine home because his white co-workers at his new job were so incensed about having a black supervisor that they destroyed everything on his

Figure 1.1. Front row: Mary Alice Mosley, Joshua Mosley Jr., Emory Mosley; Second row: Frank Mosley, Joella Mosley, Julius Mosley; Third row: Josie Mae Sneed holding Elmer Mosley. *Photo courtesy of Joella Mosley*

credenza and wall of achievements when he was out of his office one day. The bronze paratrooper was the only thing he could salvage. I grew up thinking I broke that miniature statue as a mischievous toddler until I interviewed my father for this book. While many have experienced far greater tragedies due to racism, such blatant contempt for black achievement was a common feature of racial terrorism—a form of cultural warfare meant to intimidate, humiliate, and discourage others from trying to excel.

THE EBB AND FLOW OF RACISM AND SOCIAL CHANGE

The degree to which America has resisted social change is important because it illustrates the degree of contempt a considerable number of people have for various forms of social change. Where did the elected officials go who brought court challenges against the Federal Government to prevent school and housing desegregation? Where did the constituents go who advocated legal resistance to integration? What did they teach their children and their grandchildren about people of color as these court battles were settled in the early to mid-1970s? Did they have a sudden change of heart about people of color in the 1980s and '90s? One can only hope. People who profess not to be racist often make the claim, "you cannot legislate people's hearts." Such hollow logic misses the point: for the moment, no one cares about what's in the hearts of hateful people; their actions must be in keeping with the values our society has established as law. Changing hearts and minds is a noble and essential pursuit that the nation should not give up on because an enlightened society is a better society, free to tackle other ethical challenges. At the end of the day we must respect everyone's right to believe and think as they wish, provided those beliefs do not infringe on others' protected rights. But until our hearts and minds are harmonious, we must address the actions that contradict our purported national values.

After my awakening in Atlanta's airport, I was continually reminded of how my blackness made me different in the eyes of non-blacks. I remember feeling abandoned around the age of thirteen: the birthday party invitations stopped coming and I watched my white male friends go to mixed gender dance parties and sleepovers. Once someone broke into our home and poured liquor into our fish tank, scrolling the word "Nigger" on my bedroom mirror in 1980.

In high school, I tried out for Boy's State, a Veterans of Foreign War (VFW) program designed to teach emerging young leaders about American governance. I wasn't selected through the Atlantic Beach Chapter. An elderly Filippino member of the VFW told me that I did great and that I should go to the Jacksonville Beach Chapter and try again. I did and I was selected. His encouragement was just enough validation to persuade me to keep going.

While at the Boy's State camp, I met a young man from Mulberry, Florida, a tiny town of about 4,000 where my mother grew up. The young man was a quiet, polite white teenager. I assumed he was racist because of where he was from. I imagined that he was probably like the people who scrolled the racial epithet on my mirror and poisoned my family's fish tank. I was wrong. Chris turned out to be one of the kindest people I had ever known. When I overcame my own prejudice, I introduced myself and told him that I had relatives from Mulberry. After sharing stories about our hometowns, Chris pulled a picture of my great-uncle Malvis from his wallet on the spot, a picture which he carried with him at all times. My uncle was an assistant principal at his high school and recommended Chris for the two-week summer camp. Chris and I had a great two weeks at Boy's State.

When we returned home, I was beaming with pride. As was customary the VFW convened all the boys selected from each of the beaches' chapters so we could tell of our exploits. I held the highest office, Senator. I learned three powerful lessons from that experience that I share to this day with kids whom I mentor: 1) you are not beaten until you stop trying; 2) you must be better than whatever obstacles are put in your path; and 3) everyone deserves an opportunity to define themselves based on their actions instead of their appearances.

Perhaps more poignant than my own awakening was that of my youngest daughter's. Out of the blue one day while I was stationed overseas in Germany, my precocious four-year-old daughter asked me, "Why did God make us black? I want to be white." She did not ask me what's an officer, what does rank mean, or some other question related to the military. Being a major in the Army, I had those answers at the ready. What she shared with me was an insight that at the tender age of four she could already perceive a difference in how she was treated and how her white peers were treated, and in her estimation the treatment was a little better if you were white. Comparatively, her awakening had come three years earlier than mine. Even though things had changed, the rippling effects of the unwritten truce were still very real to a preschooler in 2002. I'm sure my epiphanies are not unlike that of millions of other black Americans and other minorities. I share them for those who have not experienced such moments to illustrate how everyday of your life as a black citizen is affected, and how you must continually choose how you respond, if you respond, or even if what you perceive is due to race at all. In most instances, I tend to look to race last, after I have excluded every other possibility. In the overwhelming majority of instances, I choose to ignore the subtle micro-aggressions and daily indignities, the rude sales person, the hostess who walks past open tables to get to one tucked away in the back next to the bathroom or kitchen (I actually don't ignore that one), or the woman who smiles and clutches her purse as if you are going to try to steal it dressed in your suit and leather wing tips. Regardless of class, these are the indignities minorities, especially black Americans, confront daily—a constant reminder that for all the accomplishments secured, there is still a palpable notion that you are somehow less of an American, less deserving, inferior, or even criminal.

Despite, my own personal anguish due to racism, I am keenly aware that I had a wonderful childhood for which I am very grateful to my father and mother, the community I grew up in, and this nation that made it possible. That life would not have been possible without the passage of the Civil Rights Acts of the 1960s. In writing the opinion for their unanimous 1954 decision in *Brown vs. Board of Education of Topeka*, the Supreme Court noted that segregation of white and black children has a detrimental effect upon black children. They explained that the effect is especially pronounced when the separation is state-sanctioned because it denotes inferiority of the black group. The court went on to opine, "A sense of inferiority affects the motivation of a child to learn.... To separate them from others of similar age and qualifications solely because of their race generates a feeling of inferiority as to their status in the community that may affect their hearts and minds in a way unlikely ever to be undone."[2] This articulation by the highest court in the land specifies the great harm done to others when we discriminate based on race. I submit that the effect is similar when discrimination is based on religion, gender, country of origin, or sexual orientation.

The US Armed Forces got the policy portion right in 1948, however they dragged their feet until 1954 before fully implementing the policy. Malcontents at the highest levels and throughout the ranks did everything within their power to delay or not comply. It wasn't until the Korean War when General Matthew Ridgeway had finally had enough. "I need to place soldiers into whatever units need them regardless of the Soldier's race" or the predominant race of the unit.[3] The last all-black Army units were finally integrated in November 1954. Believing that segregation was inefficient, un-American, and immoral, General Ridgeway worked with Army Chief of Personnel, General Anthony C. McAuliffe on "Project Clear," which demonstrated the inefficiencies of a segregated force.[4] Nonetheless, the necessities of war and initiatives from figures like Ridgeway have been key factors in the military's emergence as a driver of social progress.

Despite demonstrated progress regarding social justice, there is still an ebb and flow of racism that runs throughout our national consciousness. The election of Donald Trump and the August 12, 2017 events of Charlottesville, VA, revealed a considerable number of the electorate who felt like they were losing "their country." President Trump very effectively exploited feelings that America had somehow become too politically correct (a politically correct way of saying too progressive and too diverse); he preyed on the fears of Americans who felt immigrants and terrorists were physically threatening, and convinced this many (if they weren't convinced already) that the nation was becoming too brown.

Much of Trump's campaign rhetoric, "Make America Great Again," "Build a Wall," and his generally nationalist ideology played well to millions of Americans who felt like President Barack Obama did not represent them. Despite being very intelligent, articulate, compassionate, Christian, and a family man, many Americans did not feel a connection with Obama and thought the country was becoming "too liberal." For many of them, the thought of Hillary Clinton, a woman chief executive was completely unacceptable on the heels of America's first black Commander in Chief. In a nutshell, President Obama and Hillary Clinton represented social change, expanding the tent so that all members of society have an opportunity to lead and rise to the limits of their abilities. In many ways, the 2016 election cycle was a referendum that pushed back against the advances America has made in becoming more compliant with the ideals of democracy that we espouse. Until America as a nation can come to grips with the fact that change is necessary for growth, America will always have this ideological tug of war.

NOTES

1. Erin Blakemore, "Jim Crow Laws Created 'Slavery by Another Name,'" National Geographic, February 5, 2020, https://www.nationalgeographic.com/history/reference/united-states-history/jim-crow-laws-created-slavery-another-name/#close.

2. C. J. Earl Warren, *Brown v. Board of Education of Topeka*, 347 U.S. 483 (1954).

3. Gail Buckley, *American Patriots: The Story of Blacks in the Military from the Revolution to Desert Storm* (New York: Random House, 2001), 360.

4. Bernard C. Nalty, *Strength for the Fight* (New York: Free Press, 1986), 260.

TWO

America in 1946

The Events Leading to the Desegregation of the Armed Forces

One unifying aspect of combat is that people are rarely as equal as when they serve their country. From the opportunity to serve to the opportunity to die in defense of American values, seldom are we as equal as when thrust into military service. In combat, the enemy's bullets make no distinction among class, race, gender, or sexual orientation. It has often been said that there are no atheists in foxholes. Similarly, when "things get real," racism, sexism, and homophobia also quickly go by the wayside. In that context, one is primarily concerned about whether his or her fellow service members are trained, proficient, and ready to execute their duties efficiently, lethally, and without delay.

This great common denominator has cast the armed services as an unlikely historical advocate for both equality of treatment and opportunity. The first American cited as killed in the American Revolution during the Boston Massacre was a black man, Crispus Attucks, born of an African father and a Wampanoag Indian mother. During pre-revolutionary conflicts and the Revolutionary War, whites, blacks, and in some instances natives all served together. The military was a race-neutral institution.[1] Following the Revolutionary War, Congress enacted laws prohibiting whole scale use of black Americans in the military for fear of armed slave rebellions. As American society advanced beyond slavery, the military was slow to adapt, seeking to preserve the status quo; blacks were no longer slaves, but the government was still reluctant to fully include them in the military.

By many historical accounts, life for black Americans in 1945 had not changed appreciably since the ratification of the Reconstruction Amendments, the boost provided to black Americans by FDR's New Deal notwithstanding. In fact, the number of black Congressmen decreased from nine during the height of Reconstruction (1865–1876) to two in 1945. The South and many border states, including Missouri, Kentucky, Delaware, and Maryland had legalized segregation, including the nation's capital.[2]

President Harry S. Truman succeeded Franklin Delano Roosevelt and was sworn into office on April 12, 1945. The Allied powers accepted Germany's unconditional surrender on May 8, 1945. President Truman approved the use of the atomic bomb against Japan on July 21, 1945, and the first atomic bombs were dropped on Hiroshima and Nagasaki, Japan on August 9th and August 12th, respectively. World War II ended with the official surrender of Japan accepted by the Supreme Allied Commander, General Douglas MacArthur and Fleet Admiral Chester Nimitz aboard the USS *Missouri* in Tokyo Bay on September 2, 1945.

Truman's attention then immediately turned to reintegrating the twelve million US veterans who returned home after America concluded its four-year combat involvement in World War II. As a veteran of World War I, Truman understood the enormity of the sacrifice each service member made in the preservation of the democratic way of life.

Georgetown University civil rights scholar Michael Gardner states that, "It was his belief in the equality of opportunity and civil rights for all Americans that shaped Truman's words and actions."[3] Gardner also maintains that young Harry Truman developed a fondness for man and a soft spot for the beleaguered and oppressed, having served as the commanding officer for Irish-Catholic National Guardsman during World War I. Adding to his compassion for the oppressed, the local Ku Klux Klan (KKK) opposed Truman when he ran for a county judge position after returning home from WWI. Though he won the election, the impact the Klan had on black voter turnout made a lasting impression on Truman.[4]

Of the twelve million returning veterans, over 1.2 million were black servicemen who would be reintegrated into society almost overnight. Those hoping to maintain the status quo in the South knew that blacks who fought for the freedom of others would "feel entitled" to the same liberties they experienced while abroad. Indeed, many black veterans held this same sentiment following World War I, but their hopes were doused amid an outbreak of violence against them in the summer of 1919. They experienced an unprecedented level of racial violence that permeated virtually every major American population center and came to be known as the Red Summer.[5]

The months immediately following the end of World War II were no different. They were fraught with mob violence against blacks, often led by the KKK. The racist power structure of the South doubled down on

Figure 2.1. Captain Harry Truman, Battery D, 129th Field Artillery Regiment.
Photo courtesy of the National Park Service

Jim Crow laws and other forms of systemic racism to reassert that nothing would change because of black veterans' service during World War II. The two ideologies clashed violently in bloody discord during the months following V-Day.

After the war, black veterans led the push within the black community to assert their right to vote. The southern resistance was equally determined to oppose any political or social gains as a function of black Americans' service in World War II. Racist Mississippi Governor Theodore G. Bilbo retorted in response to advocates for black voting rights: "Red blooded Anglo-Saxon Southerners must stop blacks from voting by any means. If you don't know what that means," Bilbo added, "you are not up on your persuasive measures."[6] Leading to the Georgia primaries in 1946, a sign was hung on a black church that read, "The first nigger to vote will never vote again."[7] War veteran Macio Snipes was dragged from his house and shot to death for casting the single black vote in Taylor County, Georgia.[8]

THE BEATINGS WILL CONTINUE

Two incidents in particular drew a great deal of notoriety and were linked to President Truman's timing to integrate the armed services: the

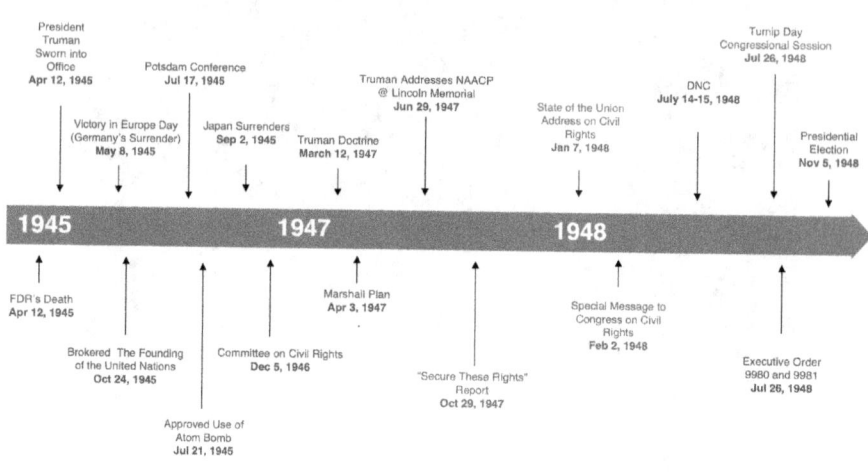

Figure 2.2. Timeline of significant events related to desegregation of the armed forces. *Created by author Troy E. Mosley*

George and Mae Dorsey case and the Lynwood L. Shull trial. On July 25, 1946, George Dorsey, his pregnant wife Mae Dorsey, and another couple, Roger and Dorothy Malcolm, were savagely murdered in Georgia because Malcolm allegedly stabbed a white man.[9]

George served five years in the Pacific Theater with the Army and had been discharged for just nine months at the time of the quintuple murder. Roger, George's friend and neighbor, was charged for killing the son of the farmer whose land they worked as tenant farmers. George posted Roger's $600 bail, and the couples were headed home when they were accosted by a white mob of 15–20 people. All four were killed. The coroner's report stated both couples were shot over sixty times and then hung. Mae Dorsey's fetus was cut from her womb. Local and federal authorities investigated but ran into a wall of silence that halted the investigation. No one was ever charged for the crime.[10]

Just a few months before the Dorsey case, on February 12, 1946, South Carolina Police Chief, Lynwood Lanier Shull, physically removed Isaac Woodward from a bus while Woodward was still in uniform, took him into an alley, beat him with a billy club, and then jailed him for allegedly disturbing the peace. Woodward was a twenty-seven-year-old Army veteran, listed on his Army discharge papers at 5'8", 148 lbs., returning home from active duty just five hours after his discharge. Shull was listed at 215 lbs. While jailed, Shull used a blackjack to gouge out both of Sergeant Woodward's eyes, leaving him blind and without medical attention for two days.

Incensed by the report on Sergeant Woodward, President Truman directed then Attorney General, Tom Clark, to employ the full authority and weight of the Department of Justice (DOJ) to investigate and bring criminal charges against any impugned. This move was unprecedented by the federal government in criminal prosecution cases, which were generally left to the states to adjudicate, particularly involving alleged atrocities motivated by racial hatred. The Federal Bureau of Investigation (FBI) investigated, and the DOJ charged Chief Shull with depriving Sergeant Woodward of constitutional rights; a white man, let alone a law enforcement official, standing trial for the assault of a black American was unheard of in 1946. An all-white jury acquitted Lynwood L. Shull on November 5, 1946, after deliberating for only thirty minutes.[11]

Truman was witnessing a repeat of some of the same events that precipitated the Red Summer, which followed his return from World War I. During the Red Summer, race riots broke out in Chicago, Washington, DC, over three dozen other US cities, and one rural Arkansas county where five whites and an estimated 100–240 blacks were killed. One can surmise that Truman recognized how history was repeating itself.

Despite Truman's efforts, this wouldn't be the last time in US history that such turmoil erupted. What would the trial outcome be if South Carolina Police Chief Shull were tried today? The Walter Scott case almost seventy years removed from Sergeant Woodward's beating provides an eerily similar case study. Scott, a fifty-year-old Coast Guard veteran was shot in the back by Charleston, South Carolina, police veteran, Michael Slager on April 4, 2015. Scott was stopped in broad day light during a routine traffic stop for a non-functioning brake light. Unarmed, Scott attempted to flee the scene, and Officer Slager shot him in the back five times.

Eyewitness Feidin Santana came forward with a video of the events, which differed from Slager's police report. Feidin presented the video to local Black Lives Matter activists, who presented the footage to Scott's family. Slager was immediately released from the Charleston Police Department and charged with murder. A five-week trial ended in a mistrial due to a hung jury. Eleven of the twelve jurors favored a guilty verdict; one juror held out, citing that he "could not in good conscience consider a guilty verdict."[12] On May 11, 2016, Slager was indicted on federal charges for violating Scott's civil rights and unlawfully using a weapon during the commission of a crime. Slager pled guilty on May 2, 2017, to the federal charges in exchange for the state charges being dropped.[13]

The difference between Walter Scott's case and Sgt. Woodward's case is there are civil rights laws in place to provide a safety net for victims when the judicial process breaks down at the state-level. The similarities are that law enforcement officials still often have a blatant disregard for the sanctity of black lives. The ripple effects of Jim Crow are still pushing otherwise good people to commit unthinkable acts. This is where America must change. This is also where the armed forces have an opportunity to continue advancing positive social change by removing the vestiges of Jim Crow and ending the unwritten truce.

TRUMAN'S CALL AND RESPONSE

Truman knew the federal government had to intervene to make equal protection under the law and other constitutional liberties a reality for all Americans. Truman was enraged by the atrocities committed against black veterans returning from victory in America's war effort and was even more incensed by the federal government's inability to provide protection, relief, or justice. In the immediate months following World War II, Truman attempted unsuccessfully to exercise federal protection when Southern States either failed to protect citizens' rights or when state-sponsored atrocities were committed against black Americans and black war veterans.

Truman met with National Association of Colored People (NAACP) President Walter White and other civil rights leaders on September 19, 1946, when Mr. White and other leaders made their case for increased federal protections. President Truman commissioned "The Presidential Committee on Civil Rights" by Executive Order 9980 on December 5, 1946, after reflecting upon the acquittal of Chief Shull and the fact that no one was charged with the Dorsey and Malcolm murders. The decree was made exactly one month after the Shull acquittal. The committee was unprecedented in its charter and composition. Even the name ". . . Civil Rights" was ground-breaking. Until that point, racially motivated violations of minority rights were more commonly referred to as "violations of civil liberties" or "violations of human rights."

The committee was chaired by Charles Wilson, President of General Electric—a liberal also concerned about the growing post-war violence perpetrated against black veterans. Other notable appointees included Sadie Tanner Alexander—an uncompromising civil rights advocate and Philadelphia Assistant City Solicitor, as well as the first black woman to earn a PhD in economics. Wilson announced FDR Jr. and Dartmouth College President John S. Dickey as co-chairs. Dickey then brought on Professor of Government Robert K. Carr as Executive Secretary of the Civil Rights Committee. The Civil Rights Committee further divided into three subcommittees: one focused on the adequacy of federal legislation; one on socio-economic and educational discrepancies; and the third on efforts of private organizations to affect social change.

Their mission was to work toward making America "free from fear" of intimidation or threat of violence in pursuit of one's rights. The committee's charter was to document the prevalence of racism both quantitatively and qualitatively, to provide insights into causality, and to suggest remedies that the president could implement. They were to recommend laws and policies that would eliminate racism, establish equal protection under the law, as well as make economic and educational opportunities afforded to white citizens a reality for all Americans.

SECURE THESE RIGHTS

The committee became affectionately known as the Noah's Ark Committee because it had two of everything: two industry captains, two labor leaders, two women, two blacks, two unionizers, etc. The committee met ten times as a complete committee and documented systemic police abuse of black citizens through research and interviews. On October 29, 1947, the President's Committee on Civil Rights delivered a 178-page report entitled, "Secure These Rights." Twenty-two pages of the report contained thirty-five recommendations, which the *Washington Post* reported on the following day. The *Post* characterized the report as "Social Dynamite" because of the urgency and immediacy with which it called upon the nation to wipe out segregation and discrimination from the American way of life. The committee surmised that only a national solution would be effective in achieving rights for all Americans in all locations.[14]

The committee recommended simultaneous action on multiple fronts including federal court rulings, congressional legislation, and presidential executive orders. When the committee's report focused on a person's right to safety and security it addressed the lingering problem of lynchings in America and described lynchings as the ultimate "terrorist device." Lynchings of black citizens in America was a common terrorist tactic perpetrated against black Americans for attempting to vote or fight for dignity—acting so-called "uppity." W. E. B. Dubois, famed black sociologist, historian, and editor of the NAACP periodical, *The Crisis*, ran an annual issue on the number of lynchings in America until 1961 when the prevalence of lynchings was deemed no longer pervasive.[15]

The report called for creating a Civil Rights Division within the DOJ, establishing a permanent Civil Rights Commission in the Executive Branch, instituting Federal anti-lynching legislation, ending poll taxes and other barriers to voting, enacting comprehensive federal rights voting legislation, and passing a federal statute criminalizing police brutality . Other recommendations included: legislation prohibiting all forms of discrimination against members of the armed services, federal laws requiring full disclosure of authorship for organizations trying to influence voters, ending segregation in the United States based on protected status, instituting federal fair employment legislation, enacting fair education laws, and outlawing restrictive real estate covenants.[16]

President Truman adopted many of the Committee's recommendations into his ten-point plan. When President Truman addressed Congress on February 2, 1948, he issued a detailed message outlining his vision for civil rights reform. This plan helped pave the way for what would later become the modern civil rights movement a full decade and a half prior to the passage of the 1964 Civil Rights Act. All but two of the President's civil rights imperatives were ultimately adopted into law: a federal law against lynching and an immigration law to equalize opportunities for residents of the US to become naturalized citizens.

One of the few recommendations from the President's Committee on Civil Rights that Truman did not advance was their recommendation to address police brutality. This omission is historically and politically significant given that police brutality remains one of our great societal ills. Unequal sentencing, the school-to-prison pipeline, and the "felonization" of petty crimes have helped spurn the current Black Lives Matter movement.

One can only wonder how much further ahead the United States would be in resolving these issues had Congress enacted the initial measures to address police brutality in 1948. These historical omissions have many lessons for us today. Still, President Truman, deserves credit for being bold, visionary, and strategic in advancing the issues he chose. Like many politicians, he advanced issues which he thought were fundamental and those he felt could garner support. The lessons for us today are that political governance matters and sweeping changes take time. Electing informed, unbiased officials can have a significant impact on how our society fares in the long term. The longer we delay addressing societal woes, the more deeply we become entrenched.

President Truman was keenly aware of the public crisis posed by unequal protection under the law and police brutality perpetrated against black Americans. He issued the following statement when he signed Executive Order 9981 into law:

> Today, Freedom from Fear, and the democratic institutions which sustain it, are again under attack. In some places, from time to time, the local enforcement of law and order has broken down, and individuals—sometimes ex-servicemen, even women have been killed, maimed, or intimated. The preservation of civil liberties is a duty of every Government, state, federal, and local. Wherever law enforcement measures and the authority of federal, state, and local governments are inadequate, these measures and this authority should be improved. The constitutional guarantees of individual liberties and of equal protection under the law clearly place the duty to act upon the federal government when state or local authorities fail to do so.[17]

Truman's comments indicate that blatant abuses against black service members and their families factored into his decision to integrate the services.

WITH DELIBERATION AND FORETHOUGHT

Although President Truman lacked formal higher education, he was a shrewd man and a voracious reader who understood people. He spoke in simple, straightforward terms, and took quick, decisive actions. He had a healthy respect for the importance of education, valued it as a means of socio-economic advancement, and recognized it as a strategic means for moving the nation forward during the quickly intensifying Cold War.

Truman also knew that he would be unlikely to advance civil rights for black Americans through the normal congressional channels because Southern segregationists would ally with northern "states' rights" Republicans to block the legislation. Nonetheless, President Truman presented his ten-point plan to Congress with the hope that they would act on his request and develop legislation to support his goals. What the members of the 80th Congress didn't know was that Truman anticipated his calls for legislation would fall upon deaf ears. He had already resolved to use his executive authority to emplace measures that would make equality under the law a reality for all Americans, but as I will show, he was also setting a brilliant political trap for those who would oppose his measures.[18]

Truman's predecessor, Franklin Delano Roosevelt, had enjoyed a greater reputation as an advocate for civil rights, while many of Roosevelt's tangible acts pale in comparison to Truman's. When staunch segregationist Senator Strom Thurmond was interviewed following his departure from the 1947 Democratic National Convention, a reporter asked why then Governor Thurmond was leaving when Truman was essentially continuing many of the civil rights proposals that FDR had advocated. Thurmond replied, "I agree, but Truman really means it."[19]

Leading up to Executive Order 9981, President Truman addressed Congress three times advocating for civil rights, the first of which was January 7, 1948, in his third State of the Union Address. In his second address to Congress on February 2, 1948, President Truman presented a plan that focused on five top priorities: 1) protect and develop America's human resources, 2) conserve and utilize the country's natural resources, 3) strengthen the economy to raise the standard of living for all Americans, 4) achieve world peace based on the principles of freedom, justice, and the equality of all nations, and 5) ensure civil rights for all Americans.[20]

During his January 7th address, Truman stated, "Any denial of human rights is a denial of the basic beliefs of democracy and of our regard for the worth of each individual. Today, however, some of our citizens are still denied equal opportunity for education, jobs and economic advancement and for the expression of their views at the polls. Most serious of all, some are denied equal protection under laws. Whether discrimination is based on race, creed, or color, or land of origin, it is utterly contrary to American ideals of democracy."[21] This statement attests to Truman's understanding that the denial of rights to any American citizen, black or otherwise, was a fundamental flaw in our expression of democracy. I would also venture to say that Truman understood this flaw had to be corrected if America was to tout itself as an exemplar of governance superior to Communism. It is striking that Truman noted as early as 1946 that black citizens did not benefit from equal protection under the law and that of all inequalities this was the "most serious of all," yet this problem still plagues America.

Many historians characterized Truman's personality as one of stubborn determination, if not outright recklessness. During the 60th Anniversary celebration of Executive Order 9981, Truman's speech writer and former West Virginia Congressman, Ken Hechler recalled how one historian described the Executive Order as "revolutionary and politically reckless."[22] After all, Truman was campaigning vigorously for the civil rights of black Americans during an election year when most of the country was either indifferent to or outright opposed to advancing the rights of black Americans.

Truman was not reckless at all. Rather, he was a shrewd, calculating politician, with the courage and moral fortitude of a combat veteran. Truman was an avid poker player, keen military strategist, and self-taught connoisseur of the literary classics. His military experience as an Army officer gave him unparalleled tactical and strategic instincts in determining "key terrain"—the ground or goal that must be secured at all costs to posture oneself for decisive victory. Truman understood that securing civil rights for black Americans was 'key terrain,' even if doing so meant risking the presidential election. Truman commented on the 1948 campaign trail, "If securing equal protections under the law for all Americans means losing the election, it is a cause worth losing for."[23] Here, Truman did not merely leverage his tactical and strategic abilities to defeat his opponents. He also did so to advance the fight for America to embody the ideals of modern democracy and to remove the embarrassing symptomology of American racism.

Another key military tenant is understanding intelligence—information about your opposition's position, capabilities, strengths, weaknesses, and tendencies. Truman knew his political adversaries were hamstrung by their racial animus; they were predictable. Southern segregationists who opposed affording black Americans Constitutional freedoms were so constrained by their own racial hatred that Truman knew they had a finite range of options for opposing his initiatives, and he knew which initiatives were likely to elicit certain responses. This intelligence gave Truman a tremendous strategic advantage over his political adversaries; it's the political equivalent of having your opponent's playbook. President Truman also knew that his political opponents' position was morally indefensible. If he could shine a light on the immorality and injustice of their actions, he could win the hearts and minds of those who were otherwise indifferent.

If Truman needed proof of concept (i.e., a test case for his strategy), he had one in his own 1940 Senate campaign when he defeated Governor Lloyd C. Stark in a bitter primary that made the two men life-long political enemies. Truman won the Missouri Democratic Senate primary by only 8,133 votes, carrying over 90 percent of the black vote in Missouri's two largest cities, Kansas City and St. Louis. Although Missouri was segregated, it was a border state that fought for the Union during the Civil War. It was also less oppressive than the Deep South where blacks were effectively prohibited from voting in the 1940s by Jim Crow laws such as poll taxes. At the same time, lynching and other terrorist tactics perpetrated by the KKK were a reality for blacks in Missouri who were especially motivated to overcome any legal barriers to their safety and equality. Truman went on to win the general Senate election against the Republican candidate, Manvel Davis by a slightly more comfortable margin: 51.2 percent of the vote to Davis' 48.7 percent. This gave Truman documented evidence that the black vote could be strategic in shaping the outcome of an election.[24]

Armed with the report that his Presidential Committee on Civil Rights delivered—which concluded that the Federal Government was the only hope for black Americans to attain the full-fledged, constitutional rights of citizenry—President Truman launched one of the most brilliantly conceived civil rights campaigns of the twentieth century. The Committee's report, "Secure These Rights," served as what is known in military parlance as Intelligence Preparation of the Battlefield—the diligence military staff put forth before embarking upon a campaign. President Truman had a detailed and comprehensive study of the racism plaguing the United States. He not only knew that Northern, "states' rights" Republicans and Southern segregationists alike would oppose this campaign plan, but he also knew how they would oppose him.[25]

FLIPPING THE SCRIPT

Truman set a trap by requesting civil rights legislation from Congress that he could sign into law, knowing Congress would not act on his requests. Republicans and Southern Democrats took the bait. Truman knew any civil rights gains would have to be passed through executive order and any other authority he could leverage unilaterally. By making the requests to Congress in a public and demonstrable fashion, he could then campaign on Congress' failure to act. This is another military tenet and a brilliant part of Truman's plan: you cannot win an engagement while in a defensive posture. To secure an objective, you must seize the initiative and go on the offensive.

After Truman proposed his civil rights plan in his January 7, 1948, State of the Union Address, he publicly issued a call to Congress about civil rights in his special message to them less than a month later. Even the timing and tempo had the pace of a "blitzkrieg" style offensive. During the Democratic National Convention, July 14–17, 1948, the Democratic Party adopted an aggressive civil rights platform spear-headed by Minneapolis Mayor Hubert Humphrey.

However, before Humphrey's plan was adopted, moderates in Truman's camp proposed a watered-down version of Truman's own civil rights plan to appease Southerners led by then Governor Strom Thurmond of South Carolina. Thurmond countered with his own compromise, later named the Moody Plank, which called for the reserved powers of the states to control and regulate local affairs and act in the exercise of police powers.[26] Thurman's version would make civil rights a state's issue and not a federal concern.

Humphrey's plan, which was adopted by the Democratic National Convention and later named the "Biemiller Plank," argued that Congress should enact legislation guaranteeing blacks full and equal political participation, equal employment opportunities, personal protection, and integration of the military. Regarding the issue of civil rights, Humphrey stated in his introduction of President Truman at the convention, "My friends, to those who say that we are rushing into this issue of civil rights, I say we are 172 years late."[27]

After the July 14th vote in which the Democratic Party voted to adopt the more aggressive "Biemiller Plank," 651 ½ to 582 ½, members of the Mississippi and Alabama delegations led a walkout of the convention. On July 15, only thirteen out of a possible 278 Southern delegates cast their votes for Truman. The other 263 Southern delegates cast their votes for racist Senator Richard Russell of Georgia. Truman was nominated by a 947 ½ delegate margin. Many of the delegates who walked out of the DNC gathered in Birmingham, Alabama two days later to form the Southern States Rights Party, the "Dixiecrats," and voted Strom Thurmond as their presidential nominee.[28] Truman's plan was brilliant because he caught his adversaries by surprise. The Dixiecrats did not have a well-conceived counter attack and were made to look small over an immoral position. They were stammering out of the convention trying to figure out what to do while Truman sped towards the presidential nomination with a huge victory in his back pocket: the desegregation of the armed services. This move also stole the moral-high ground from his

Republican challenger and began to build Truman up in the eyes of black voters who held the swing vote in the Northeast and Midwest.

In a fiery acceptance speech, President Truman—dressed in a dapper, all-white linen suit, perhaps as a nod to his earlier days as a Kansas City Haberdashery owner—shrewdly attacked the GOP (and not his fellow Southern Democrats) for failing to move on the civil rights legislation he had requested on multiple occasions. By going on the offensive, Truman again exhibited tactics drawn from military science to seize the initiative. For example, he preemptively handcuffed his GOP opponent Thomas Dewey, a reputed socially progressive governor of New York who himself advocated for equal rights of blacks and other minorities in New York.[29]

President Truman kept the promise he made at the DNC and called a special "Turnip Day" Congressional session, giving Congress yet one more opportunity to blunder the development of civil rights legislation. Knowing that Congress would again fail to deliver, Truman was already prepared to issue Executive Order 9980 and 9981. He did so on July 26, 1948, delivering the political equivalent of a nuclear bomb to his political adversaries. These executive orders were widely regarded as unprecedented for the advancements they provided for civil rights. Not since the time of Lincoln had one executive order done so much to re-baseline the rights of black citizens under law. Instead of being out on the campaign trail, Republican congressmen and Democratic Southerners alike were in Washington, DC with egg on their faces, caught flat-footed, and sent reeling back to their home states to campaign for the November elections. They were left playing defense, and while they desperately tried to calculate their next moves, Truman continued his offensive.

Taking credit for being a visionary champion of civil rights, he embarked upon a whistle-stop tour of the Midwest and West to secure the other two segments of his strategic block: Western farmers and Midwestern organized labor. To win the 1948 presidential election, Truman calculated that he needed progressive western farmers, the unions (i.e., big city labor), and Southern conservatives. These three groups ensured FDR's election, and Truman was fully committed to securing their support.

It's also likely that Truman anticipated further black migration and factored it into his campaign strategy. Following the end of World War II, one in three black veterans expressed a desire to relocate to another state, while nine out of ten white veterans intended to stay in the state where they joined the service. In an April 8, 1945, survey, an *Atlanta Constitution* article forecasted that returning black veterans would lead a northern migration, predicting that thousands of black soldiers would move to northern and north-central states.[30]

In the 1940s, twenty states had segregation laws for public accommodations, and eighteen prohibited discriminatory practices in public accommodations. The latter were primarily Northern and Northeastern.

Ten states including Missouri had no laws either way, but Missouri's State Constitution called for segregated schools unless otherwise mandated by state law, which effectively made Missouri as segregated as the rest of the South. So, it is no wonder that the years following World War II would usher in a second great migration of black Americans to urban areas in the North, Northeast, and Midwest.

Truman's campaign strategy evidenced an understanding of the changing demography. Most likely, he understood that losing support from Southern States' rights groups due to his civil rights platform meant he would have little margin for error with Western farmers and big-city labor. His strategy also implies that he understood how pivotal the growing black urban vote would be in winning Midwestern and Northeastern cities. Truman's strategy for simultaneously prioritizing civil rights and winning the election proved to be effective. Brilliantly conceived with great deliberation and relentlessly executed, it paved the way for his dramatic desegregation of the military through Executive Order 9980. Although often overshadowed in the history books by Executive Order 9981, Executive Order 9980 was just as significant. Executive Order 9980 made it illegal to discriminate in hiring federal employees based on race, religion, gender, creed, or national origin.

This executive order set the stage for the Civil Rights Act of 1964, which prohibited discrimination based on race and sex in hiring, promoting, and firing. President Truman detailed his expectations of Cabinet Members and Agency Directors, laying out a process for measuring success, as well as a system of redress for prospective employees who were aggrieved by violators of Executive Order 9980. For the first time in US history, blacks and other minorities had a reasonable chance of securing federal employment in broad numbers.

President Truman understood that freedom from tyranny and terror, economic opportunity, educational opportunity, and the ability to exercise civic duty were essential components to being a part of the American experiment in democracy. Anticipating resistance, the executive orders spelled out how managers and agency heads were to go about integrating the federal work force, monitoring the program, and processing grievances. Aggrieved employees or potential employees were given recourse and possible remedies for discrimination. Each department was to hire a Fair Employment Officer who could be petitioned if prospective employees encountered discrimination, or individuals could go directly to the head of the agency or department for help. Full operational responsibility was given to the Fair Employment Officer who reported directly to the department or agency head.

Truman put the heads of each federal department and agency on notice that he would be holding each personally accountable for implementation and he expected progress. He also sent a shot over the bow to the nation at large that he was serious about civil rights; those senior managers who refused to move out on the directive were removed from office.

THE CHECK IS IN THE MAIL

Although Executive Order 9981 was issued on July 26, 1948, the execution of that order was protracted and implemented with great reluctance; full compliance would not come until 1954. The very next day following the order, the *Washington Post* quoted Four Star General Omar Bradley, then Army Chief of Staff, saying, "The Army is not out to make any social reforms. The Army will put men of different races in different companies. . . . Desegregation will come to the Army only when it becomes a fact in the rest of American society."[31] Such a statement by a uniformed military official following an executive order by the President of the United States acting in his capacity as Commander in Chief was unheard of, and it flew in the face of one of the fundamental principles upon which this country was founded: subjugation of the military to civilian authority. Members of the US Armed Forces could classify such behavior as insubordination and a violation of Article 88 of the Uniformed Code of Military Justice, which prohibits uniformed military officials from using contemptuous language against government officials.

General Bradley's comment prompted Truman to issue the following statement in a press conference on July 29, 1948: "the intent of Executive Order 9981 is to end segregation in the armed forces."[32] Behind closed doors, General Bradley was most likely reprimanded severely and offered his mea culpa. Following the 60th Anniversary Celebration of Executive Order 9981, Truman speech writer Ken Hechler stated in an interview at the Pentagon that Truman's reaction to the Army Chief of Staff's *Washington Post* remarks "was blunt . . . Believe me, he was called onto the carpet–Harry Truman talked to him in good old Missouri-English and Omar Bradley changed his position pretty quickly."[33] Truman must have accepted Bradley's apology as General Bradley later received his fifth star from Truman before being named the first Chairman of the Joint Chiefs of Staff.

The last black, segregated unit in the Army was not integrated until a full six years after Truman's executive order.[34] President Truman certainly could not be faulted for the defense department's delay tactics, given that he had several other pressing issues to attend to, such as the burgeoning Cold War, the Korean War, the progress of the fledgling North Atlantic Treaty Organization (NATO), and the formation of the new Jewish State, Israel. As foreign policy battles raged, Southern segregationists continued to threaten funding for the Marshall Plan, which would provide economic aid to war-torn Europe. Threats to defund the Marshall

Plan were routinely levied in exchange for a reversal on Truman's civil rights mandates; he relented on neither.

As a follow-up to his executive orders, Truman's administration created the Committee on the Equality of Treatment and Opportunity in the Armed Services—a seven-member, multiracial panel—to further study integrating the armed services and to advise the armed services. Two nationally prominent blacks were appointed, Jesse Mitchell, President of Industrial Bank, and the Urban League's Eugene Kinkle Jones. This board became known as the Fahy Committee, named after its chairman, former Solicitor General Charles Fahy. The President and the three Armed Services Secretaries attended the first meeting. Perhaps anticipating the angst and delays that would occur, President Truman set the tone by stating, "I want the job done, and I want it done in a way so that everyone will be happy to cooperate to get it done."[35]

Yet, it's doubtful that even Truman could have known the extent to which the services, primarily the Army and Marine Corps, would push back; in some cases, they even insisted that segregation be maintained as a personnel management policy. During the Fahy Committee's first hearings on January 13, 1949, representatives from the Army attempted to defend segregation. Secretary of the Army Kenneth Royall argued before the Fahy Committee on March 28, 1949 that the Army was in favor of maintaining segregation, testifying that the Army was not "the instrument for social evolution."[36]

The Marine Corps attempted to defend its segregation policy and admitted that only one of its 8,200 officers was black. By contrast, Secretary of the Navy John L. Sullivan and Secretary of the Air Force Stuart Symington testified that they were opposed to segregation in the armed forces and were actively pursuing policies to integrate the services.

On April 1, 1949, Secretary of Defense Louis Johnson issued a Department of Defense memorandum, which stated that the DoD's policy going forward was to ensure equality of treatment and opportunity for all in the armed services and that "qualified Negro personnel shall be assigned to fill any type of position without regard to race."[37] On May 11, 1949, Secretary Johnson approved the integration plans of the Air Force but rejected the plans of the Army and the Navy. Later that month, the Fahy Committee recommended changes to the Army and Navy for their integration plans, specifically advising the Army to desegregate its units and abolish its ten percent enlistment cap for black recruits. In June 1949, Louis Johnson accepted the Navy's revised integration plan.[38]

Secretary of the Army Kenneth Claiborne Royall was ultimately forced into retirement for essentially refusing to desegregate the Army a year after the issuance of the Executive Order. Under Royall's leadership as the civilian executive head of the Army, the Army submitted two separate plans that both sought to maintain the status quo. Gordon Gray replaced Royall, but also submitted a plan that was deemed inadequate.

On July 25, 1949, the Fahy Commission recommended to Truman, Johnson, and Gray that the Army's plan submitted on July 5, 1949, also be rejected.

As the summer closed, the Fahy Commission and Department of the Army continued discussions that yielded no resolution to the Army's insistence on various aspects of desegregating existing units, as well as capping the percentage of black recruits at ten percent of total annual recruits. On September 27, 1949, the Army informed the Fahy Commission that it was submitting a revised plan to Johnson but did not provide the Fahy Commission with a copy.

On September 30, 1949, Secretary Johnson approved the Army's latest version of its integration plan, which still included the ten-percent cap on black recruits and provisions that maintained segregated units. President Truman held a press conference on October 6, 1949 in which he called the Army's integration plan "a progress report" and reiterated that his executive order was to integrate the Army. The Army completed another revision of its integration plan and submitted it for approval in late November 1949. Once again, the plan included provisions that allowed for segregated units and the ten-percent cap on black recruits. The Fahy Committee admonished the Army for this last report and threatened to issue a press release strongly condemning the Department of the Army if they did not remove the provisions supporting segregation and capping annual black recruits.[39]

In April 1951, General Matthew Ridgeway, Commanding General of United Nations Peacekeeping forces in Korea, requested the Army allow him to integrate all black soldiers within his command. The Army announced that the integration of all Army units in Korea and Japan (including Okinawa) would be completed within six months. Finally, in October 1953, the Army announced that 95 percent of African American soldiers were serving in integrated units, five years and five rejected integration plans later. The Army disbanded its last segregated unit, the 94th Engineer Battalion in the European Command in November 1954.[40]

THE AFTERMATH OF EXECUTIVE ORDER 9981

Such wanton disregard for presidential executive orders and the advice of presidentially appointed committees with subpoena authority was unprecedented. Yet, American history is replete with examples of outright defiance regarding the implementation of policy and law designed to end state-sanctioned violations of constitutional and civil rights.

This type of struggle is emblematic of the nation's evolution toward equal rights for all Americans. Blinded by eventual adaptation of progressive policies and practices, many historians and members of our society in general fail to acknowledge the lasting impact of such obstinance and insubordination on present day race relations. A general reluctance to fully recognize the effects of resistance to equality perpetuates the cycle of believing we are further along than we are, goading many otherwise reasonable people into believing we live in a "post-racial" society.

How can we be post-racial when, at each critical juncture in the struggle for equality, opponents of federal laws designed to promote equality have flagrantly disobeyed the law, failed to enforce the law, or actively opposed the law?

Even our late twentieth-century history is littered with examples of opposition to equal protection under the law. Take for instance when Governor George Wallace activated the National Guard to prevent the federally mandated integration of the University of Alabama in 1963, or when South Carolina voted to raise the Confederate battle flag on state grounds in defiance of the Civil Rights Act of 1964. Society's failure to acknowledge the degree of opposition to equality, and its willingness to accept and even glorify those who have opposed equality glosses over the extent to which America still struggles with equality and racism. US Army installations and public schools bear the names of historical figures primarily known for opposing the values of the Constitution and taking arms against the United States and its citizens.

It comes as no surprise that when the GOP is absent from milestone celebrations of America's triumph over injustice and inequality, they resemble the unrepentant segregationists who fought integration in the courts and delayed full implementation of court ordered school segregation for twenty years. For instance, the Republican Party was virtually unrepresented at the 50th Anniversary celebration of the passage of the 1964 Civil Rights Act.[41] The history of race relations in America does not permit such a conspicuous absence to be coincidental. This brand of politics and failed leadership perpetuates long-standing divisions. I'm certainly not suggesting how people should think or behave, just advocating that racist behavior should be characterized accordingly.

Americans shudder at the very thought of characterizing anything as racist. People recoil at the possibility that anything could be racist; after all, America has elected a black president. Even the term, "playing the race card" denotes a certain underhandedness. In failing to accept that racism exists, we perpetuate the false notion that we live in a post-racial society. As a general societal norm, the moniker "racist" is almost exclusively reserved for those who pejoratively use the word "nigger." Many Americans are offended by the notion that racism exists, but somehow are less bothered by the statistic that ninety percent of white people in America who take the Implicit Association Test show an inherent racial bias for white people and against black people.[42] Similarly, a study by Pro Publica released in the fall of 2014 found that black males are twenty-one times more likely to be shot dead by police than their white male counterparts.[43]

Harboring different feelings based upon racial identity or another form of bias in and of itself doesn't make someone a bad person; it makes them human. The failure to consider our own implicit biases and how these deeply seated feelings impact our behavior is a moral failure. Everyone can do better in this regard. We should first consider the possibility that we are biased and reflect upon our feelings before we act, particularly when our actions have the potential to affect others in a significant or meaningful way.

When President Obama used the word "nigger" during a June 21, 2015, "WTF Podcast" hosted by Marc Maron, it touched off a fire-storm of controversy; some analysts even accused the President of being racist for using the N-word, which is preposterous and goes to my earlier point about America's fixation with the N-word. Like many words in the American English lexicon, the N-word has multiple definitions and it is the context in which it is used that determines its meaning; hence, some blacks use it as a term of affiliation or even endearment in an attempt to reclaim or redefine the word. While I am not condoning the routine use of the N-word, we as a society must move beyond these topical issues and dig deeper into the facts that suggest we are still struggling with the legacy of slavery; an incomplete reconstruction; and the legacy of Jim Crow laws, mores, and customs.

Many suggested that President Obama's mere existence as Commander in Chief was proof that America was in a post-racial society. More concerning than that is the fact that many of President Obama's political opponents have argued that he created an even greater racial divide than previously existed. Such analyses fail to account for the sordid history of America's struggle for legal equality, not to mention the injustices that persist outside of the law.

A simple scan of the demographic breakdown of the 2008 presidential election exposes this pre-Obama divide. 45 percent of the white electorate cast a ballot for President Obama, while 53 percent of white Americans voted for John McCain; conversely 95 percent of black Americans voted for Barack Obama compared to only 5 percent who voted for John McCain. If you are still not convinced of this pre-Obama divide, a review of the electoral map compared to a map of the United States during the Civil War shows that the Republican states match the states that left the union over the issue of slavery except for Virginia, North Carolina, and Florida. The Democratic states reflect the makeup of the Union states during the Civil War except for Missouri, Kentucky, and West Virginia, which were border states that didn't secede but had slavery. While this illustration is anecdotal in some regards, it poses a serious question as to how much race factored into voters' choices in 2008 and how regional attitudes about race have evolved over time.

My point is simple: the military has historically, even if begrudgingly, led the way in the struggle for equal rights, a term I prefer to civil rights.

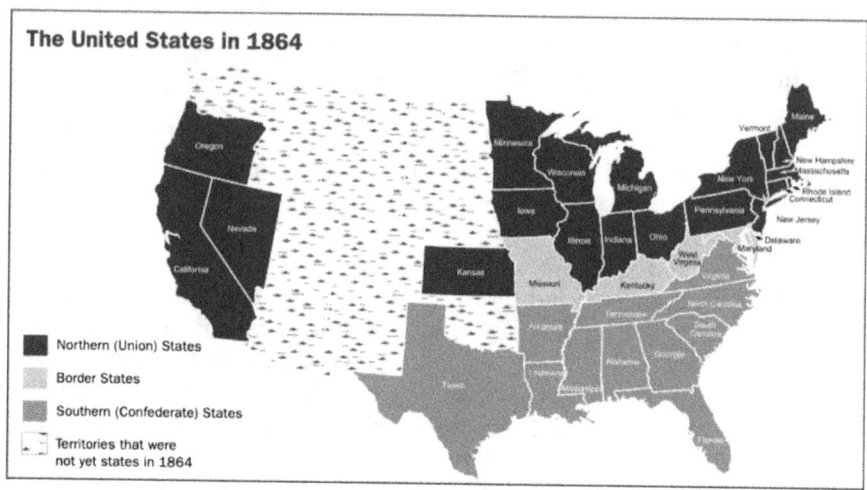

Figure 2.3. 1864 Map of United States and Confederate States. *Photo courtesy of U.S. Citizenship and Immigration Service*

Rather than reject the concept that the military can be an institution that supports social change and equality in American society, the Department of Defense should fully embrace this historical legacy and the precedents it has established, not only because it's the right thing to do, but because America's diversity represents a potentially tremendous strategic advantage over its adversaries.

As one of the world's few multi-ethnic republics, the US has the potential to infiltrate any adversarial group, Al-Qaida and other terrorist organizations included. But to do so, America and the DoD must truly embrace diversity and not just pay lip service to it. No one race, gender, sex, sexual orientation, or socioeconomic class of people has the exclusive privilege to serve our great nation in direct combat. In this simple regard, the opportunity to serve America is one instance in which we are all truly equal. This has only recently become true with the Pentagon allowing women to serve in combat roles effective December 3, 2015 and the DoD allowing transgender persons to serve openly effective June 30, 2016.

Human resources, like any other resource, represents potential energy. Until this potential is embraced, cultivated, and harnessed, it remains a theoretical strategic advantage. Rather than having disillusioned, marginalized Muslims, or any other minority group recruited by our adversaries, we should be training Americans to infiltrate such organizations to gather intelligence that can be used to America's advantage. Such programs require a commitment to diversity as a strategic, operational, and even tactical advantage, establishing programs that support these concepts and living this concept in both policy and practice.

Figure 2.4. 2008 Presidential Election Electoral College Map, Republican states in light gray, Democratic states in dark gray. *Source: Library of Congress*

Although the Army was dragged kicking and screaming into an integrated force, the entire Department of Defense was still fifteen years ahead of corporate America, which didn't remove its barriers to opening management positions for blacks and other minorities until passage of the Civil Rights Act of 1968, which prohibited the use of race, gender, creed, or national origin in hiring decisions. Following that landmark legislation, many Fortune 500 companies installed recruitment programs to diversify their management and executive positions. It should come as no surprise that companies seeking vast numbers of college-educated professionals with leadership experience then targeted military officers.

The US military has paved the way in desegregation, equal pay, marriage equality, and the removal of barriers to women serving as equals in combat, which surely casts dispersions on corporate America's glass ceiling. Rather than resist or minimize this aspect of military service, we should continually weave diversity and the promotion of diversity into the very fabric of our military culture. Millions of famous and unsung Americans (majority and minority) have benefitted from the education, structure, discipline, and opportunities provided through our armed services, and in turn countless American communities have benefitted from their continued service as civilians. In embracing this heritage, the military gives strong cause for the rest of America to follow.

NOTES

1. Gail Buckley, *American Patriots: The Story of Blacks in the Military from the Revolution to Desert Storm* (New York: Random House, 2001), 3–4.
2. Michael Gardner, *Harry Truman and Civil Rights: Moral Courage and Political Risks* (Carbondale, IL: Southern Illinois University Press, 2002), 11–13.
3. Ibid., 6.
4. Ibid., 6–8.
5. "The Great War: A Nation Comes of Age," *PBS*, Public Broadcasting Service, Aired July 3, 2018, https://www.pbs.org/wgbh/americanexperience/films/great-war/.
6. Buckley, *American Patriots*, 337.
7. Ibid.
8. Ibid.
9. Gardner, *Harry Truman and Civil Rights: Moral Courage and Political Risks*, 132.
10. Ibid., 132–137.
11. Ibid., 18–20.
12. Elizabeth Chuck, "Lone Juror Says He Can't Convict Ex-Cop in Walter Scott Killing," *NBC News*, December 5, 2016, https://www.nbcnews.com/news/crime-courts/jury-says-it-s-deadlocked-trial-officer-who-shot-walter-n691291.
13. Kevin Johnson, "Michael Slager, Former South Carolina Cop Who Killed Walter Scott, Pleads Guilty on Civil Rights Charges," *USA Today*, Gannett Satellite Information Network, May 2, 2017, https://www.usatoday.com/story/news/2017/05/02/ex-sc-cop-plead-guilty-civil-rights-charges/101194668/.
14. Rawn James, Jr., *The Double V: How Wars, Protest, and Harry Truman Desegregated America's Military* (New York: Bloomsbury, 2013), 224.
15. Taylor Branch. *Parting the Waters: America in the King Years 1954–63* (New York: Simon & Schuster, 1988), 61.
16. President's Committee on Civil Rights, *To Secure These Rights: The Report of the President's Committee on Civil Rights*, Internet Archive, (New York: Simon and Schuster: 1947), https://archive.org/details/tosecuretheserig00unit.
17. Raymond Geselbracht, *The Civil Rights Legacy of Truman* (Kirksville, MO: Truman State University Press, 2007), 156–158.
18. James, *The Double V: How Wars, Protest, and Harry Truman Desegregated America's Military*, 225.
19. Geselbracht, *The Civil Rights Legacy of Truman*, 57.
20. Ibid., 156–158.
21. Harry S. Truman, "On the State of the Union," (speech, Washington, DC, January 6, 1947), History, Art & Archives: United States House of Representatives. National Archives, https://history.house.gov/Media?mediaID=15032450453.
22. Kenneth Hechler, *Working with Truman: A Personal Memoir of the White House Years* (Columbia, MO: University of Missouri Press, 1996), 72–80.
23. Gardner, *Harry Truman and Civil Rights: Moral Courage and Political Risks*, 100.
24. James, *The Double V: How Wars, Protest, and Harry Truman Desegregated America's Military*, 102.
25. Willliam C. Binning, Larry E. Esterly, Paul A. Sracic. *Encyclopedia of American Parties, Campaigns, and Elections* (Westport, CT: Greenwood Press, 1999), 57–60.
26. Geselbracht, *The Civil Rights Legacy of Truman*, 23.
27. Gardner, *Harry Truman and Civil Rights: Moral Courage and Political Risks*, 98.
28. Ibid., 99.
29. Ibid., 93.
30. Ibid., 93–94.

31. Hank Burchard, "Omar N. Bradley, 'GIs' General,' Is Dead at 88," *The Washington Post*, WP Company, April 9, 1981, https://www.washingtonpost.com/archive/local/1981/04/09/omar-n-bradley-gis-general-is-dead-at-88/7f187d1a-9867-4cf5-ba93-246f3cd45ad5/.

32. William A. Taylor, *Every Citizen a Soldier* (College Station, TX: Texas A&M University Press, 2014), 163.

33. Kenneth Hechler, "Military and Federal Services Integration 60th Anniversary," (speech, August 6, 2008), C-Span, National Cable Satellite Corporation, 2016, https://www.c-span.org/video/?280333-1/military-federal-services-integration-60th-anniversary.

34. James, *The Double V: How Wars, Protest, and Harry Truman Desegregated America's Military*, 239.

35. Gardner, *Harry Truman and Civil Rights: Moral Courage and Political Risks*, 115.

36. Richard M Dalfiume, "The Fahy Committee and Desegregation of the Armed Forces," *The Historian* 31, no. 1 (1968): 1–20, www.jstor.org/stable/24440952, 5–6.

37. "Desegregation of the Armed Forces," Harry S. Truman Library and Museum, National Archives, accessed July 7, 2014, https://www.trumanlibrary.gov/library/online-collections/desegregation-of-armed-forces.

38. Ibid.

39. Ibid.

40. Morris J. MacGregor. *Integration of the Armed Forces, 1940–1965* (Washington, DC: U.S. Government Printing Office, 1981), 17–45.

41. Jaime Fuller, "Four Presidents are converging on Texas to celebrate the 50th anniversary of the Civil Rights Act, " *Washington Post*, April 8, 2014, https://www.washingtonpost.com/news/the-fix/wp/2014/04/08/four-presidents-are-converging-on-texas-to-celebrate-the-50th-anniversary-of-the-civil-rights-act-heres-what-you-need-to-know/.

42. Jeff Nesbit, "America, Racial Bias Does Exist," *U.S. News and World Report*, January 13, 2015, https://www.usnews.com/news/blogs/at-the-edge/2015/01/13/america-racial-bias-does-exist.

43. Ryan Gabrielson, Eric Sagara, Ryann Grochoski Jones, "Deadly Force in Black and White," *ProPublica*, October 10, 2014, http://www.propublica.org/article/deadly-force-in-Black-and-white).

THREE
A Brief History of Diversity in America's Armed Forces

The American military has contributed as much to the notion of American exceptionalism as the leaders of American industry and artistry. Since its inception, the US military has established a proven record of winning America's wars—the standard by which all militaries are measured. When called upon to defend the nation or to do its bidding in combat or field of competition, the US military has been second to none. What is unique about the American military is that it has provided America with numerous examples of the merit of inclusiveness, albeit reluctantly or even serendipitously at times. The Department of Defense's policy regarding the use of black men for most of the 19th and early 20th centuries could best be described as an awkward attempt to balance the requirement to win America's wars with the desire to support the sociopolitical caste system that relegated black Americans to second-class citizenship. This caste system known as "Jim Crowism" was like an unspoken Civil War truce between northerners and southerners—'You can no longer have slaves, but we will leave you to "manage" the aftermath of the war in a manner that Southerners deem appropriate.' This largely silent agreement permeated the DoD as policy makers were afraid to challenge the status quo by giving black citizens more options and opportunities within the military than they had in broader civilian society. Such policy promulgated inequality in the private sector because private employers surely couldn't be asked to do what the federal government was unwilling to do: treat all Americans equally under the law.

Even when necessity forced marginalized groups into action, political opposition, in and out of uniform, undermined the significance of their accomplishments and even exhibited outright hatred at the sight of minorities in uniform. The mere presence of people of color wearing the nation's colors as decorated war heroes was a threat to the status quo. It is important to recognize these sacrifices appropriately and to humanize those who chose to serve despite facing the indignities of racism. We must honor the sacrifices they made to protect the freedoms of all Americans, including racists who actively denied them their own freedoms.

BLACKS IN THE REVOLUTIONARY WAR—TWISTED IRONY

During the Boston Massacre, a man named Crispus Attucks became the first recorded American to die in the American Revolution who was described as black or mulatto, having had an African father and a Wampanoag Indian mother.[1] On the eve of the American Revolution, roughly twenty percent of the twenty-two million colonials were of African descent. The initial US forces, militiamen organized and partially equipped

Figure 3.1. Cripus Attucks, first American killed in the American Revolution.
Source: Bridgewater State College Archive.

by the thirteen colonies, fought as racially integrated forces. Despite black volunteers having acquitted themselves during the French and Indian Wars in the 1750s and '60s, employing blacks in the revolution was controversial due to fear of large numbers of armed, trained black soldiers potentially instigating slave revolts.

In May 1775, the Committee of Safety of the Massachusetts legislature presented the following resolution: "that no slaves be admitted into this army upon any consideration whatever." However, black freed men were permitted to fight for the Continental Army as well as state militias. An estimated 9,000 black soldiers participated in the War with England on the side of the colonies.[2]

This controversy foreshadowed growing dissension between abolitionist northern states, especially New England, and the slave-laden Southern States where slave owners often used slaves as their proxies instead of serving themselves. Black freedmen, also known as black "minute men," fought at Lexington and Concord as early as April 1775. Law initially prohibited slaves from serving in the Continental Army based on the ethical precedent set by New Englanders that no man could be compelled to fight for a cause he did not believe in or could not benefit from. Such law also deferred to white southern fears of armed slave revolts. At its core, the belief in freedom was the cause of the American Revolution and the institution of slavery was inconsistent with the Declaration of Independence. Therefore, slaves were excluded from serving in the Continental Army.

The British were sensitive to the fact that slavery was becoming a divisive issue among the colonies and began to enlist black soldiers to serve and fight for the crown in exchange for their freedom. Suffering from his own manpower shortages, and desiring a swift end to the conflict, John Murray, Earl of Dunmore and Royal Governor of Virginia, issued a proclamation on November 7, 1775, which stated: ". . . and I do hereby further declare all indentured servants, Negroes, or others, (appertaining to rebels,) free, that are able and willing to bear arms, they joining His Majesty's Troops, as soon as may be, for the more speedily reducing the Colony to a proper sense of their duty, to His Majesty's crown and dignity." By December 1775, almost three hundred blacks, paying this price for freedom, with "Liberty to Slaves" inscribed on their uniforms, were members of Lord Dunmore's "Ethiopian Regiment."[3]

As the war raged and both sides were desperate for soldiers, early restrictions were largely ignored. Aside from whether to include blacks in defense of the colonies, no organizational distinction or segregation was made based on race. Black freedmen, and in some instances black slaves when directed by slave owners, fought alongside white Americans or instead of their slave owners. It wasn't until the American Civil War that the US military began to segregate units based on racial affiliation.

The issues of emancipation and military service were intertwined from the onset of the Civil War.

BLACKS IN THE CIVIL WAR: TURNING THE TIDE

"Once let the Black man get upon his person the brass letter, U.S., let him get an eagle on his button, and a musket on his shoulder and bullets in his pocket, there is no power on earth that can deny that he has earned the right to citizenship" (Frederick Douglass).[4]

Early in the Civil War, news from Fort Sumter set off a rush by free black men to enlist in Union military units. They were turned away, however, because of the federal Militia Act of 1792, which barred the descendants of Africans from being enlisted into the US Army in large numbers. Black Americans had served in the American Revolution and in the War of 1812 but on a smaller scale. In Boston, disappointed would-be volunteers met and passed a resolution requesting that the government modify its laws to permit their enlistment as state militia volunteers.[5]

The Lincoln Administration initially wrestled with the idea of authorizing the recruitment of black troops, concerned that such a move would prompt the border states to secede. By mid-1862, the escalating number of former slaves (contrabands), the declining number of white volunteers, and the increasingly pressing personnel needs of the Union Army pushed the government into reconsidering the ban.[6] On July 17, 1862, Congress passed the Second Confiscation and Militia Act, freeing slaves who had masters in the Confederate Army. Two days later, slavery was abolished in the territories of the United States, and on July 22nd President Lincoln presented the preliminary draft of the Emancipation Proclamation to his cabinet. After the Union Army turned back General Robert E. Lee's first invasion of the North at Antietam, MD, the Emancipation Proclamation was announced. By May 1863, the government established the Bureau of Colored Troops to manage the burgeoning numbers of black soldiers.[7]

The movie *Glory* depicts the exploits of the 54th Massachusetts Infantry Regiment, part of more than 179,000 black soldiers who served as state militia (10 percent of the Union Army). Another 19,000 black sailors served in the US Navy. Black soldiers were statutorily prohibited from serving in the Regular Army (federal forces) until 1866.[8] Nearly 40,000 black service members died over the course of the war, while another 30,000 died from infection or disease. Black soldiers served in artillery and infantry and performed all noncombat support functions that sustain an army. Black carpenters, blacksmiths, chaplains, cooks, guards, laborers, nurses, scouts, spies, steamboat pilots, surgeons, and teamsters also contributed to the war effort. There were nearly eighty black commissioned officers by the end of the war. Black women, who could not formally join the Army, nonetheless served as nurses, spies, and scouts—the most famous being Harriet Tubman who scouted for the 2nd South Carolina Volunteers.[9]

THE "BUFFALO SOLDIERS": ROUGH AND READY REGULARS!

Following the US Civil War, the Senate passed a bill establishing the regular army at sixty-seven regiments. Six were to be comprised of black troops with white officers. A further reorganization in 1869 reduced the six black regiments to four, the 9th and 10th Cavalry Regiments and the 24th and 25th Infantry Regiments. Their mission was to protect settlers moving west, suppress hostile Indian tribes, guard the mail, and protect railroad construction. In addition, they often had to build their own quarters and forts.

These black regiments were equipped with "broken down" horses rejected by white cavalry units, deteriorating equipment, and grossly inadequate rations. Despite the adversity, the morale in these units was high and they enjoyed the lowest desertion rate of all the Army units.[10] Life on the western frontier was harsh and monotonous. Boredom was a continual problem for all soldiers, but particularly for black soldiers because many towns refused their business. On paydays, there were few places to spend their money. Even if a town was near a black garrison, the townspeople generally refused service to blacks and heaped abuse upon them, even though the soldiers constituted the town's only defense. In 1881, after several years of conflict with the citizens of San Angelo, Texas, Buffalo Soldiers posted the following handbill in town: "We, the soldiers of the United States Army, do hereby warn cowboys, etc., of San Angelo and vicinity, to recognize our rights of way as just and peaceable men. If we do not receive just and fair play, which we must have, someone will suffer; if not the guilty, the innocent. It has gone too far; justice or death. U.S. Soldiers, one and all."[11]

In addition to a hostile climate and a hostile citizenry, black soldiers faced numerous Indian tribes who resented the encroachment of the "civilizing" influence from the East. In over one hundred battles, black soldiers clashed with Indian warriors. Their bravery earned them the moniker "Buffalo Soldiers" from the Indians. The US Government awarded 18 of the 416 Medals of Honor awarded for the "Indian Wars" to soldiers from black regiments.[12]

The first black American to receive the Medal of Honor during the Indian Campaigns was Sergeant Emanuel Stance, Company F, 9th Cavalry. Stationed at Fort McKavett, Texas, in 1870, Sergeant Stance and nine troopers commanded by Captain Henry Carroll left the fort on routine patrol. They were searching for Indians who had kidnapped two children during a raid. Approximately fourteen miles from the fort, they observed a party of Indians escorting nine horses. They attacked and engaged in a running fight for eight miles until the Indians broke contact, abandoning the animals. After camping overnight, the soldiers were taking the captured horses back to the fort when they encountered about twenty Indians who were stalking a herd of government horses and a small detachment of guards. Again, Stance and the men attacked. The Indians retreated, regrouped, and counterattacked. Stance and several men constituted the left flank of the Army column, outflanking the Indians who fled. Captain Carroll was full of praise for Sergeant Stance and recommended him for a medal, which he was awarded in June.[13]

WEST POINT FOLLIES: THE SILENT TREATMENT

Twenty black cadets were admitted to West Point between 1870 and 1899. Only three graduated: Henry O. Flipper in 1877; John H. Alexander graduated ten years later in 1887; and Charles Young in 1889. All black cadets faced some degree of hazing, harassment, and torment, as well as social isolation for their entire tenure at West Point. These men were gifted mentally and physically, and possessed a high degree of emotional intelligence to withstand the rigors they faced. The very first black cadet admitted to West Point, James W. Smith of South Carolina, reached his breaking point, struck back at his assailants, and was expelled. Three years after Flipper's graduation, Cadet Jonathon C. Whitaker was found tied to his bed with his ears "slashed" in his junior year. Whitaker was accused of inflicting the wounds himself and was dismissed from West Point under Court Martial proceedings. The case drew notoriety and President Chester A. Arthur was asked to review the case as Commander-in-Chief. President Arthur determined that the evidence was inconclusive and Cadet Whitaker's dismissal was upheld.[14]

CADET HENRY OSSIAN FLIPPER

In July 1877, 2nd Lieutenant Henry Ossian Flipper reported to Fort Sill, Oklahoma Territory for assignment to the 10th Cavalry Regiment. Since the 10th was no longer at Fort Sill—they were on maneuvers at Fort Concho, TX—2nd Lieutenant Flipper was assigned to what are known as "garrison duties" (appropriate for his rank and position) until his unit returned. He supervised work such as irrigation projections and the construction of roads and telegraph lines until he finally received orders to report to Fort Concho in October 1877 where he was assigned to A Troop. Henry was the first nonwhite officer to lead the Buffalo soldiers of the 10th Cavalry.[15]

As the commanding officer of A Troop, Captain Nicholas M. Nolan was responsible for continuing the development of young Flipper and

Figure 3.2. First Black West Point Graduate, 1877. *Photo courtesy of National Park Service*

the other lieutenants placed under his charge, teaching them the craft of being cavalry officers. Nolan was censured by several white officers for allowing Flipper into his quarters for dinner while his daughter Kate was present. Nolan defended his action by stating that Flipper was an "officer and a gentleman" just like any other officer present.[16]

After Captain Nolan married his second wife, Anne Eleanor Dwyer, Anne's sister, Miss Mollie Dwyer, arrived in Fort Elliott in Texas where A Troop was stationed in 1879. Mollie Dwyer and Flipper became friends and often went riding together. Nolan was the de facto commander of Fort Elliott, and he made Flipper his adjutant, giving him high marks. Many historians believe 2nd Lieutenant Flipper's relationship with Mollie Dwyer was the cause of professional backlash he encountered shortly thereafter.[17]

In late 1880, Flipper was transferred to Fort Davis in West Texas and assigned as the post quartermaster and commissary officer. Colonel William Rufus Shafter assumed command at Fort Davis in March 1881. Shafter had been the commander of the First Infantry Regiment at Fort Davis and had a reputation for harassing officers he disliked. While he tolerated Buffalo Soldiers, he did not endorse the use of black officers. Within days, Flipper was dismissed as quartermaster. Then, Shafter "asked" Flipper to keep the quartermaster's safe in his quarters. Being "asked" by a superior officer was a de facto order and Flipper complied. In July 1881, Flipper found a shortage of over $2,000. He realized Shafter's intent to force him out of the Army and knew Shafter could use this shortage of money against him. Flipper attempted to hide the discrepancy, but it was later discovered. Flipper lied about it when confronted, and eventually Shafter arrested him for embezzling government funds. Word quickly spread about the missing money. Many felt it was a setup, so soldiers and the community gathered enough money to replace what was missing within four days. Shafter accepted the money, but still convened a court martial on September 17, 1881.[18]

In December 1881, the court martial found Flipper innocent of embezzlement, but another charge was added during the trial. He was found guilty "of conduct unbecoming an officer and gentleman," and sentenced to be "dismissed from the service of the United States." It was more than a harsh sentence. In two prior situations involving white officers who were found guilty of embezzlement, neither officer was dismissed nor dishonored. The letters exchanged between Mollie Dwyer and Flipper were obtained and used against Flipper. Relationships between whites and blacks were strictly forbidden in the viewpoint of the white officers on the board. Flipper was drummed out of the Army on June 30, 1882, with a court martial dismissal—the officer equivalent of a dishonorable discharge. Appeals to the Army for a more appropriate sentence and an appeal to President Chester Arthur were denied. Flipper went on to have a successful career, carving out a niche as a bilingual engineer. He took mining, petroleum, and civil engineering jobs in the West, Mexico, and Venezuela. Nonetheless, Flipper spent the rest of his life contesting his dismissal from the Army.[19]

Henry O. Flipper's descendants applied to the Army Board for the Correction of Military Records on his behalf in 1976, and they eventually won a change to the characterization of his service from dishonorable to good conduct discharge. After reviewing the case, the board concluded that the conviction and punishment were "unduly harsh and unjust." A bust of Flipper was unveiled at West Point on May 3, 1977. Since then, an annual Henry O. Flipper Award has been granted to graduating cadets at the academy who exhibit "leadership, self-discipline, and perseverance in the face of unusual difficulties." On October 21, 1997, a private law firm, Arnold & Porter, secured a full pardon from President Bill Clinton on February 19, 1999.[20]

CADET JOHN H. ALEXANDER

John Hanks Alexander was the second black West Point graduate. He graduated thirty-second out of his class of sixty-four cadets in 1887.

Figure 3.3. Second Black West Point Graduate, 1887. *Photo courtesy of the National Park Service*

While Flipper was born into slavery, John Alexander was born January 6, 1864, to former slaves, James Milo Alexander and Fannie Miller Alexander. James was an astute entrepreneur who owned a successful barbershop in Helena, Arkansas. All seven of the Alexander children graduated from high school, and three attended Oberlin College in Ohio, including John H.[21]

At West Point, Alexander was generally accepted by the other cadets and he was not subjected to as much intolerance as previous cadets.

Alexander was known as an excellent student, particularly in math and languages. Strikingly handsome, he was also a skilled boxer. His official academic records described him as a "splendid scholar" who had "achieved an enviable record." Upon graduation, 2nd Lieutenant Alexander was assigned to the 9th US Cavalry and reported for duty on September 30, 1887. Eventually, Alexander was appointed as a commander in the 9th Cavalry, making him the first black officer to command soldiers in the regular Army. Command of soldiers is a high honor reserved for the most capable officers. The first US Army command is at the company or "troop" level, which is commanded by a captain or senior first lieutenant. The commander has the responsibility to train, equip, and protect those under his or her charge. Commanders at each level have legal responsibilities and authority over those under his or her command, and are responsible for the good order and discipline of the unit.[22]

Lieutenant Alexander held various other duties including garrison duties, fighting fires, escorting prisoners, supervising construction projects, and erecting telegraph lines. Alexander also served in court martial proceedings. He was detailed to Wilberforce University, Ohio—now considered a historically black college—where he took a position as Professor of Military Science on October 12, 1893. On March 26, 1894, he died suddenly of a heart aneurism while serving in that position. Many speculate about the ways he would have impacted the armed services given his charisma and ability to avoid some of the pitfalls that plagued his black contemporaries.

CADET CHARLES YOUNG

Charles Young was the third black Cadet to graduate from West Point, and the last of the black West Point graduates who was admitted during Reconstruction. After Young's graduation, the next black cadet would not graduate from West Point for another forty-seven years. Charles was born into slavery in 1864 to Gabriel Young and Arminta Bruen in Mays Lick, Kentucky. His father escaped from slavery early in 1865 and enlisted in the 5th Regiment of Colored Artillery (Heavy) near the end of the American Civil War. Gabriel's service earned the freedom of Arminta and Charles, and Gabriel saved enough money from his service to purchase land and buy a house in Ripley, OH. Charles Young attended the only high school in Ripley, which was otherwise all-white. He graduated in 1880 at the top of his class. He then taught school for several years in Ripley's new black high school.[23]

Young earned the second highest score in his district on a competitive examination for appointment as a cadet at West Point in 1883. Young failed an engineering class late in his career at West Point, but he passed the second time when he was tutored during the summer by George

Figure 3.4. Third Black West Point Graduate, 1889. *Photo courtesy of the National Park Service*

Washington Goethals—the same George Goethals who later became the lead engineer for the Panama Canal. Goethals was an assistant professor at West Point at the time and took an interest in Young. Cadet Young's strength was languages, and he learned to speak several.[24] After graduating in 1889, Young took his commission as a Second Lieutenant and reported to the 9th US Cavalry Regiment, in Fort Robinson, Nebraska. Second lieutenant Young had the most distinguished military career of the three black cadets who were commissioned from West Point, rising to the rank of full colonel. He was the first black officer to achieve this rank—only one rank below general.

Young had various assignments on the American western frontier while serving with the 9th Cavalry. He stayed with them until 1894 when he was reassigned to Wilberforce College as Professor of Military Science, replacing Captain Alexander. There, Young befriended W. E. B. Du Bois, and the two became close, life-long friends. Together, they were among the early leaders of the NAACP.[25] When the Spanish–American War broke out, Young was temporarily promoted to the rank of Major and reassigned to lead a group of black Ohio Volunteers on May 14, 1898. He commanded a battalion in the 9th Ohio Infantry Regiment, but the short war ended before Young and his men could be sent overseas. Young returned to his post at Wilberforce University on January 28, 1899, and reverted to his regular rank, first lieutenant. He was promoted to captain and sent back to the 9th Cavalry Regiment on February 2, 1901.

While commanding a troop in the 9th Cavalry, Young was appointed acting Superintendent of Sequoia and General Grant National Parks, making him the first black superintendent of a national park. Young's greatest impact on the park was managing road construction, which helped improve the underdeveloped park and allowed more visitors to enjoy it. Young's men accomplished more that summer than any other officers assigned to the park during the previous three summers. Captain Young's troops completed a wagon road to the Giant Forest, home of the world's largest trees, and a road to the base of the famous Moro Rock. By mid-August, wagons of visitors could enter the mountaintop forest for the first time. Young was reassigned as the troop commander of the 10th Cavalry at the Presidio of San Francisco on November 2, 1903. He recommended the government acquire privately held lands in Sequoia Park as a preserve for future generations in his final report. The report was provided to the Secretary of the Interior, and Young's recommendation was noted in legislation introduced in the House of Representatives.[26]

Young served in the Army's newly formed Military Intelligence Department in 1904, becoming one of the first military attachés. He served in Port-au-Prince, Haiti where he collected intelligence on different groups in Haiti who were trying to destabilize the Haitian Government. This is but one example of how the US military has used its ethnic diversity as a strategic advantage in a multicultural, geopolitical environment.

Had Captain Young been statutorily prohibited from attending West Point and unable to complete the training he received as an officer, his efforts in this important role would have been improbable. These same principles—leveraging ethnic diversity to achieve a strategic advantage—can be applied across multiple geopolitical fronts in today's Global War on Terrorism.

Young spent time representing American interests in the Philippines and Liberia, where he became the first African American military attaché assigned to Liberia. For three years, he served as an expert adviser to the Liberian government and took a direct role in supervising construction of the country's infrastructure. The NAACP awarded Young the Spingarn Medal in 1916 for his military contributions.[27] Young published *The Military Morale of Nations and Races* in 1912, a study of the cultural sources of military power. Though Colonel Young achieved a very successful military career, like his black West Point predecessors, his thirty-three years of uniformed military service were inhibited by bias and prejudice.

BLACKS IN THE SPANISH–AMERICAN WAR

The 9th and 10th Calvary Regiments also fought with distinction in the Spanish – American War, as did the 24th and 25th Infantry Regiments. On February 15, 1898, over 266 American sailors were killed when the battleship *Maine* blew up and sank in Havana harbor; 250 of them were black sailors serving as stevedores. The war with Spain began in April 1898 when Major General William Shafter, a former commander of the 24th Infantry, led an expeditionary force of over 17,000 men, including nearly 3,000 black regulars, into Cuba.[28]

Although the Spanish–American War was ostensibly fought to liberate Caribbean and Philippine islanders from Spanish oppression, the participation of African American troops was very controversial within their own community. Black Americans were dissatisfied with the lack of progress made towards granting them their full Constitutional rights. Some black civic leaders urged blacks to boycott the war to protest lynchings, segregation, inferior education, and relegation to second-hand citizenry, while other black Americans believed the war presented an opportunity to prove their mettle in battle and therefore advance the cause for equal rights under the rule of law.

All four black regiments were reassigned to the southeastern United States for the first time in their history.[29] In preparation for the Cuban invasion, these units were billeted near Tampa, Florida, where overt racial discrimination was the norm. Local white citizens made no distinction between colored troops and colored civilians, and tolerated no infractions of local, discriminatory laws or customs. Despite this prejudice, the troops of the 9th and 10th Cavalry, and the 24th and 25th Infantry served with distinction on the battlefields of Las Guasimas, El Caney, and San Juan Hill.

Led by white officers, the 9th and 10th Cavalry and 24th and 25th Infantry were perhaps the most integrated battle forces of the nineteenth century. The troops of the 24th Infantry and the 9th and 10th Cavalry fought in the successful charge up San Juan Hill along with white regular Army regiments and volunteer units, including Teddy Roosevelt's 1st Cavalry volunteers, the Rough Riders. Roosevelt commented ". . . no one can tell whether it was the Rough Riders or the men of the 9th who came forward with the greater courage to offer their lives in the service of their country." Despite this praise, Roosevelt later wrote: "Negro troops were shirkers in their duties and would only go as far as they were led by white officers." One would expect the Buffalo Soldiers to be a superior, battle-tested force, having come from the western frontier where they fought Native Americans, and having gained experienced in other military operations. Their officers were West Point trained—the finest training the US military had at the time. It is unclear whether Roosevelt's later comments were political assertions pandering to voters by preserving notions of the status quo, or if they represented his true feelings about what happened during the battle of El Caney and the charge up San Juan Hill. Yet, the 25th Infantry is credited with playing a significant role in saving the Rough Riders from significant casualties and possible mission failure.[30]

One of the officers of the 10th Cavalry who would go onto great distinction, then Lieutenant John Pershing, commented following the battle of San Juan Hill that, "They [Buffalo Soldiers] fought their way into the hearts of the American people."[31] Twenty-Six Buffalo Soldiers died that day, and several men were officially recognized for their bravery, including five Medal of Honor winners. Quarter Master Sergeant Edward L. Baker, Jr., 10th Cavalry emerged from the battle wounded by shrapnel and was awarded the Medal of Honor for his heroism. Following the war, the Buffalo Soldiers returned to their posts in the US western states and territories where some would later become among the first US Park Rangers. Over 450 Buffalo Soldiers are buried at the Presidio of San Francisco. It is also noteworthy that when Truman integrated the US Government through Executive Order 9981, the Department of the Interior, to which the National Park Service and Park Rangers belong, was the only department that was already integrated.

AMERICA'S EMERGENT GLOBAL FORCE AND THE DELICATE BALANCING ACT

In 1910, the US military concluded an unprecedented modernization effort that began in the 1880s, replacing old wooden ships with steel battleships.[32] Secretary of War Elihu Root led the Army's reorganization efforts. He transformed the Army to resemble more advanced European-style armies with general staffs capable of the detailed planning needed for large scale combat operations. These two burgeoning institutions [the Army and Navy] combined to accomplish a feat of which no other nation in the world had been capable: the construction of the Panama Canal. The French attempted the engineering marvel in 1884 but failed primarily because of the effects of Yellow Fever on their work force. To complete the canal, the Theodore Roosevelt Administration relied on military lessons that Major Walter Reed and Colonel William C. Gorgas learned during the Spanish–American War about minimizing the effects of Yellow Fever on troops.

West Point trained engineer George W. Goethals, was appointed as the Lead Engineer of the Panama Canal construction project in 1907 and saw the project through to its completion in 1914.[33] Despite the advances the American military demonstrated in its war-fighting and civil engineering exploits, its policies pertaining to non-white personnel were still that of the 18th century; blacks were precluded from serving in any naval positions other than mess-men, and the Army restricted black enlistment to ten percent of the total force. Black soldiers were not permitted to be commissioned as officers unless they graduated from the US Military Academy at West Point—a concession made during the turbulent Reconstruction Era following the Civil War.

PRE-WORLD WAR I YEARS

From 1910–1919, the US Army was involved in a border war with Mexico that spun off from the Mexican Revolution. Mexico's bloody civil war killed hundreds of thousands of noncombatants and displaced several thousands of US and Mexican citizens. President Woodrow Wilson sent US forces to occupy the Mexican city of Veracruz for six months in 1914. The move demonstrated to the Mexican government that the US was keenly interested in matters affecting its interests and would not tolerate attacks on Americans, such as the "Tampico Affair," in which members of Mexican President Victoriano Huerta's regime arrested American sailors on April 19, 1914.[34] In early 1916, Mexican General Pancho Villa ordered 500 soldiers to conduct a murderous raid in Columbus, New Mexico, robbing banks to fund his army. The German Secret Service encouraged Villa, attempting to involve the US in an intervention in Mexico. They hoped the intervention would distract the US from Germany's growing involvement in the Great War and lead the US to divert aid from Europe to support an American intervention in Mexico. President Wilson sent state militias (National Guard) and the US Army under General John J. Pershing's command to punish Villa in the Pancho Villa Expedition. During the pursuit of Villa, Major Charles Young led 2nd Squadron, 10th Cavalry Regiment on a successful pistol charge at Agua Caliente on April 1, 1916, and thoroughly routed Villa's forces without losing a single soldier. Villa fled deep into Mexico with the Americans in pursuit. By early 1917, President Venustiano Carranza had contained Villa and secured the border. Wilson ordered Pershing to withdraw.[35]

Colonel Young stood a good chance of being promoted to brigadier general. However, there was widespread resistance among white officers, especially those from the South, who did not want to be outranked by and have to report to a black officer. Once, while serving as Squadron Commander, a white lieutenant who served under Young complained to the War Department. Secretary of War Newton Baker replied that the lieutenant should "either do his duty or resign." John Sharp Williams, a Mississippi US Senator, complained to President Woodrow Wilson on the lieutenant's behalf. Wilson overruled Baker's decision and had the lieutenant transferred.

Based on the precedent of reassigning the first white officers who complained about having to report to a black superior officer, other white officers in the 10th Cavalry were encouraged to apply for transfers as well. It is well established that Wilson was a staunch segregationist. In 1913, Wilson established segregated federal offices and other discriminatory federal policies. During his first term in office, the House passed a law making interracial marriage a felony in the District of Columbia. Wilson's new Postmaster General also ordered that his Washington offices be segregated, with the Treasury and Navy soon to follow. Going forward, photographs were required of all applicants for federal jobs, and for the first time racial segregation in public accommodations became the norm in our nation's capital—a practice that proved to be an embarrassment for every administration with foreign dignitaries until the Supreme Court struck it down in 1954. The Wilson administration's willingness to apply Jim Crowism to military policy created a dilemma. Because white officers were the only ones assigned to all-black regiments, it meant that black officers could not rise to a rank higher than full colonel—the rank at which a regiment is commanded—without placing them in charge of significant numbers of white officers.

This period following America's "Reconstruction" from the Civil War was a mixed bag. Black citizens could vote, and in several cases black congressmen were elected to Congress. Just as figures like Young were making extraordinary strides for themselves, their country, and the advancement of black Americans, Southerners—who were returning to West Point for the first time since the Civil War—openly challenged America's turn toward a more inclusive society.

In the Army, there was only one black Infantry Regiment (9th Infantry) and one black Cavalry Regiment (10th Cavalry); the Navy had no black officers or sailors filling combat roles, and there were no black Marines. Midway through the first decade of the twentieth century, Antebellum law was still driving the personnel policy of the armed forces. The military is a subset of the larger American populous, and although it has led advancements in equal treatment, the attitudes and opinions of its collective are largely a reflection of the attitudes and opinions of all segments of the broader society—a theme that persists in today's all volunteer force.

PRE-CURSORS TO WORLD WAR I

Leading up to America's participation in World War I, most Americans could trace their lineage to some European nation, all of which had a stake in the outcome of the war. In hindsight, America's eventual involvement in World War I appeared to be inevitable: German submarine activity in the Atlantic, Germany's increased involvement with Mexico, and brewing hostilities between the US and Mexico were all indicators. On the outset of the war, thousands of German American citizens left the US to join or attempt to join the German Army.

Yet many more German American citizens remained in the US and were committed to American values that opposed the German army's efforts. Nonetheless, anti-German sentiment arose among Americans, similar to anti-Islamic views that reached a fever pitch in 2015 following ISIS inspired terror attacks around the world. Unlike President Trump, President Wilson issued a statement drawing distinctions among German citizens, American Citizens of German ancestry, and the German Imperial Government. President Woodrow Wilson's response to Germany's unrestricted warfare against American vessels carefully identified the German Imperial Government as the appropriate target for the US response. Wilson also called for legislation criminalizing sympathizers or outright supporters of Germany and German allied causes.

In his 1915 State of the Union address, Wilson asked Congress for legislation criminalizing certain forms of opposition to the war:[36]

> There are citizens of the United States, I blush to admit, born under other flags but welcomed under our generous naturalization laws to the full freedom and opportunity of America, who have poured the poison of disloyalty into the very arteries of our national life; who have sought to bring the authority and good name of our Government into contempt, to destroy our industries wherever they thought it effective for their vindictive purposes to strike at them, and to debase our politics to the uses of foreign intrigue....
>
> I urge you to enact such laws at the earliest possible moment and feel that in doing so I am urging you to do nothing less than save the honor and self-respect of the nation. Such creatures of passion, disloyalty, and anarchy must be crushed out. They are not many, but they are infinitely malignant, and the hand of our power should close over them at once. They have formed plots to destroy property, they have entered conspiracies against the neutrality of the Government, and they have sought to pry into every confidential transaction of the Government to serve interests alien to our own. It is possible to deal with these things very effectually. I need not suggest the terms in which they may be dealt with.[37]

The prevailing public opinion was for the US to remain neutral, but Germany announced it would commence unfettered torpedoing of merchant ships believed to be carrying supplies to support Great Britain and France. The Germans followed through on their threat by sinking seven American vessels, at which point America could no longer remain neutral and declared war on Germany on April 6, 1917. Though Wilson did not vilify German Americans, he was aware of the vulnerability to German espionage posed by large populations of recent German and Italian immigrants. Wilson lobbied Congress for federal laws to deter espionage.

At Wilson's behest, congress passed both the Espionage Act of 1917 and the Sedition Act of 1918. The latter covered a broader range of offenses, notably speech and the expression of opinion that cast the government or the war effort in a negative light or interfered with the sale of government bonds.[38] Ironically, black Americans were perhaps the only segment of Americans with no European allegiance and no suspicion of dual allegiance to America or one of the warring European factions. This irony wasn't lost on black Americans, and many demonstrated their patriotism by reaffirmed pledges of allegiance to the United States. Black civic leaders called for black Americans to hang the American Flag on their front porches.³⁹

The German Imperial Government was not blind to the paradox facing black Americans, and launched its own propaganda campaign to diminish black American's support for the war:

> To the Colored Soldiers of the U.S. Army,
> Hello boys, what are you doing over there? Fighting the Germans? Why? Have they ever done you any harm? Do you enjoy the same rights as the white people do in America, the land of freedom and democracy? Or aren't you rather rated over there as second class citizens? Can you go to a restaurant where white people dine; can you get a seat in a theatre where white people sit? And how about the law? Is lynching and the most horrible cruelties connected there with a lawful proceeding in a democratic country?
>
> No all of this is entirely different in Germany, where they do like colored people, where they do treat them as gentlemen and not as second class citizens. . . . To carry the gun in [America's] defense is not an honor but a shame. Throw it away and come over to the German lines. You will find friends who will help you along.⁴⁰

On the one hand, black Americans were subject to state-sanctioned subordination and second-class citizenship: not allowed to enter the front door of establishments such as restaurants or theaters, and in the south, blacks were statutorily prohibited from voting. On the other hand, black Americans were one of the few components of the melting pot that had no genealogical allegiance to any European nation. Despite the potential benefits of welcoming their unique perspective, they still were not embraced in America's effort to build a modern fighting force. This lack of inclusivity was largely due to Southern elected officials fearing being indebted to the service and sacrifice of black service members and feeling compelled to grant them full citizenry. Knowing this indebtedness was an unacceptable outcome, Southerners also feared the discipline and worldliness gained from bearing arms in combat, which they feared black service members would bring to bear on the US caste system.

German spies infiltrated the South, imploring black Americans to sabotage the war effort and "raise up" against the perpetrators of lynchings and state-sponsored oppression once enough white men shipped off for war. In response to these stories and rumors, black pastors, civic leaders, and other intellectuals held church and school rallies in support of black men fighting for democracy alongside white soldiers in the Great War. Although not in a state of declared war, the US was providing an enormous amount of war supplies to Great Britain and France daily. The 1915 sinking of the *Lusitania* by German submarines almost assured the US would eventually enter the war on the side of France and England, and sparked a national debate about the size and role of America's military, as well as the role ethnic minorities should play in the war effort.

Prior to America's entry into World War I, the United States' standing army consisted of 100,000 soldiers. Even augmented by 112,000 National Guardsman, the American army was still outnumbered by the German army twenty to one. Fortunately, the US was able to delay its entry into World War I until the slow-moving democratic process and public opinion shifted towards establishing a larger army. War had been raging in Europe for almost four years before the US declared war on Germany on April 6, 1917. British and French allies were in desperate need of manpower as both had lost millions preceding America's involvement in the war. British and French leaders wanted America to join in the fighting under their leadership. American Armed Expeditionary Forces Commander General John Pershing urged Secretary of War Baker and President Wilson to reject this arrangement and convinced the administration to allow the War Department time to build a credible army. To that end, the first national draft was instituted through the Selective Service Act of 1917.[41]

Although white supremacist politicians such as Sen. James K. Vardaman (D-Mississippi) and Sen. Benjamin Tillman (D-South Carolina) staunchly opposed the military training of blacks, African Americans were included in the 1917 draft. Their inclusion had two benefits: it ensured the military could draft enough able-bodied men to fight, and it ameliorated political pressure from black community leaders. Ultimately, a total of 290,527 black Americans registered for the draft during the three calls of June 5, 1917, June 15, 1918, and September 12, 1918, comprising 9.6 percent of the total American pool for potential conscription. Draft board officials were instructed to tear off the lower left-hand corner of the Selective Service forms filled out by black registrants to tag them for segregated units.[42]

Two camps developed on the type of military force the US should develop: the Preparedness Movement, and the Small Standing Army Supporters. The Preparedness Movement—espoused by Northeast Republicans such as Theodore Roosevelt, Elihu Root, and Henry Stimson—maintained that economic strength and military muscle were more decisive foreign policy than idealistic crusades to spread democracy. They called upon prominent families from the banking, steel, and coal industries to ally with them.

Democrats were suspicious of the motivations behind growing America's military and saw the Preparedness Movement as a thinly veiled excuse to line their own pockets. Instead, the Democrats preferred a military that relied upon a large National Guard force that could be quickly mobilized, and an industrial complex that could turn out war machinery in the event of major global war. The result was compromise legislation passed in May of 1916 that doubled the size of the army's officer corps to 11,300 and grew the army to 208,000 men. The National Guard grew to 440,000 men and $3.5 million was spent on naval aviation. Germany did not take these measures seriously; discounting the influence of America's potential involvement in the Great War, they resumed full scale torpedo warfare of civilian vessels in January of 1917.[43]

BLACKS IN WWI, BUT FIRST YOU HAVE TO PICK THE COTTON!

Mob violence directed against b lack Americans had become an extension of the formal criminal justice system in the deep south and in many of the border states. From 1914 to 1916, white mobs lynched 126 black Americans. Black Americans fled to cities in the North, Midwest, and West to escape the brutal oppression and hatred for their mere existence. This flight was not only from oppression but toward hope for a better future, better jobs, education, and better housing for their children. This exodus began in 1910 and continued until well after World War II, demarcated by most social scientists as ending in 1970. However, if you carefully examine the micro-dynamics of the migration, you can further separate that Great Migration into two separate movements: the first from 1910 to 1930, and the second from around 1946 to 1970.[44]

The Great Migration was shaped by a flight from rampant lawlessness perpetrated against black Americans in the form of lynchings, beatings, disenfranchisement, substandard housing, inferior education, and virtually no protection of rights under the rule of law. Sharecropping included and perpetuated many such injustices, and became pervasive throughout the former slave states. At best, it was an opportunity for former slaves to rent 'shares' of land to work from their former slave owners. In exchange for use of the land, the landowner would get a share of the crops raised on it or a share of the revenue from the sale of those crops. The sharecropper could then use any earnings to buy the land outright.

At its worst, sharecropping was an exploitive extension of slavery or indentured servitude. Former Confederate state legislatures passed laws or "black codes" that forced former slaves to sign sharecropper labor contracts or be jailed for vagrancy. Labor contracts between the landowner and the sharecropper were frequently one-sided. The contract could be structured in a way that was virtually impossible for the sharecropper to generate enough revenue to pay for the land rental, use of tools, routine health care, seed, fertilizer, and other farming needs. The sharecropper always ended up on the short end of the balance sheet, and was forced to re-enter another contract, hoping for better luck the following year.[45]

Booming industrialization and the consequent economic growth added to the impetus for black Americans to migrate north. WWI also slowed a large amount of non-Irish, European immigration, which created job opportunities for black Americans. The US immigration policy prohibited new Italian, German, and Austrian immigrants from coming to America because the US was at war with these Axis powers. Expanding factory production to support the US and allied war effort, combined with fewer white immigrants to work these jobs, opened even more job opportunities for black Americans and provided greater incentive to move near Northern and Midwestern factories. All told, 1.6 of the 6 million black Americans who migrated to the North, Midwest, and West did so within the first ten years of the sixty-year migration. The demographics of the nation shifted from ninety-one percent of black Americans residing within fourteen Southern States, to only fifty-three percent of black Americans residing in those same states.[46] The black labor force was still so vital to the Southern economy that fifty years after the Civil War, Southern politicians had to lobby the Army to delay the training of the black draftees from Southern States until after completion of the 1917 cotton harvest. The Army acquiesced and those men didn't report to Camp Upton, SC, until November 1917, and shipped out to France on April 23, 1918.[47]

THE BLACK MILITARY EXPERIENCE IN WORLD WAR I

America entered World War I with firmly entrenched policies that excluded minorities from combat roles. The original rationale for limited use of blacks as combatants provided when the US was founded, was fear of large numbers of armed black servicemen inciting or carrying out slave rebellions. Nearly fifty years after the Civil War had ended, such policies were obsolete. Yet, those policies remained in place because they were essential to the preservation of the unwritten truce. The incoherent "logic of Southern racism" maintained that black men were prone to violence, dangerous, and therefore in need of suppression, yet at the same time cowardly and probably ineffectual in combat. Both contradictory arguments were used to justify the complete exclusion of black men from US military policy.[48] These excuses persisted across all armed services and affected everything from personnel policy to individual citations for bravery until well after the passage of EO 9981.

Today, there is a proclivity to view black men as violent. Sadly, some law enforcement officials even use this to justify confrontations and assaults against unarmed black citizens—a well-documented phenomenon in American history.

With the United States about to enter WWI, the War Department was faced with a curious dilemma. On the one hand, it needed large numbers of able-bodied men to engage in the modern warfare being waged in Europe. Therefore, it could not afford the political luxury of excluding black soldiers from the war effort as the number of black conscripts outnumbered that of white draftees in some Southern States.

Table 3.1 missing

The War Department carefully navigated this precarious situation (balancing of social norms vs the need for manpower) by subscribing black draftees almost exclusively to labor battalions that did the work of off-loading ships, digging trenches and fighting positions, shoeing horses, cooking, laundry, and burying the dead. Only two black combat divisions were formed from the 290,000 plus black draftees.

Despite having served as an officer in the 10th Cavalry Regiment, General John Pershing, Commander of the Army Expeditionary Force (AEF) did not want to use black units in combat operations. General Pershing's nickname "Black Jack" is said to have come from his time as a West Point Instructor where cadets jokingly referred to him (behind his back) as "Nigger Jack" for serving in the Buffalo Soldier unit.[49] Over time, the moniker softened to "Black Jack." The 9th and 10th Cavalry Regiments and 24th and 25th Infantry Regiments remained on the Western borders during World War I while General Pershing built a larger US force through the draft. America declared war on Germany and Austria in April 1917. The US instituted a draft with the passage of the Selective Service Act of 1917, which netted ten million registrants between the ages of 21–31. The first draft was deemed inadequate. The conscription age range was then extended to ages 18–45, resulting in twenty-four million additional registrants, 2.2 million of whom (13 percent black and 86.9 percent white) were inducted into service.[50]

Because the US was unwilling to put American fighting forces under foreign command, all black units were offered as a concession to Great Britain and France, and in response to political pressure from black civic leaders. Despite their need for manpower, Great Britain declined the use of black soldiers while the French accepted. World War I was the deadliest war in French history, at the height of which, the French army numbered more than eight million men. During the war, around one million French soldiers were killed, and the French army was plagued by desertion.[51]

Black leaders and activists resisted the administration's exclusionary policies as they had in the Spanish–American War and the US Civil War. Such policies were largely matters of political expediency that inhibited the military's ability to wage successful campaigns against its adversaries. Booker T. Washington, W. E. B. Dubois, and numerous other church and civil leaders vociferously opposed black Americans' involvement in the war if black soldiers were given exclusively non-combat roles and no leadership opportunities. As a concession to vocal black opposition and in acknowledgement of the large numbers of soldiers who would be required to tip the scales against Germany and its allies, Secretary of War Newton D. Baker authorized the creation of two black infantry divisions. Black civic leaders wanted Colonel Young to be placed in charge of one of the divisions and promoted to Brigadier General. Yet Baker disagreed and instead accepted Emmett J. Scott as his "Special Adviser on Black

Affairs." This made Scott—who had previously served as Booker T. Washington's Administrative Assistant at Tuskegee Institute—the highest ranking black in Wilson's administration.[52]

Black training units were assembled from the existing "Buffalo Soldier" regiments, and the Army designated a base at Fort Des Moines, Iowa to receive the trainees. Prominent black leaders wanted the training to be conducted at Howard University in Washington, DC, but the War Department did not want the media distraction that would ensue in a major east coast city. The black community, led by Randolph and W. E. B. Du Bois, continued to resist discrimination, threatening to lobby against black volunteerism if blacks weren't allowed into combat roles and commissioned to lead all-black units. The 92nd and 93rd Infantry Divisions were organized to receive black draftees, and the remaining draftees would be assigned to various non-combat roles.

Baker considered sending Colonel Young to Fort Des Moines. However, Baker realized that if Young was allowed to train these units, Baker would be pressured to allow Young to lead them into battle in Europe. That decision would make Young eligible for promotion to brigadier general, and it would be impossible not to have white officers serving under him. The War Department instead removed Young from active duty, claiming it was due to his high blood pressure. Young was placed temporarily on the inactive list (with the rank of colonel) on June 22, 1917.[53]

In May 1917, Young appealed to Theodore Roosevelt for support of his application for reinstatement. Roosevelt was then campaigning to form a volunteer division for early service to France in World War I. Roosevelt appears to have planned to recruit at least one and perhaps two black regiments for the division, something he had not told President Wilson or Secretary of War Baker. He immediately offered Young command of one of the prospective regiments, writing, "there is not another man who would be better fitted to command such a regiment."[54] Roosevelt also promised Young "carte blanche" in appointing staff and line officers for the unit. However, Wilson refused Roosevelt permission to organize his volunteer division. Young returned to Wilberforce University where he was a professor of military science during most of 1918. On November 6, 1918, after he had traveled by horseback from Wilberforce, Ohio, to Washington, DC, to prove his physical fitness, he was reinstated on active duty as a colonel, although Baker did not rescind his order that Young be forcibly retired. Young was allowed to complete his assignment at Wilberforce but was not a candidate to serve in the war with his pending retirement.[55]

In 1919, Young was reassigned as military attaché to Liberia. Young died January 8, 1922 of a kidney infection while on a reconnaissance mission in Nigeria. His body was returned to the United States where he was given a full military funeral and buried at Arlington National Cemetery. Young had become a respected public figure because of his unique achievements in the Army, almost like an earlier version of General Colin Powell. His obituary was carried in the *New York Times*.

RIOTING IN TEXAS

A clash between armed civilians and black soldiers training outside of Houston, dubbed the "Houston Mutiny and Riot," undoubtedly shaped the War Department's decision regarding the number of black combatants permitted to fight for the United States. Accusations of police brutality and dogged imposition of Jim Crow laws upon black soldiers—many of whom were from the North and not accustomed to blatant segregation—precipitated the rebellion. On August 23, 1917, roughly one hundred members of 3rd Battalion 24th Infantry Division, Camp Logan, Texas marched into Houston, killed fifteen citizens, and wounded another twelve in only two hours. Reports of a black mother of five, Sarah Travers, being dragged down the street and arrested after complaining of police brutality sparked the riot. Private Alonzo Edwards witnessed the incident and offered to take Travers in his custody. He was pistol whipped by the arresting officer, Lee Sparks, and arrested himself. Sparks had a reputation for being especially violent to black soldiers and citizens alike. Word of the incident got back to the base and Corporal Charles Baltimore, a black soldier, left the base camp to try and win Edwards' release. Baltimore met the same fate as Edwards and the impetus for the riot was underway.[56]

The rumors reached a fever pitch; many soldiers believed Corporal Baltimore had been lynched. The commanding officer attempted to calm the troops, but as a precaution he ordered that all weapons be turned in. Corporal Baltimore was released that afternoon, but this did little to assuage the soldiers who by now felt as if their dignity and that of other blacks in the community had been spat upon. That evening, the approximately one hundred wayward soldiers from the 24th, most of whom were recent draftees, reclaimed their weapons and marched into town in formation, targeting police officers and innocent bystanders alike. A junior NCO, who had been promoted to lead the newly forming 92nd division, led the charge. When the dust settled, the Army immediately moved the 24th Infantry Division to Columbus, New Mexico, to complete their training.

During the court martial trials that followed, thirteen mutineers were executed, and dozens of other soldiers were sentenced to long prison terms even though many of them were completely innocent. A media firestorm resulted. In the black community, civic leaders covering the mutiny, such as W. E. B. Dubois and editors of black newspapers like the *Baltimore Sun*, deliberately avoided espousing lawlessness like the lynchings they railed against regularly. Yet, they also did not dismiss the dehumanizing treatment of the black soldiers that instigated the hostilities.

One of the more famous editorials on the riots was in the *San Antonio Inquirer*. Sara Threadgill-Dennis, a Texas school teacher, wrote about a soldier of the 24th Infantry who rose to protect the honor of a black woman who was attacked by a white police officer. She wrote, "rest assured every [Negro] woman in the land reveres you and honors you."[57] After expressing her regret that the soldiers mutinied, she went on to state, "It is far better that you be shot for having tried to protect a Negro woman, then to have died a natural death in the trenches of Europe, fighting to make the world safe for democracy that you can't enjoy."[58] G. W. Bouldin, the editor of that article, was then convicted of violating the Espionage Act and sentenced to two years in prison at Fort Leavenworth Federal Penitentiary.[59] Ironically, Congress had passed the Espionage Act in 1917 to prevent German and Italian Americans from undermining the US war effort by voicing disapproval for the draft or expressing support for the Germans or Italians. In Bouldin's case, the act was being used to punish him for publishing an editorial that supported the defense of black womanhood.

Southern politicians used the Houston riots as rationale not to train large numbers of black Americans for war. Plans to establish sixteen black combat regiments were immediately abandoned in the wake of the Houston Mutiny and only half that number were formed.[60] The 93rd Division was hastily comprised of existing National Guard units and reorganized into four regiments. The 369th, 370th, 371st, and 372nd Infantry Regiments shipped to France in December 1917. Initially, the 93rd worked as labor units, unloading ships, providing port security, and digging trenches, while being trained for trench warfare. The 369th Infantry Regimental Commander, Colonel Heyward, characterized the 93rd Division's early entry into the war as General Pershing leaving a black orphaned infant on France's doorstep. General Pershing sent a secret communique for the French, detailed care instructions, cautioning them not to treat the black troops as equals, that "the vices of the Negro are a constant menace to the American who has to repress them sternly."[61] The French ignored this admonishment, but it illustrates the degree of commitment US institutions had for preserving the status quo following WWI.[62]

The Houston Mutiny also influenced the War Department's decision to relegate the majority of black soldiers to the building of roads, unloading of shipping, and other forms of common labor. Blacks were entirely excluded from the US Marine Corps and consigned to menial labor in the U S Navy for the duration of the war.[63]

Public opinion within the black community was that war provided an opportunity for black Americans to demonstrate their patriotism and mettle in battle. Many believed that these achievements could be leveraged to secure equal rights at home, and to reshape the hearts and minds of Americans who wished to preserve Jim Crowism and the oppression of blacks.

The state of New York grew its National Guard by reorganizing its forces. On June 29, 1916, the 15th Infantry Regiment was reformed into the 369th Infantry Regiment (Colored) following the model used in the Civil War to create fighting units for black soldiers. The 369th was called onto active-federal service on July 25, 1917. They guarded rail lines and ports until they were shipped to Spartanburg, South Carolina, on October 8, 1917 to train for fighting overseas in the Great War. Once again, training all-black forces in the Deep South caused friction. Contrasting cultures and differing societal norms set the stage for tensions between Southerners working on the bases and black soldiers from the New York National Guard who were accustomed to integrated schools and not to the stifling racial oppression common in the south. This contrast of cultures made for a volatile combination, and demoralized the former fighting 15th.

Their commander secured orders for the 369th to ship to France along with the other black infantry regiments that comprised the 93rd Division in December 1917. These National Guardsmen were among the first Americans to fight in World War I as a regimental sized unit in a French Division.[64] Several factors made the 93rd Division ripe for early deployment to Europe. These factors included pressure from the black community to create black combat divisions, England and France's demand for manpower, and General Pershing's unwillingness to provide American forces piece-meal. The 369th spent more consecutive days in combat than any other US combat unit in WWI. The Main Armed Expeditionary Forces arrived in July 1918, and most combat units didn't fight until October 1918, ten months after the 93rd Division arrived in France.

Prior to March 1918, there were not enough ships to simultaneously move combat supplies and import American manpower, which thwarted efforts to build the American Expeditionary Force presence on European battlefields. British and French leaders wanted American material first to shore up their forces already engaged in combat. Europeans also didn't trust that American officers were seasoned in what was, at the time, modern warfare, so they preferred American Troops minus the American military leadership. As a result of these strategic stalemates, the US offered the 93rd to the British and French, though only the French accepted.[65] Great Britain refused to have black men fighting as combatants in their Army. From March through May 1918, there were only 183,000 American troops in Europe, including seven combat divisions, one of which was the 93rd Infantry Division. By June 1918, there were over 900,000 American troops in Europe with 10,000 arriving daily in France. Twenty-three combat divisions were organized from these 900,000

American soldiers, but only seven of them had seen actual combat over the previous three months—the 93rd Division was one of them.[66]

THE 93RD INFANTRY DIVISION

The troops of the 93rd never fought together as a division; its brigades were broken up and the regiments were brigaded with French Army divisions. In fact, the 93rd was treated completely different from any other US AEF unit until they had firmly established a stellar combat record. They did not return to US command and control until after the armistice.

The 93rd was issued French equipment and arms but wore US uniforms. Their "blue hat" nickname was derived from the blue French Casque Adrian helmets they wore. Each regiment remained brigaded with French forces for three periods: July 1–21, 1918; August 1, 1918; and October 24, 1918 to the armistice on November 11, 1918. The 93rd Infantry was comprised of four regiments (369th, 370th, 371st, and 372nd) organized into two brigades, and the largest unit of organization they fought was at the regimental level. This piecemeal implementation differed from all other American combat divisions, highlighting that the 93rd was among the first—if not the first—American ground combat units to engage the enemy in World War I, prior to America forming its organized AEF.[67]

369TH INFANTRY REGIMENT (HARLEM HELLFIGHTERS)

The 369th Infantry Regiment was no ordinary unit; they were the equivalent of the New York Yankees of National Guard units. Their Regimental Commander, Colonel William Hayward, was a dapper attorney and former Secretary of the Republican National Committee. Other members with great notoriety included Paul Roberson's brother, Benjamin Roberson who served as a Lieutenant, and Captain Napoleon Bonaparte Marshall, a Harvard-educated attorney. It was the only black National Guard unit in the state of New York and one of only six black National Guard units in the United States.[68] Its members hailed from all parts of New York but mainly Harlem. By day, many of its officers were prominent black businessmen, lawyers, educators, and entertainers.

The 369th organized a regimental band from the professional musicians that played storied venues in Harlem. Many of them eventually returned home to lead the Harlem Renaissance, telling stories of their time in France and inspiring other authors, singers, and performers to travel to France and Great Britain. Its band director was Big Jim Reese Europe who served as a lieutenant. In February and March 1918, he led his military band over 2,000 miles in France, performing for British,

French, and American military audiences as well as French civilians. Europe's experience in France and Great Britain led him to conclude, "We won France by playing music which was ours and not a pale imitation of others, and if we are to develop in America we must develop along our own lines."[69]

370TH INFANTRY REGIMENT

The 370th Infantry Regiment was originally the 8th Infantry Illinois National Guard. Like the 369th, they were one of six existing black National Guard units who were federalized at the beginning of the war and redesignated the 370th Infantry Regiment. Unlike the 369th, they were the only regiment of the four that comprised the 93rd Infantry Division exclusively led by black officers. Members of the 370th were drawn from Chicago's elite, educated professionals. With former Chicago Assistant City Prosecutor Colonel Franklin Denison leading them, they unsurprisingly compiled an exceptional combat record, much like the 369th.[70]

371ST INFANTRY REGIMENT

The 371st Infantry Regiment was the only regiment in the 93rd Division that was formed almost exclusively from draftees. Mostly sharecroppers and other manual laborers, the men of the 371st were drafted from Georgia, Alabama, Tennessee, and the Carolinas. The Army expected little of the 371st in the way of combat success. The officers of the 371st were white Southern officers who were believed to be better suited to "deal with" black soldiers. Initially, most of the white senior officers who led them resented their appointment to command black soldiers.

372ND INFANTRY REGIMENT

The 372nd regiment was made up of troops from the 1st Separate Battalion, District of Columbia National Guard; the Separate Company, Connecticut National Guard; Company L, Guard; the 9th Separate Battalion, Ohio National Guard; the 1st Separate Company, Maryland National Guard; and 250 draftees from Camp Custer, Michigan.[71]

The 93rd Infantry Division compiled a remarkable combat record, while the sister all-black division met with mixed results fighting alongside other American divisions that were resistant to their inclusion. Unlike the Spanish–American War, black leaders successfully insisted that black officers be trained and allowed to lead black units into combat. Consequently, 1,250 black officer candidates were trained and assigned to the 92nd and 93rd Divisions. The 93rd Infantry Division is credited with many noteworthy accomplishments, including:

- the most consecutive days (191) of any American unit in combat during WWI;
- the 369th Infantry Regiment never lost a foot of ground;
- the enemy never captured a prisoner from the 369th Infantry Regiment;
- the 93rd was the first allied unit to reach the Rhine River on the border between France and Germany;
- they saved the town of Séchault, France, from German capture;
- the 369th Infantry Regiment Band introduced the American art form of jazz to European audiences, where it was wildly popular in both Great Britain and France;
- the 93rd boasted three out of the forty-four total Congressional Medal of Honor winners from WWI: First Lieutenant George Robb 369th Infantry, Corporal Freddie Stowers 371st Infantry (awarded posthumously by President George H. W. Bush), and Sergeant Henry Johnson (awarded posthumously by President Barrack Obama);
- Private Henry Johnson was the first American soldier to receive the Croix de Guerre (the French equivalent to the US Medal of Honor) for heroism in the Argonne Forest in the Champagne region.[72]

Private Henry Johnson was awarded the Croix de Guerre for his heroism during a German attack in which a German raiding party of fourteen to twenty-four soldiers attacked him and Private Needham Roberts at 2 am on May 14, 1918. Roberts was injured during the first few minutes of the attack and Johnson fired his weapon until it jammed, then lobbed grenades at the enemy as Roberts fed them to him until the enemy was upon them. He used the butt of his rifle until he splintered it on one of the enemy soldiers, then killed four attackers using his US Army–issued Bolo knife. Johnson was injured twenty-one times during the attack, and still managed to rundown the fleeing enemy who had taken Roberts prisoner. Johnson fought off the German attackers, regained control of Roberts and returned to their outpost where reinforcements rescued him and Roberts.

When discharged, Private Johnson was denied military disability and a Purple Heart due to lack of documentation of his injuries. This incident speaks to the degree of inequity black soldiers faced during this era. Nonetheless, Private Johnson became an American war hero. Nicknamed "Black Death," tales of his exploits were widely publicized in American radio and print media. In 2003, the Defense Department posthumously awarded Johnson the military's second highest honor, the Distinguished Service Cross, but they wanted more documentation to award the Medal of Honor. Senator Chuck Schumer of New York stayed on the case for more than fifteen years, and in 2011 discovered correspondence signed by the Armed Forces Expeditionary Commander, General Pershing, which documented both Private Johnson's heroics and Pershing's intent that Johnson be recognized with the Nation's highest military honor.

On September 25, 1918, the French 4th Army went on the offensive in conjunction with the American drive in the Meuse–Argonne region. The 369th captured the important village of Séchault during this campaign. At one point, the 369th advanced faster than French troops on their right and left flanks and risked being cut off. By the time the regiment pulled back for reorganization, it had advanced 14 kilometers (8.7 mi) through severe German resistance. To this day, a monument dedicated to the heroics of the 369th stands in Séchault. A replica was later built and dedicated in Harlem, NY.

I first became aware of the 369th Infantry Regiment's exploits while serving as a US Army captain assigned to Landstuhl Regional Medical Center, Germany. My commander, Colonel Elder Granger, made me the special projects officer for the hospital's annual Black History Month celebration. Colonel Granger charged me with doing something unique, more than just the assembly and luncheon we held for the German American Community. He requested something unique to our geography that would honor the memories of black service men and women who fought for their country. Colonel Granger offered the services of the hospital historian, Bill Adkins. Adkins and I presented Granger with a menu of options. At that time, I had not been exposed to the history of contributions that black servicemen and women made in support of freedoms they themselves did not enjoy. I thought it was an impossible task. I met with Bill Adkins and the hospital's Public Affairs Officer, Ms. Marie Shaw who was a native of Belgium. Both knew of these units, but I—a seasoned military officer who had been hand-picked to teach my contemporaries at the United States Infantry School—had never heard of them.

My ignorance of this significant aspect of American history provides insight into a glaring gap not only in what is taught in formal education, but also how the American historical apparatus compartmentalizes the feats of minorities into singular months (e.g., Native American Heritage Month, Black History Month, Hispanic Heritage Month, Asian Pacific Islander Month, Women's History month, etc.) rather than including these accomplishments in the greater narrative of American history. This history belongs to all of us. Greater inclusion of the accomplishments of minorities in core curricula provides a more realistic picture of our history and a richer context for our present.

On February 19, 2001, members of the Landstuhl Regional Medical Center Black History Month Observance Committee led 110 employees of the hospital and members of the Kaiserslautern Military Community on a staff ride to the Village of Séchault, France. Unit Historian Bill Adkins took us on a battlefield tour of the Battle of Séchault. We laid wreaths at the monument and on the grave site maintained by the

A Brief History of Diversity in America's Armed Forces 75

Figure 3.5. Captain Troy Mosley delivers welcome address Landstuhl, Regional Medical Center Black History Month Celebration 2001, Landstuhl Germany. *Photo courtesy of author.*

American Battle Monuments Commission and the townspeople. A champagne brunch followed, hosted by the Mayor of Séchault. It was a time of great pride and professional satisfaction to see American and European communities come together to honor a shared past. The members of the

369th Infantry Division successfully defended the town from enemy aggression. These brave black soldiers overcame numerous obstacles for the opportunity to potentially give their lives to protect the freedom of our French Allies—freedoms they didn't enjoy in America themselves.

THE 92ND INFANTRY DIVISION

Conversely, the 92nd Infantry Division was comprised mostly of draftees. Its junior officers, captains and lieutenants, came from the officer training camps run by Colonel Young. NAACP Chairman Joel Spingarn and The Central Committee of Negro College Men (CCNCM) secured the right for black officers to serve in segregated combat divisions through the protest of efforts. Spingarn, himself a Major in the Army reserves, thought it was patently unfair that the Army planned to open fourteen training camps for white officers, but no such provisions were made for black officers. The exclusion of black officers couldn't even be defended under the *Plessy vs. Ferguson* law that maintained segregation because there was no equal status for black officers. These two forces combined, embarked on letter writing campaigns to elected officials and collected 1,250 signatures on petitions from black college students who committed to volunteering for officer training if the Army made it available. Spingarn left his position as a tenured professor at Columbia University in 1911 to lead this campaign. He was determined not to allow the Great War to go by without black officer involvement. Spingarn also successfully lobbied for congressional support of the measure. These efforts were similar to those the black community embarked upon prior to the Spanish–American War. This time, the Army acquiesced, in part because of their shameful treatment of COL Young when they effectively excluded him from participating in the war through forced retirement.[73]

Of the 290,527 black men who signed up for the draft, 40,000 were selected for assignment to the 92nd Infantry Division. Some of those who were not assigned to labor units were assigned as replacements in the 93rd Infantry Division. The men drafted into the 92nd Division were mainly from Alabama, Georgia, Mississippi, Florida, Louisiana, and South Carolina. Upon their arrival in November 1917, Emett J. Scott, the Secretary of War's Special Assistant for Negro Affairs, described the chaos of conscripting hundreds of thousands of mostly sharecroppers into the Army like this, "Hundreds [were] coming directly from the cotton and corn fields or the lumber and mining districts—frightened, slow-footed, slack-shouldered, [and] many underfed."[74] Some were unaware of why they were brought together, others were unconcerned, and all of them were received by relatively inexperienced officers.[75]

The task of making soldiers of these men not only required formal education, but their entire demeanor and affect had to be transformed.

They were raised in an oppressively subservient environment where they were prohibited from looking white men in the eye and speaking. They had to relinquish the sidewalk if a white person was walking the other way. They were forced to use back entrances to conduct routine business, and they were taught to be non-threatening. All of this would have to change if they were to be thrust into combat against a seasoned enemy who had been at war for over three years.

The black officers of the 92nd Infantry organized night school to follow combat training. They began with the bare rudiments of elementary education and held talks on the simple rules of better living and Army sanitation. The second- and third-order effects of training these men to be soldiers was to learn how to occupy a larger place in their community lives. Almost without exception the men showed that they were eager to learn: Emmett J. Scott captured the pride and enthusiasm with which the black soldiers engaged their training in his book *The American Negro in World War I*. These men understood the opportunity before them. They knew wearing uniforms with "U.S. Army" embossed upon them meant they were becoming a part of something greater than themselves. They recognized they were being afforded the opportunity to better themselves, prove their worth, and attain a higher place in society.

Scott captured the convergence of this opportunity and their training with this assessment: "as the stoop came out of their spines, the shamble from their gait, they learned to read and write their names."[76] On the first payday of one regiment of the 92nd Division, ninety percent of the men were unable to write and made their marks. Yet, "Five months of night school eliminated this condition and in its place came smartness in drill, cleanliness in billets, discipline, a pride in the uniform, respect for the flag, and the ability to sign their names to the pay-rolls."[77] When the men returned to the South, they were almost unrecognizable.[78] This newfound self-esteem made it impossible for these black men to go back to the foot-shuffling, word stammering shells of themselves they once were. The divergent expectations of the black soldiers and the Jim Crow establishment then set the backdrop for a reintegration fraught with tumult and violence.

REINTEGRATION AND DISILLUSIONMENT

The black soldiers who fought in World War I returned home to the same conditions they left. The 2016 GOP Presidential Candidate Donald Trump infamously stumped for the black vote by arguing things were bad enough that black people in America had nothing to lose by voting for him. Although that approach is fraught with fundamental errors, such a statement would have applied for black Americans in 1918. The quality of life for a great deal of blacks and poor whites had not substantially changed since the mid-1800s. The photos of a typical residence for black Americans just before the Civil War and from the early twentieth century bear witness to that reality.

When black GIs returned home from the Great War, they literally had nothing to lose. The tables had been set for an epic clash of ideals: staunch segregationists didn't want blacks to serve in the Great War in any meaningful way for precisely some of the same reasons blacks wanted to fight—to disprove notions of African Americans not being worthy of equal rights and equal protections under the law. The summer of 1918—also known as the "Red Summer"—bore witness to numerous riots across the nation, not only in the South, but also in Midwest and East Coast cities. Adding to the tension, growing numbers of black migrants caused severe housing shortages and greater competition with recent immigrants for jobs. Many black migrants from the Deep South and immigrants were forced into cramped, urban housing ghettos by restrictions or covenants that prevented landlords from renting to minority groups, specifically blacks, Jews, and Asians. Race riots erupted in over three dozen cities, most notably, Chicago, IL; Washington, DC; and Omaha, NE. In 1919, seventy-eight black citizens were lynched in riots, including eleven veterans, some of whom were hung in their uniforms. The bodies of fourteen of the lynched were burned.[79]

Figure 3.6.　Slave quarters, circa 1863. *Photo courtesy of National Archives.*

Figure 3.7. Share Cropper's quarters, circa 1916. *Photo courtesy of National Archives.*

THE GREAT MIGRATION

Herein lies the historical context for the Great Migration, the Black Lives Matter Movement, the Back to Africa Movement, the Black Power Movement, and virtually every other movement intended to bring relief from the violence of racial oppression and Jim Crowism. They were all embarked upon to achieve equality of opportunity and treatment under the law, to affirm black people, and to make the provisions guaranteed under the Constitution a reality. In his last book, *Where Do We Go from Here: Chaos or Community?*, Dr. Martin Luther King Jr. lamented that white supremacy is so ingrained into American culture that white America cannot even begin to fathom true equality. He wrote:

> Negroes have proceeded from a premise that equality means what it says, and they have taken white Americans at their word when they talked of it as an objective. But most whites in America . . . proceed from a premise that equality is a loose expression for improvement. White America is not even psychologically organized to close the gap—essentially it seeks only to make it less painful and less obvious but in most respects to retain it.[80]

At the core of Dr. King's assertion is the notion that most white Americans do not see blacks as equals. Although it is socially unacceptable in today's America to openly hold or espouse racist ideology, many white Americans don't want to face the fundamental racial inequities that still exist, for to acknowledge them requires change.[81]

Even the way people peaceably protest or call attention to racial inequity is subject to criticism. In the fall of 2016, several professional sports figures began taking a knee during the National Anthem, customarily played before the start of each game, to protest police brutality. These short, peaceful protests drew a firestorm of criticism from mainstream America, the type of outrage one would expect from witnessing unarmed people being killed at the hands of police. Ironically, many white Americans who don't understand the black community's resentment of police brutality were more disturbed by the peaceful protest than the actual killing of unarmed citizens. This paradox illustrates the inferiority with which black Americans are regarded, and the lack of empathy American society has been programed to have at the sight of police violence perpetrated against blacks. Though we have honored Dr. King and millions of other brave Americans who gave their lives to secure equal rights for all Americans, American society has never apologized for the physical violence perpetrated against peaceful protestors. In failing to acknowledge the state sanctioned use of force against black Americans as wrong, we have normalized this behavior. Today, when we see videos of police abusing black people in the street, such as Rodney King or the numerous shootings of unarmed black citizens, this historic lack of empathy for victims of state-sponsored police violence causes many present-day white Americans to rationalize such violations: "they must have done something wrong," "if they would only follow the police commands," and so on. While police shoot and kill black citizens because "he had a gun," there are mountains of qualitative and quantitative evidence that white Americans are not treated with the same hostility and use of deadly force when they are confronted by police, do not obey police "commands," or are seen openly carrying guns and assault weapons. Because American society rarely questions or apologizes for how black Americans have been lynched by mobs, beaten by police, hosed, had dogs put upon them, and more, they effectively "preserve" this gap.

Many African Americans know bits and pieces of this history and the plight for equality through oral traditions, but if it is addressed in schools it is often glossed over or sugar-coated. The curricula and texts used in American public schools even minimizes the harshness of slavery and its legacy, calling slaves "workers" in some textbooks and even ignoring the unbridled violence perpetrated against black Americans simply for seeking equal rights. Some school districts do a phenomenal job, but for those that do not, this history is too important for our nation to teach sporadically. Eddie S. Glaude Jr., endowed professor of Religion and African American Studies at Princeton University, takes King's thesis one step further by asserting that when most Americans think of "equality as a loose expression for improvement," they reduce racial justice to a charitable enterprise—a practice by which white people "do good" for black people. That is not equality, and to confront this fact would cause America to confront another fact: there is a gap in how all things black and all things white are valued. Acknowledging and addressing these realities would take America a long way toward achieving racial justice.[82]

On the surface, the events discussed here seem like ancient history but they are not. As a fifty-year-old black male I am not so far removed from these events. My mother and father, born in 1946, lived through Jim Crow, desegregation, and the passage of civil rights legislation. My grandparents could not vote most of their adult lives. My great-grandfather, whom I knew as a young child, was draft eligible in 1917. His grandparents were born into slavery and worked for free to generate wealth for their owners. In turn, that wealth was taxed to build financial, educational, and political institutions. The black people who helped make America an international power and their decedents were statutorily prohibited from the fruits of their labor in an effort to make them a permanent underclass until 1968, one year after my birth.

In effect, there was no money, land, or education to pass on to future generations of former slaves. Not only did these black Americans suffer enslavement, their children couldn't benefit from the colleges and universities in the South whose endowments were created in part from revenue generated by slave labor. While many of the same injustices are no longer in place, contemporary black Americans are competing against those who have had a 250-year head start. Most Americans lack knowledge of this painful history, in part because their experiences have not been shaped by the violence and oppression of Jim Crow. Most non-black Americans know what we are taught in school, which is often sanitized—a white-washed, distorted version of events. It seems too painful and too recent for America as a society to deal with earnestly. As a result, the chasms, policies, and sentiments that were born of white supremacy still fester in kind though not degree. Differing views of the Confederate Battle Flag exemplify this social disease: what many white Americans (even those without direct ties to the South) view as a symbol of Southern heritage, remains a symbol of racial hatred to most black Americans.

In the summer of 2015, a deranged racist murdered nine black Americans who welcomed him into their bible study at Mother Emanuel African Methodist Episcopal Church. Authorities found pictures of him on his computer and Facebook pages parading the Confederate flag as a symbol of his hatred for black Americans. Despite this evidence, many elected officials of South Carolina were unmoved in their position that the flag should remain in a position of prominence on the capital grounds. This standoff sparked a nationwide debate that pitted opponents of the flag against its advocates. It wasn't until the surviving members of the slain responded to the assailant with such grace and dignity that those elected officials who previously opposed the removal of the Confederate flag from the capital grounds were essentially shamed into changing their positions.

The saying, hindsight is 20/20 is never more poignant than when it is applied to matters of race. The overwhelming majority of Americans can look back on slavery, lynchings, and segregation and agree on the abhorrent nature of these atrocities. Yet we still diverge in our ability to see racism as it applies to today's society. Consequently, even a simple slogan like "Black Lives Matter" has become controversial. It is in the context of American history that this campaign has validity, because historically there is a significant body of evidence to suggest that black lives too often have not mattered to the rest of American society in a manner commensurate with their humanity.

NOTES

1. "Crispus Attucks," *Biography.com*, January 19, 2018, https://www.biography.com/people/crispus-attucks-9191864.
2. "Africans in America: The Revolutionary War," *PBS*, April 9, 2015, http://www.pbs.org/wgbh/aia/part2/2narr4.html.
3. Ibid.
4. Frederic M. Holland, *Frederick Douglass: The Colored Orator* (New York: Funk and Wagnalls, 1891), 301.
5. Roger Butterfield, *The American Past* (New York: Simon and Schuster, 1957).
6. "Black Soldiers in the U.S. Military During the Civil War." *U.S. National Archives and Records Administration*, September 1, 2017, https://www.archives.gov/education/lessons/blacks-civil-war.
7. Budge Wiedman, "Black Soldiers in the Civil War: Preserving the Legacy of the United States Colored Troops." *U.S. National Archives and Records Administration*, March 19, 2019, https://www.archives.gov/education/lessons/blacks-civil-war/article.html.
8. "Black Soldiers in the U.S. Military During the Civil War," *U.S. National Archives and Records Administration*, September 1, 2017, https://www.archives.gov/education/lessons/blacks-civil-war.
9. Sara Kettler, "Harriet Tubman's Service as a Union Spy," *Biography.com*, February 12, 2017, https://www.biography.com/news/harriet-tubman-biography-facts.
10. United States Office of the Deputy Assistant Secretary of Defense for Equal Opportunity and Safety Policy, *Black Americans in Defense of Our Nation* (Washington, DC: DoD, 1985), 25.
11. James N. Lieker, *Racial Borders Black Soldiers Along the Rio Grande* (College Station, TX: Texas A&M University Press, 2002), 91.
12. Gail Buckley, *American Patriots: The Story of Blacks in the Military from the Revolution to Desert Storm* (New York: Random House, 2001), 112.
13. Buckley, *American Patriots*, 114.
14. John Marszalek, *Assault at West Point, The Court Martial of Johnson Whitaker* (New York: Atheneum Books for Young Readers, 1984), 115.
15. Henry O. Flipper, *The Colored Cadet at West Point* (New York: Start Publishing, 2012), 172.
16. "Lieutenant Henry O. Flipper," *Mobeetie Jail Museum*, accessed September 5, 2015, http://www.mobeetie.com/pages/flipper.htm.
17. Marvin Fletcher, *The Black Soldier and Officer in the United States Army: 1891–1917* (Columbia, MO: University of Missouri Press, 1974), 178.

18. "Lieutenant Henry O. Flipper," *Mobeetie Jail Museum*.
19. Henry Ossian Flipper, "The Colored Cadet at West Point. Autobiography of Lieut. Henry Ossian Flipper, U.S.A., First Graduate of Color from the U.S. Military Academy," *The Multiracial Activist*, January 1, 2001, https://multiracial.com/index.php/2001/01/01/the-colored-cadet-at-west-point-autobiography-of-lieut-henry-ossian-flipper/.
20. Ibid.
21. Willard B. Gatewood, "John Hanks Alexander (1864–1894)," *Encyclopedia of Arkansas*, September 18, 2009, https://encyclopediaofarkansas.net/entries/john-hanks-alexander-46/.
22. Patricia A. Pearson, "John Hanks Alexander 1864–1894," *Encyclopedia.com*, April 20, 2020, https://www.encyclopedia.com/african-american-focus/news-wires-white-papers-and-books/alexander-john-hanks.
23. Brian G. Shellum, *Black Cadet in a White Bastion: Charles Young at West Point* (Lincoln, NE: University of Nebraska Press, 2006), 56.
24. Ibid.
25. Ibid., 7.
26. Col. Charles Young, Leader and Builder," *National Park Service: Sequoia and Kings Canyon*, October 30, 2019, http://www.nps.gov/seki/learn/historyculture/young.htm.
27. Brian G. Shellum, *Black Officer in a Buffalo Soldier Regiment: The Military Career of Charles Young* (Lincoln, NE: University of Nebraska Press, 2010), 226–67.
28. "Buffalo Soldiers and the Spanish-American War," *National Park Service: Presidio of San Francisco*, February 28, 2015, https://www.nps.gov/prsf/learn/historyculture/buffalo-soldiers-and-the-spanish-american-war.htm.
29. Ibid.
30. Ibid.
31. Carl M. Cannon, *On This Date: From the Pilgrims to Today, Discovering America One Day at a Time* (New York: Twelve Hatchett Book Group, 2017), 460.
32. James L. Yarrison, "The U.S. Army in the Root Reform Era, 1899–1917," *U.S. Army Center of Military History*, May 3, 2001, https://history.army.mil/documents/1901/Root-Ovr.htm.
33. "Contagion: Historical Views of Diseases and Epidemics," *Harvard Library*, accessed April 19, 2015, https://library.harvard.edu/collections/contagion-historical-views-diseases-and-epidemics.
34. Friedrich Katz, *The Life and Times of Pancho Villa* (Stanford, CA: Stanford University Press, 1998), 147, 908.
35. Successfully defeating Villa led to other accomplishments for Young and the "Buffalo Soldiers." On March 23, 1907, the US military academy decided to make noncommissioned officers from the 9th and 10th Regiments the principal cavalry instructors to cadets at West Point to teach mounted combat skills. Major Young was promoted to Lieutenant Colonel in September 1916 because of his exceptional leadership of the 10th Cavalry in the border war with Mexico. Young was then reassigned as commander of Fort Huachuca, Arizona, the base for the 10th Cavalry until mid-1917. There, he was promoted to the rank of full Colonel. Young was the first African American to achieve the rank of colonel in the US Army, making him the highest-ranking black officer in the armed forces at that time. Gail Buckley, *American Patriots: The Story of Blacks in the Military from the Revolution to Desert Storm* (New York: Random House, 2001), 360.
36. S. Mintz, and S. McNeil, "The Espionage and Sedition Acts," *Digital History*, accessed June 7, 2016, http://www.digitalhistory.uh.edu/disp_textbook.cfm?smtID=2&psid=3479.
37. Woodrow Wilson, "Third Annual Message to Congress" (speech, Washington, DC, December 7, 1915), *The American Presidency Project*, UC Santa Barbara, accessed April 17, 2016, https://www.presidency.ucsb.edu/documents/third-annual-message-19.

38. Geoffrey R. Stone, *Perilous Times: Free Speech in Wartime from the Sedition Act of 1798 to the War on Terrorism* (New York: Norton, 2004), 541.

39. Rawn James, Jr., *The Double V: How Wars, Protest, and Harry Truman Desegregated America's Military* (New York: Bloomsbury, 2013), 25.

40. Ibid.

41. Richard W. Stewart, ed., "Peace Becomes Cold War," in *American Military History*, 2nd ed., Vol. 2, *The United States Army in a Global Era, 1917–2008*, 203–220 (Washington, D.C.: Government Printing Office, 2010), 12–23.

42. James, *The Double V*, 28–29.

43. Michael Kazin, *War Against War: The American Fight for Peace, 1914–1918* (New York: Simon & Schuster, 2017), 95–97.

44. Yohuru Williams, "Great Migration," *History.com*, retrieved May 5, 2016, https://www.history.com/topics/black-history/great-migration-video.

45. History.com Editors, " Sharecropping," *History.com*, June 24, 2010, http://www.history.com/topics/.

46. Williams, "Great Migration."

47. Ibid.

48. Buckley, *American Patriots*, 164.

49. Buckley, *American Patriots*, 163–164.

50. Scott, *History of the American Negro in the Great World War*, 66–67.

51. Martin Kitchen, "The Ending of World War One, and the Legacy of Peace," *BBC*, February 17, 2011, http://www.bbc.co.uk/history/worldwars/wwone/war_end_01.shtml (accessed April 12, 2016).

52. Buckley, *American Patriots*, 178–179.

53. Ibid., 175–176.

54. The correspondence among Roosevelt, Young, and F. S. Stover (who was raising money for the regiment) is in the John Motley Collection, Tredegar Museum. A fuller account is in Richard Slotkin, *Lost Battalions: The Great War and the Crisis of American Nationality* (New York: Holt, 2005), 41–42.

55. James, *The Double V*, 50.

56. Ibid., 32–34.

57. Ibid., 35.

58. Ibid.

59. Adreane D. Lentz-Smith, *Freedom Struggles African Americans and World War I* (Cambridge, MA: Harvard University Press, 2009), 71–80.

60. James, *The Double V*, 58.

61. Ibid., 64.

62. Buckley, *American Patriots*, 61–62.

63. James, *The Double V*, 29.

64. Ibid., 65.

65. Richard W. Stewart, ed., "Peace Becomes Cold War," 27.

66. Ibid., 35.

67. James, *The Double V*, 62.

68. Ibid., 55.

69. Buckley, *American Patriots*, 203.

70. James, *The Double V*, 63.

71. Ibid.

72. Erick Trickey, "World War I: 100 Years Later: One Hundred Years Ago, the Harlem Hellfighters Bravely Led the U.S. into WWI," *Smithsonian Magazine*, May 14, 2018, https://www.smithsonianmag.com/history/one-hundred-years-ago-harlem-hellfighters-bravely-led-us-wwi-180968977/ (accessed May 27, 2016).

73. Robert H. Ferrell, *Woodrow Wilson and World War I: 1917–1921* (New York: Harper and Row, 1985), 214.

74. Scott, *History of the American Negro in the Great World War*, 78.

75. Ibid.

76. Ibid.

77. Ibid.
78. Ibid.
79. "The Great War: A Nation Comes of Age," *PBS*, Aired July 3, 2018, https://www.pbs.org/wgbh/americanexperience/films/great-war/.
80. Wolfgang Mieder, *"Making a Way Out of No Way": Martin Luther King's Sermonic Proverbial Rhetoric* (New York: Peter Lang Publishing, 2010), 539.
81. Martin L. King, Jr., *Where Do We Go from Here: Chaos or Community?* (Boston: Beacon Press, 2010), 37.
82. Eddie S. Glaude, *Democracy in Black: How Race Still Enslaves the American Soul* (New York: Crown, 2017), 5.

FOUR

Minorities in World War II

Sowing the Seeds for the Civil Rights Movement

When Japan attacked Pearl Harbor on December 7, 1941, the Department of Defense's policy regarding black Americans was the same as during WWI. Blacks were restricted to the same four segregated combat regiments in the Army (9th and 10th Cavalry and 24th and 25th Infantry), and black servicemen in the Army not assigned to those regiments were restricted to segregated service, supply, and labor units. The Navy employed black sailors exclusively as cooks and mess men. The Marines excluded blacks all together, and the Air Force (then the US Army Air Corps) only employed blacks in supply and labor roles. Black journalists from prominent black newspapers, such as the *Pittsburgh Currier* and the *Baltimore Afro-American*, characterized black sailors of the day as seagoing bell hops.[1]

Just as the previous chapter on black Americans in World War I began with vignettes of individuals, so too does this one. The status of a few individuals serves to exemplify the collective impact of black Americans within the armed forces. This scarcity of black influence within the military was by design a way to preserve the socio-economic status quo within and outside of the military. The great unwritten truce between Northern and Southern states regarding treatment of blacks was so ingrained in US military policy that individual exploits were more or less the extent of black Americans' impact within the armed forces prior to the attack on Pearl Harbor. There were two black officers on active duty prior to America's second Selective Service Act just before World War II. One of those officers was Benjamin O. Davis Senior, a former enlisted orderly room clerk who served under Colonel Charles Young, whom Colonel Young tutored to pass the Officer Candidate School exam. The other was

Davis' son, Benjamin O. Davis Jr., who graduated thirty-fifth of 276 cadets at West Point in 1936.[2] Benjamin O. Davis Jr. endured the same hazing and silent treatment that the three black graduates before him suffered forty-seven years prior. There were fewer than 5,000 black soldiers on active duty at the time, comprising less than three percent of the total force. Black Americans made up ten percent of the population.

There were some societal gains made in the black community, tangential to the experiences and contributions of black veterans from WWI. The Great Migration continued and grew after The Great War. Black veterans who experienced life in England and France were convinced more than ever that Southern customs, mores, and Jim Crow laws allowed no future for them or their children.

The plight of the average black American improved considerably between World War I and World War II in part due to the provisions implemented in President Roosevelt's New Deal in the 1930s. Black Americans were not excluded from this landmark legislation. The baseline living standards for both average black Americans and poor whites appreciated considerably, especially in the Southern States, just as a rising tide lifts all boats. More unencumbered from the weight of meeting life's bare necessities, black Americans were able to give more thought to their futures and to those of their children for the first time since Reconstruction. They relocated to cities in the Northeast and Midwest by the millions, reshaping the political landscape and giving the black community a considerable voting bloc, which black civic and community leaders leveraged for continued progress. The black press, church, and civic leaders coalesced into a formidable, like-minded triumvirate whose top priority was desegregation. Better educational opportunities for black Americans in integrated schools in the Northeast and Midwest meant the educational gap between black and white draftees, though still significant, had narrowed considerably since the First World War.

The degree to which racial segregation cast a suffocating shroud on the entire black collective cannot be overstated. Segregation as a policy limited educational and professional opportunities for black Americans, and had a devastating effect on their emotional and psychological well-being. "Separate but Equal" as public policy inherently meant inferior, not good enough, smart enough, clean enough for the mainstream. As a strategy for achieving equality, black leaders knew their best hope was to advocate for equality of opportunity through the federal government. Bound by the Constitution, the federal government had a much more difficult time justifying racial segregation from legal and moral perspectives because the two ideals were antithetical to the Constitution's specified protected rights. What better institution to lead America's foray into desegregation than the military, given that they were bound by strict regulations? First Lady Eleanor Roosevelt also proved to be an influential ally in the black community's plight to advance opportunities for black Americans in the armed forces.

The special cabinet position created under the Wilson Administration, Special Assistant to the Secretary of War, carried over from World War I. The position was filled by William Hastie, Dean of Howard Law School and the first African American federal judge. At that point, instead of arguing for the existence of leadership opportunities for black officers, black community leaders could argue for integrated officer training programs for black and white officers.

Hastie served as Henry L. Stimson's special assistant, just as Emmett J. Scott did during World War I for Secretary of War Newton Baker. By the time the US initiated its second national conscription of the century, the black triumvirate was fully mobilized and had launched a multi-pronged attack against segregation in the armed services. The NAACP continued the work it began during World War I, this time under the leadership of NAACP President Walter White. They lobbied Congress to include language in the pending Selective Service Law (crafted in response to Germany's invasion of France) that would outlaw racial discrimination in the armed services. Lieutenant Rayford W. Logan, World War I veteran and professor at Howard University, testified before Congress in June 1940 that blacks should be given "equal opportunity to participate in the national-defense program . . . and to serve in the naval and military services of this country in proportion to their numerical strength in the whole population." Charles Hamilton Houston also testified fervently before the House Armed Services Committee on behalf of the NAACP, stating, "Negroes want some of the Democracy they fought for in 1917 this time, and the sooner the better."[3]

New York senior Senator Robert F. Wagner proposed an amendment to the already proposed selective service legislation that would out- law race-based discrimination in any of the military services. Wagner was directly opposed by Texas Senator Tom Connally, who argued that adopting such a bill would mean surrendering to bourgeois black Americans "who want continually to agitate, disturb, stir up discussion, and raise the devil about what they speak of as their political and social rights." Despite Connally's objection, the bill passed the Senate by a vote of 53 to 21. A similar amendment passed in the house, led by New York Congressman Hamilton Fish. In the black press, the NAACP hailed the bill as a landmark victory, which Roosevelt signed into law on September 14, 1940.

Doris J. Miller was one of the early heroes of World War II. Miller was a Navy Messman Third Class aboard the USS *West Virginia* on December 7, 1941. Miller was onboard when the ship was attacked and helped move his mortally wounded commanding officer and other comrades to safety, then manned a .50-caliber machine gun, downing three Japanese fighter aircraft. Miller was awarded the Navy Cross for his bravery, which at the time was the Navy's third-highest award. Miller's accomplishments flew in the face of Navy policy that restricted black sailors as cooks and messmen.

How many more aircraft might Messman Third Class Miller have shot down if he had been trained to use the Browning .50 caliber machine gun? How many more potential "Doris Miller's" might there have been at Pearl Harbor if blacks were allowed to serve as combatants? A Navy press release listed some heroes of Pearl Harbor, which included one "unnamed" black messman third class who distinguished himself in the face of enemy fire through conspicuous acts of bravery. It's unclear if the Navy deliberately or inadvertently attempted to suppress the story of Miller's heroics. The black news media seized on this moment and pressed the Navy for a name, instantly making Doris Miller one of the war's early heroes, as well as the darling of the black news media and war effort.[4]

Again, the black media and black civic leaders were unified in their belief that segregation and equality were mutually exclusive. The NAACP's ranks and sphere of influence had grown significantly since World War I; its ranks numbering in the hundreds of thousands, growing as high as 450,000 by 1946. As the number of black men who enlisted in the Army grew, Pentagon officials could no longer ignore the mounting pressure for the Army to end segregation in its units. Even within the Army, some of the senior brass were bothered by the fact that racial segregation in the American military mirrored the racist fascism against which they were fighting.[5]

The Pentagon knew very early that the single most important factor in predicting a soldier's readiness for combat training was education. The Army developed the Army General Classification Test (AGCT), which divided recruits into five categories, I through V. The AGCT was one of the very first "intelligence tests." The test was first developed during World War I to determine the level of literacy (Alpha test) within a heterogeneous group. Those who were illiterate were given another test (Beta test), and some enrollees were interviewed. Subsequent testing targeted aptitude to better fill roles, or to meet the need for increasingly complicated skills that came along with technological progress, especially after World War II.[6]

Soldiers who scored in categories I through III were identified as potential leaders, or specialists capable of grasping technologically oriented warfare and concepts. Soldiers who scored on the lower end of the scale—categories IV and V—were relegated to semi-skilled labor.[7] In 1941, nearly fifty percent of black recruits drafted between March and December of 1942 scored in the lowest category of the AGCT, compared to eight and a half percent of white recruits who tested during the same period. Eighty percent of all black recruits scored in categories four and five. The test was a better predictor of overall education level than raw intelligence. The Army fully recognized the high correlation between test score and education level, yet their policies were based on race. White Southern leaders more likely to buy into the racist theory were disproportionately represented among policy-making, military brass, and this correlation contradicted their widely held, racist ideology. As a result, the performance gap on the AGCT among black and white soldiers was attributed to black recruits being, supposedly, inherently inferior intellectually and therefore unsuited for combat, rather than these differences being correctly attributed to educational disparities.[8]

The other problem with segregating units was that it forced a disproportionate number of recruits from the lowest AGCT categories into significantly fewer units. The raw number of white recruits who scored in the lowest categories was higher, but because the rates were lower in relation to the number of white units, the white recruits who were not as combat ready could be more easily absorbed by the greater number of units. Dispersing these white soldiers in such a way prevented them from overwhelming and therefore hindering any single unit in terms of training or overall readiness. Conversely, there were very few black units to absorb a significantly higher proportion of category IV and V recruits, thus segregation compounded the detrimental impact on training black units.[9]

Two credible efforts were made to desegregate the Army during World War II. NAACP President Walter White led the first effort, enlisting the help of William Hastie, Civilian Aide to the Secretary of War Henry Stimson. Hastie then recruited senior Pentagon officials who disliked the notion that the US Armed forces were engaged in discriminatory practices similar to the fascism against which they were waging war. Robert P. Patterson, Undersecretary of the War Department, was one such leader. These men were "gravely bestirred by the conflict inherent in their country's declaration that it was fighting a war against dangerous Nazi racial theories, while a similar racial philosophy dominated our Army and Navy." White effectively organized bilateral support from both Northerners and Southerners, civilians and military officials who supported desegregating the armed services. Frank P. Graham, then President of the University of North Carolina Chapel Hill and Howard Kester, General Secretary of the Fellowship of Southern Churchmen were among Mr. White's civilian supporters. With this diverse group of supporters, White proposed an experimental, integrated combat division composed of volunteers who agreed to serve together.[10]

General George Marshall, US Army Chief of Staff rejected the plan, stating that the urgency of the war effort was too critical for social experimentation. Col. Edwin W. Chamberlain, a staff planner in the Army's G-3 Directorate made a similar proposal that drew interest from Pentagon insiders. Col. Chamberlain argued that segregating soldiers by race aggravated, if not caused, racial friction and flash points. Moreover, he argued that segregation hindered mission readiness because it wasted manpower and added an unnecessary variable for Army manpower managers to accommodate, over-complicating an already difficult task. Instead of filling a vacancy with the correct skill set based on the AGCT, Army officials had to determine if the recruit was the right color for the unit in need. If not, they had to place the recruit in a position for which he may not have been qualified. Regarding black recruits, this often meant placing men with college degrees or high AGCT scores in service roles because there were not enough combat assignments for them in the limited number of black combat units. Consider for instance, that the 93rd Infantry division was one of only two black army divisions activated for combat service during WWII. It was comprised of black and white officers, but only consisted of 10,000 men—a very small number of combat roles given that 2.5 million black men were registered for the draft during World War II.[11]

THE BLACK AND MINORITY COMBAT EXPERIENCE IN WORLD WAR II

Just as in World War I, the 92nd and 93rd Infantry Divisions (ID) were the only African American infantry divisions to fight in World War II. The 92nd "Buffalo Soldier Division" and the 93rd "Blue Helmet Division" took their lineage from the famed 9th and 10th Cavalry and the 24th and 25th Infantry Regiments, which were among the best units in America's active force during the expansion of the western territories. The 93rd Infantry Division fought in the Pacific Theatre while the 24th Infantry Regiment remained activated as part of the US occupational force in Japan following World War II.

The 92nd Division fought as an entire Division on the US Italian front under Major General Edward Almond's command. Almond was a graduate of the Virginia Military Institute (VMI) like then Army Chief of Staff George C. Marshall. General Marshall held Almond in high regard and selected him as the 92nd ID Commanding General, immediately following Almond's promotion to Major General. The 92nd Infantry Division's combat record was a mixed bag and the subject of great debate. Historians' accounts on the 92nd's performance range between them being adequate to poor. The reasons for their questionable performance have also been hotly debated. Some historians attribute the 92nd's poor performance to the poor leadership that bordered on contemptuous. Other reasons include: an overabundance of illiterate soldiers forced into positions because of segregationist war policy, failure to allow black officers to command above company grade level, and disparate support from higher military brass.[12]

Given the political sensitivity of blacks in combat, those who were against using black men in combat or integrating the services had a biased slant to ensure the 92nd was unsuccessful. Therefore, the veracity of their reports of the 92nd must be regarded with some skepticism. There are numerous examples of soldiers of the 92nd demonstrating acts of bravery that were not fully recognized until decades later.

MG Almond blamed his division's performance in command on black troops being "unreliable in battle." Yet, other military leaders assigned to the 92nd Infantry Division, such as Colonel Howard Donovan Queen, countered Almond's claims. Queen stated, "whatever shortcomings the 92nd had, it rested entirely on the shoulders of Major General Almond. His entire staff was incompetent, excepting for Brigadier General (William H.) Coburn, the artillery commander, whose artillery was rated among the best on the front."[13] The 92nd ID fought a series of attacks and counter attacks against the Italians, supported by Germans until the Italian surrender on May 2, 1945.

Two soldiers from the 92nd were awarded the Congressional Medal of Honor: First Lieutenant John R. Fox, 366th Infantry; and First Lieutenant Vernon Baker, a Heavy Weapons Platoon Leader in the 370th Infantry Regiment. Fox was killed in action when he deliberately called for artillery fire on his own position to prevent the German's from overrunning it. Thirty-eight years later, Fox was awarded the Distinguished Service Cross for his actions. Both Fox and Baker were awarded the Medal of Honor following the determination that there had been systematic racial discrimination in the criteria for awarding decorations during World War II. During the war, no Medals of Honor were awarded to black Americans who served in World War II. After an exhaustive review, a commission recommended that ten black recipients of the Distinguished Service Cross have their awards upgraded to the Medal of Honor. President Bill Clinton awarded the Medal of Honor to seven of the ten World War II veterans on January 13, 1997; Baker was the only living recipient at the time.[14]

THE 442ND "GO FOR BROKE" INFANTRY REGIMENT (JAPANESE AMERICAN)

Black and other minority participants in both world wars would shape the social, economic, and political fabric of the US for the next hundred years. Many great American social and political figures came out of military service. People such as Medgar Evers, Daniel Innoyuae, and Carl Rowan are but a few minority figures who served in the military during that time. The story of the 442nd "Go for Broke" Combat Regiment is another prime example of how minority participation in the armed services has shaped American Society.

The 442nd was attached to the 92nd ID towards the end of the war. The 442nd was comprised of Japanese Americans, "Nisei," who volunteered to fight despite having family members interned in "relocation" camps along the west coast. The 442nd was so courageous and disciplined that they earned the nickname of the "Purple Heart" Battalion as so many of their members were wounded in action.[15] It is also credited with being the most decorated unit in the history of American warfare for its size and length of service. The 442nd earned eight Presidential Citations, including five in one month.[16]

The 442nd Regimental Combat Team rescued the "Lost Battalion," the 141st Infantry Regiment, Texas National Guard. Against the advice of superior officers, Major General John E. Dahlquist, Commanding General of the 36th Infantry Division, committed the "Texas Battalion" to an attack against a dug-in enemy. Companies A, B, C and a platoon from Company D, forming the right flank of the regimental attack, were outflanked and cut off from the rest of the regiment. Once they realized the enemy had surrounded them, they were forced to dig-in and pool their supplies. Two other battalions tried unsuccessfully to extract the 275 men of the Texas National Guard unit. After several days of bitter fighting, the 442nd broke through enemy lines and rescued the remaining men at an extremely high cost; they lost 800 men in five days of fighting.[17]

As I consider the tremendous bravery and selflessness displayed by the 442nd, sacrificing their lives while their loved ones were interned in detainment camps, I can't help but point out the amazing parallels between how these Japanese Americans fought—perhaps more bravely than anyone, enduring almost unprecedented casualty rates—and the selfless sacrifices of black Americans in all previous wars, giving life and limb for America abroad while being persecuted at home. Though the US recognized the very real and looming threat of German and Italian immigrants with dual allegiance, sympathies for their mother land, or outright spy missions, the Japanese Americans bore a much greater burden. Only about 11,000 German Americans were interned compared to 110,000 to 120,000 Japanese Americans—the majority of Japanese Americans in California. Another 130,000 Japanese Americans were relocated to the American interior.[18] Ironically, German Americans faced far fewer restrictions and probably posed a far greater threat because they were physically indistinguishable from the majority of Americans. This is another characteristic of racism: it causes people to act irrationally.

In 1980, under mounting pressure from the Japanese American Citizens League, the Carter Administration opened an investigation to determine whether the decision to put Japanese Americans into internment camps had been justified. He appointed the Commission on Wartime Relocation and Internment of Civilians (CWRIC) to investigate. The Commission's report, titled Personal Justice Denied, found little evidence of Japanese disloyalty at the time. It concluded that the incarceration of

Japanese Americans had been the product of racism, and recommended that the government pay reparations to the survivors. President Ronald Reagan signed the Civil Liberties Act into law in 1988, which apologized for the internment on behalf of the US Government, and authorized a payment of $20,000 to each individual camp survivor. The legislation admitted that government actions were based on "race prejudice, war hysteria, and a failure of political leadership." The US government eventually disbursed more than $1.6 billion in reparations to 82,219 Japanese Americans who had been interned and their heirs.[19] By contrast, the United States has never issued an apology for 400 years of slavery and Jim Crow laws, nor ever attempted to entertain the idea of reparations for its black citizens since the end of Reconstruction. Perhaps the closest the US ever came in attempting to right these injustices was in 1996 when President Bill Clinton appointed famed historical scholar John Hope Franklin to chair the Advisory Board on One America in the 21st Century: The President's Initiative on Race. This project was crucial in President Clinton's effort to prepare the country to embrace diversifying American society. Sadly, the timing of the One America Initiative coincided with the Monica Lewinsky scandal, and the initiative never gained the attention or traction it deserved.

Following World War II, the Japanese American experience was similar to that of black Americans who returned to the United States. They returned to an ungrateful nation who refused to serve them in some places of business; some businesses even posted signs in their front windows stating, "No Japs" or "Japs not served here." Despite the fact that Japanese Americans were not the only ethnic minority in America's melting pot with native origins from enemy soil, they were disproportionately singled out for internment, which underscores the racially charged discrimination they experienced.

As with many of World War II veterans of America's "Greatest Generation," many of the surviving veterans of the 442nd "Go for Broke" Regiment went on to serve their country with distinction out of uniform. One of its notable alumni included the late Senator Daniel Inouye who served the great state of Hawaii for over forty-nine years. The Army's first Asian American Army Chief of Staff and former Veteran's Administration Secretary, Erick Shinseki had three uncles that served in the 442nd.

761ST TANK BATTALION (BLACK PANTHERS)

The 761st Tank Battalion was activated on April 1, 1942 at Camp Claiborne, Louisiana, two years after Congress passed the Selective Service Act of 1940 (SSA). The SSA stated, "In the selection and training of men under this act, there shall be no discrimination against any person on account of race and color." In October, however, the Roosevelt Administration issued a statement that declared, "while the services of Negroes would be utilized on a fair and equitable basis," the policy of segregation in the armed forces would continue.[20] The battalion began training in M5 Stuart light tanks as the country's only segregated tank battalion. They nicknamed themselves "Black Panthers," and their motto was "Come Out Fighting."

The 761st Tank Battalion trained for two years and completed their training at Fort Hood, TX. After a special review, General Ben Lear, commander of the US Second Army, rated them "superior" and deemed the unit "combat ready."[21] Shortly thereafter, famed General George S. Patton summoned the 761st to fight under his 3rd Army Command to exploit the success of the Normandy Offensive. After a brief deployment to England, the 761st landed in France via Omaha Beach on 10 October 1944. General Patton had lost 1/3 of his tanks by that time and was bogged down in the hedgerows of France.

The unit arrived with six white officers, thirty black officers, and 676 black enlisted men. They were commanded by Lieutenant Colonel Paul L. Bates, a 1931 graduate of Western Maryland, now McDaniel College. LTC Bates was widely regarded as a fair man and was very instrumental in fostering the 761st's drive for excellence. He allowed the men to train as long and as hard as they were willing, and pushed them to strive for greatness. Though Lieutenant Colonel Bates had a long and distinguished military career, he is perhaps best known for refusing to court martial the unit's most famous member, Jackie Robinson, for refusing to move to the back of the bus when ordered to by a white civilian bus driver. Second Lieutenant Jackie Robinson was, however, transferred to the sister unit, 784th Tank Battalion, and forced to stand trial (court martial) for two charges: 1) a violation of Article of War No. 63, which accused him of "behaving with disrespect toward Capt. Gerald M. Bear, his superior officer," and 2) a violation of Article No. 64, in this case "willful disobedience of lawful command of Gerald M. Bear, his superior."[22]

Three other charges were dropped before the trial began. Testimony reveals how bravely Robinson had fought to defend himself on the evening of the incident, including reportedly saying quite heroically, "Look here, you son-of-a-bitch, don't you call me no nigger!" After a four-hour trial, Robinson was exonerated: "Robinson secured at least the four votes (secret and written) needed for his acquittal. He was found 'not guilty' of all specifications and charges."[23]

Robinson did not deploy to Germany with the 761st who were attached to the 26th Infantry Division for the duration of the war, including the Battle of the Bulge. The 761st served 183 consecutive days in combat. Like many of the all-black units that served in WWII, the 761st wouldn't be recognized for their feats until decades later. In 1978, President Jimmy Carter awarded the 761st Tank Battalion the highest unit award, the Presidential Unit Citation. President Bill Clinton awarded Sergeant Ruben

Rivers, who was killed in the 761st's second week of fighting, the Congressional Medal of Honor by Bill Clinton in 1997.[24]

Major General E. Hughes recommended the 761st for the Distinguished Unit Citation, but General Eisenhower refused to sign the recommendation. Twelve other units whom the 761st was attached to and fought alongside were recommended for the award and received it in May of 1945. The 761st Tank Battalion was instrumental in disproving the 1920s Army War College Report, which stated black men were ill suited for combat due to lack of intelligence and cowardly tendencies. This doctrine set the tone for the War Department's policy on the use of black service men for over twenty years and two world wars.[25]

New York Public Television station WNET debuted a documentary in October 1991 entitled, *Liberators: Fighting on Two Fronts in World War II*. The TV studio brought together thirty concentration camp survivors and forty black veterans to see the film. The film's creators, William Miles and Nina Rosenblum, made the film to document the plight of the 761st Tank Battalion, and to highlight the role these men played as unsung if not ironic heroes in freeing Jewish men, women, and children from some of the worst atrocities known to man in the twentieth century.[26] The film was released at a time when black and Jewish Community relations, which had been close and collegial during the civil rights movements of the sixties, had become strained. The film was moving and met with a great deal of fanfare and critical acclaim; it was nominated for Best Documentary Feature by the Academy of Motion Pictures in 1992.

Yet, by September of 1993, the film had come under great criticism for claiming that the 761st liberated the infamous Dachau and Buchenwald Concentration Camps, and intimating that one of its then surviving members, E.G. McConnell, was present at the liberation. Official Army records indicate the 4th Armored Division liberated Dachu and Bauchenwald on April 11, 1945. Though the 761st was assigned to the 4th Armored Division at different times during their march to Germany, and survivors of the Buchenwald Concentration Camp recount being rescued by black soldiers, it is unclear if those soldiers were members of the 761st Tank Battalion.

What is clear is that the 761st Tank Battalion participated in the liberation of smaller camps in Austria and outside Straubing, Germany. Buchenwald survivor and Nobel Laureate Elie Wiesel recounted his memory in a 1989 *New York Times* editorial: "It was the morning of April 11, I will always remember with love a big black soldier. He was crying, like a child, tears of all the pain in the world and all the rage. Everyone who was there that day will forever feel a sentiment of gratitude to the American soldiers who liberated us."[27] Regardless of which camp was liberated, the great irony remains that black soldiers fighting for the right to serve their nation would help freeing another group of people who have also been the victims of unconscionable racial hatred and torture.

THE 333RD FIELD ARTILLERY REGIMENT (COLORED)

The 333rd Field Artillery Regiment was one of the first experimental, black combat units. The 333rd was trained for what is known in the military as indirect fire or artillery fire. They used cannons to target the enemy targets many miles away. Field artillery is usually employed in support of infantry or armored units to break down enemy defenses before ground troops commit to an assault.

The 333rd landed on Utah Beach on June 19, 1944. They were a part of the US Army Eighth Corps, a corps-level asset to be used at the discretion of the corps commander. They were part of the larger US and allied forces that landed on the beaches of Normandy, France. They successfully fought their way inland through the hedgerows of French farm country before getting bogged down in Belgium with other rapidly advancing US Forces. The 333rd was among other US Forces who outpaced their surrounding units and were cut-off by the last major German counterattack of WWII in the Battle of the Bulge.[28]

During the Ardennes Offensive, the 4th Battalion of the 333rd Field Artillery was in direct support of the 106th Infantry Division, eleven miles behind them situated on both sides of the North-South running Ohr River. The unit arrived in the small village of Schonberg, near St. Vith, Belgium, in October 1944. The firing batteries A, B, and C were oriented east of the river while the headquarters and service battery was west of the river. A very dense fog rolled in the evening of December 16th, which concealed the advancing German counter attack. Conversely, the fog limited air support to US and allied ground forces. The 106th Division was ordered to withdraw to the west of the river, anticipating they would be overwhelmed by numerically superior German forces, and left without the aid of bomber or close-air support.

The 4th Battalion 333rd Field Artillery Battalion was ordered to stay in place and provide indirect fire for the retreating 106th Infantry. Missions where one unit is directed to remain in place to cover a retreating unit are known by the individual soldiers to be fraught with peril. In the loose battlefield vernacular of soldiers, this is also known as a "Die In Place" or "DIP" mission because there is little time for the covering force to withdraw after the safe relocation of the unit it covers.[29] On the evening of December 16th the Germans initiated a directed and sustained artillery barrage into the 106th and the 333rd's sector. By the morning of December 17, C Battery was flanked and overrun. Most of the troops were killed or captured, and eleven soldiers were separated from the unit. Attempts to find their way back to friendly lines failed and they hunkered down in Wereth, Belgium where they evaded enemy patrols. Though Belgium was a neutral country, many Belgian men were forced into serving in the German Army. Allegiances were mixed and there was no way to be certain of individual sympathies. Eventually, the soldiers—exhausted, hungry, some of them wounded, and all without water—sought the shelter of a local farmer. Mathias Langer offered them shelter at great risk to himself and his family. The Wereth/St. Vith portion of Belgium had been German territory prior to World War I and three of the nine homes in the village were loyal to Germany. It is believed that the wife of a German soldier who lived in the town told members of the 1st SS Division about the black American GIs hiding in the town.[30] The Germans captured the eleven soldiers and took them to a nearby field, where they tortured, maimed, and eventually shot them. Six weeks later, Mathias Langer found the remains of the eleven soldiers after the Allies re-captured the area. The Germans had battered the soldiers' faces, cut their fingers off, broken their legs, and used bayonets to stab them in the eyes. None of the Wereth 11 survived. Mathias Langer took a headstone from his family's cemetery plot and marked their grave with it.[31]

I first heard about the Langer Family and the Wereth 11 while serving overseas at Landstuhl Regional Medical Center. The Black History Month Staff Ride we organized for the 369th was so popular, and generated such feelings of goodwill, that the German and American military community was anxious for a new experience into the untold exploits of black patriots. Ms. Marie Shaw, who was Belgian, knew of this history and organized a meeting between the Langer Family, the unit historian, and me. There, the seeds were sown for a different European program involving unheralded black Americans' patriotism.

The Langers told us of how they have maintained the burial site ever since the discovery. They attempted to have the site established as an overseas American Battle Monument, like some of the other cemeteries of great notoriety in Normandy and Belgium. Once again, we organized as a committee and took a group of participants to the tiny village to pay homage to their sacrifices. The group raised donations to have the site gated, a fence emplaced, and a Belgian and American flag pole erected. On May 23, 2004, Lieutenant General William "Kip" Ward, the Deputy Commanding General of all Army forces in Europe conducted a dedication ceremony to these fallen soldiers who had been excluded from the annals of history.

General Ward dedicated the official American Battle Monuments site in their memory, and I was honored to be the moderator for the ceremony. The committee found a surviving relative of one of the Wereth 11, Ms. Gloria Barrow. Ms. Barrow and General Ward laid a wreath on the headstone to commemorate the dedication. The Langer family asked General Ward if he would also be willing to lay a wreath in memory of the Belgian soldiers who fought for their families in the German Army. LTG Ward graciously honored their requests and extemporaneously delivered a flawless tribute to their sons in fluent German.

The Wereth 11 were part of a larger group of American soldiers who were massacred during the last German counteroffensive—atrocities that came to be known as the "Malmedy Massacres." Yet, for some seventy-three years, the story of the 333rd Field Artillery was conspicuously omitted from the documentation of the Malmedy Massacres, as well as subsequent war trials for perpetrators. In omitting the sacrifices of these brave men, the Army and the War Department were in keeping with a larger narrative of that time: the denial of any positive achievement by black Americans in service to their country. In military circles, the term "stolen honor" exists. It is used to describe men and women who attempt to pass themselves off as war veterans, despite never having served in uniform. This definition should be expanded to include the systemic denial of achievements and sacrifices of men and women of color in an effort to diminish the accomplishments of minorities. This systematic delay of accolades is evidence that segregation was never really about beliefs of ability or operational efficiency, but about subjugating an entire race of people and maintaining a system of oppression.

THE TUSKEGEE AIRMEN "BLACK PANTHERS"

The Air Force can attribute changes in its policies regarding segregation to legislation perhaps more than any other armed service. Executive Order 8802, issued in 1941, made it possible for black construction companies to participate in building airfields and barracks to facilitate the training of black pilots. Public Law 18 mandated that flight training opportunities be made available for black pilots in addition to the white pilots already being trained in the lead up to WWII. Black civic leaders and the black media converged to push for the development of legislation meant specifically to end race-based discrimination.[32] The Tuskegee Airman were constituted because of the black media and back civic leaders' collaborative lobbying campaign. Black civic leaders had been lobbying for black admission to the Army Air Corps since it formed in 1917.[33] President Roosevelt was seeking an unprecedented third term in office in 1939. Roosevelt was an astute politician, particularly skilled at reading the political tea leaves and assessing what he could sell to members of Congress and the American people. The black political machinery was also politically savvy, and was fully aware of the political power its bloc wielded in large Midwestern and Northeastern cities following the Great Migration.

President Roosevelt knew he needed this bloc of votes to secure the Democratic nomination and win the presidency. Black Americans believed that, as Commander in Chief, Roosevelt could easily direct the Armed Services to integrate or create pilot positions for black Americans. Roosevelt resisted pressure from the black media and black civic organizations to integrate the armed services in 1940, though he did acquiesce by including language in the 1940 Selective Service Act that indicated desegregated armed forces could be on the horizon. The legislation read, "any person between the ages of 18 and 35, regardless of race or color, shall be afforded an opportunity voluntarily to enlist and be inducted into the land or naval forces of the United States for the training and service prescribed . . . if he is acceptable to the land or naval forces for such training or service."[34] Yet, the draft law still contained language that left the door open for the armed services to continue to segregate draftees: no man could be admitted unless he was "acceptable" and "adequate provision" had been made for his "shelter, sanitary facilities, medical care and hospital accommodations."[35] The intimation here, regarding accommodation's, was that a lack of separate facilities could be grounds for rejecting a draftee.

When black political factions learned that the language was misleading and that the services had no intention of desegregating, they engaged Eleanor Roosevelt's sympathetic ear in the early Fall of 1940 to leverage a meeting between President Roosevelt, Assistant Secretary of War Robert Patterson, Secretary of the Navy Frank Knox, and black civic leaders: T. Arnold Hill, National Urban League officer; Walter White, President of the NAACP; and A. Phillip Randolph, President of the Brotherhood of Sleeping Car Porters—a powerful black labor union.[36] The black delegation provided a list of demands to Roosevelt prior to the meeting. Among them were: an end to segregation in the military, and the opportunity for black clergy and medical professionals to serve as officers like their white colleagues.

The services dug-in their heels, refusing to budge on integration, stating, "Every effort should be made by the War Department to maintain in the Army the social and racial conditions which exist in civil life in order that normal customs of white and colored personnel now in the Army may not be suddenly disrupted."[37] Roosevelt was firm on his position while being sympathetic. He assured the black civic leaders that he would lessen discrimination in the armed services, and that black draftees would be afforded the same opportunities as white draftees with the caveat that only Medical Corps officers and chaplains would be allowed to serve in regular Army units. All black officers called from the reserves would be restricted to serving in the only two black National Guard Regiments.[38] The navy's conditions were that all black draftees would have to serve as messmen because the navy had no all-black ships. The War Department did not want black officers in charge of white officers, and only white officers were assigned to the four regular Army black regiments, with the exception of Benjamin O. Davis Jr.

The solution presented by Roosevelt, Patterson, and Knox was bleak. This policy represented a step backward from WWI when you consider black officers served in the regular Army 92nd Division, which was created through the draft. As news of the outcome of Roosevelt's meeting with White, Arnold, and Randolph spread, black celebrity figures, the black middle class, and the press began to shift support to Roosevelt's Republican opponent, Indiana-born lawyer and businessman, Wendell Wilkie.[39] Wilkie was boisterous in his support of integration, "under my administration, there will be no discrimination between people because of race, creed or color in the appointments to federal positions . . . Colored citizens [will be] appointed to any branch of the Civil Service to which they are qualified."[40]

Days before the 1940 election, Roosevelt was concerned about this shift in black popular opinion and granted black civic leaders three concessions to demonstrate he was serious about minimizing discrimination in the Army and Navy: 1) He promoted Benjamin O. Davis Sr. to Brigadier General. This helped appease the black community who was still upset about how Colonel Charles Young was forced from active duty prior to the start of WWI. 2) William Hastie, a Harvard Law School trained attorney and Dean of Howard Law School, was appointed as Special Assistant to Secretary of War Henry Stimson. 3) A reserve officer, Major Campbell C. Johnson was appointed Assistant to the Selective Service Director to help ensure equitable treatment for black recruits in the draft process.[41]

In December of 1941, the Army Air Corps submitted a plan for an experiment that would establish an all-black fighter squadron. The press release stated that the 99th Fighter Squadron would consist of between thirty-three and thirty-five pilots and 278 ground crew members. The senior officers who led the unit, however, were still going to be white. *The Crisis* magazine praised the establishment of the 99th Fighter Squadron as a step in the right direction.[42]

Continuing on the theme from the 1920s War College Report that black men lacked the intelligence, courage, and mental agility to be successful in combat, the Tuskegee Airmen were born as an experiment to test this notion. By the late 1930s, the War Department had to establish a systematic response for the steady barrage of inquiries from the black national press corps, civic organizations, church groups, and trade and labor units regarding defense policy on the use of black manpower. These groups formed a powerful bloc, applying concerted pressure on elected officials and the War Department. They disagreed on how progress should be achieved, but they all agreed that the status quo of limited use of 'Negro manpower' had to end.

Tuskegee Army Air Field was built by a black-owned architectural and construction company out of Nashville, TN. McKissack and McKissack Inc. won one of the largest government contracts ever awarded to a minority owned firm at that time to build not only the runways and control towers, but all the administrative and support buildings. President Roosevelt instituted Public Law 18 at the behest of his military advisors in 1939. Germany's invasion of Poland in 1938 prompted Roosevelt's military advisors to recommend large scale pilot training programs in the event war broke out in Europe. Congress instituted the Civilian Pilot Training Program (CPTP), which set aside funds to train twenty thousand college students per year at colleges and universities across the country using existing facilities. The program consisted of seventy-two hours of ground training and thirty-five to fifty hours of flight instruction to issue a private pilot's license. African American leaders insisted that black colleges be included among these institutions.[43]

However, at the time, the Army Air Corps had no plans for ever creating black fighter or bomber squadrons, or for establishing any other flying roles for blacks. Segregation was so ingrained that policy makers couldn't conceive of a time when the armed forces would ever be integrated, so they didn't see the need to establish CPTP programs at black colleges.

No service benefited more quickly or more directly than the War Department's newly reorganized Army Air Force. World War I and World War II were somewhat unique in that both efforts required what is referred to as full-scale mobilization—a complete and total effort involving a military draft for personnel and a partnership between commercial and defense industries. To fund the mass production of military hardware, as well as rapidly expanding and fielding military units, war bonds were sold primarily to raise capital, and secondarily to generate public morale behind the war effort.

The black press, plus church and civic leaders, seized upon this total reliance on public goodwill to point out glaring gaps in America's policy regarding both the use of black manpower in the war effort, and its zeal for their hard-earned dollar. Black World War I veterans testified before Congressional committees, met with black civic organizations, and underscored that there could be no repeat of the failures of World War I with respect to black inclusion in the full military effort. William Hastie, then Dean of Howard University Law School, declared in his testimony before a Congressional committee, "We will be American soldiers. We will be American ditch diggers. We will be American laborers. We will be anything that any other American should be in this whole program of national defense. But we won't be black auxiliaries."[44]

To decrease the gap between the military's stated policy of separate but equal, Congress put provisions into Public Law 18, designating one commercial aviation school for training black pilots. Yet, the military had no intention of training black pilots or creating black units to receive black pilots, mechanics, and ground crews. Senator Harry H. Schwartz of Wyoming proposed that of the civilian aviation schools designated by the Secretary of War to receive military equipment for training US combat pilots, one or more should be ear-marked for training by the Civil Aeronautics Authority (CAA) to train black pilots who met the qualification standards.[45] The measure was adopted and passed into law, setting the stage for what would become the "The Tuskegee Airmen."

Perhaps the demand from the black community for inclusion in the Air Corps was the greatest of all these services because it was the newest and most modern of the three armed services. Not only were the tax dollars of black Americans being used to literally build a modern flying force, but the black community was actively being recruited to fund new aircraft, air bases, and training facilities through the aggressive war bond campaign. The July 1940 issue of the NAACP's *The Crisis* magazine ran a photo on its cover of an airplane assembly line with the words, "FOR WHITES ONLY." The caption at the bottom read, "Warplanes, Negro Americans may not build them, repair them or fly them, but they must help pay for them."[46]

The black community pounced on this glaring double standard to insist that the newly forming Air Force be progressive. Given that the Air Corps was being built party from black capital, they felt it should be built with progressive policies that prohibited segregation. At the very least, there should be a mandated role for black service members at every level of service, especially pilots. Separate but equal was the law of the land at that time, and many politicians tried earnestly to ensure that there was equal opportunity in an effort to diminish the demand for a completely integrated society. A significant number of black men, such as Eugene Bullard, lobbied unsuccessfully to serve as aerial observers in the Army during World War I, but they were denied due to overtly racist policies.

THE BEGINNING OF THE TUSKEGEE EXPERIMENT

Although the press release stated the Army Air Force was seeking thirty-three to thirty-five pilots, the first class began at Tuskegee with thirteen: twelve cadets and one officer trainee. By the end of the course, only five successfully completed the requirements to become pilots: Cadet George Roberts, Lieutenant Benjamin O. Davis, Jr., Cadet Charles DeBow, Cadet Lemuel Curtis, and Cadet Mac Ross. As the first wave of pilots ended their training, America entered World War II following the attack on Pearl Harbor. The first class of black pilots earned their wings in a formal ceremony on March 7, 1942.[47] The cadets were promoted to lieutenant, and Benjamin O. Davis was promoted to captain, having already been commissioned as a second lieutenant following his graduation from West Point.

Black men signed up for the Army Air Corps in record numbers following the declaration of war against the axis powers. There were so many applicants for the pilot training and airplane maintenance courses that the Army Air Corps could afford to be very selective. Only the best of the best were chosen for pilot training. Effectively, the selection process for the 99th became almost as rigorous as the selection process for astronauts during the space race of the 1950s and '60s. One Tuskegee

Airman commented that there was always the underlying reminder that they were an "experiment." Every black pilot knew when they wore those wings, donned the uniform, or climbed into the cockpit they weren't just operating complex, dangerous equipment; they were representing an entire race of people fighting for a seat at the table of equality.

So many men trained and the experiment grew so rapidly that a second pursuit squadron, the 100th was formed on May 23, 1942. Skipping the rank of major entirely, in July 1942, Captain Davis was promoted to lieutenant colonel (along with his entire West Point class) in preparation for accelerated recruitment to meet the war's manpower requirements. Once promoted to lieutenant colonel, Davis took command of the 99th Pursuit Squadron. The Army Air Corps was now at a crossroads. Initially, the Army Air Corps never intended to train black pilots or form black fighter squadrons, but political pressure compelled them to do so. They had stalled and delayed as long as they could. Now that they had formed and trained black aerial combat units, they had to figure out how to employ them.

In April 1943, the 99th shipped out for the African Campaign where British and US forces were trying to push the Germans away from the oil-rich region of the Sudan and back into Italy. This was the beginning of the US's fight to push the Axis powers back to Europe and finally into Germany. Initially, the 99th patrolled the coast of Liberia for German submarines off the coast of West Africa.[48] The limited range of the aircraft assigned to the 99th would not allow them to fly significantly beyond the coast-line to perform this mission and have enough fuel to return to base. The 99th's mission was a fool's errand and became a cruel joke in US military circles. William Hastie resigned his position as Special Assistant to the Secretary of War in part to protest the treatment of the 99th and 100th Pursuit Squadrons.[49]

The 99th was assigned to the 33rd Fighter Group, which Colonel William Momyer commanded. Momyer was not a fan of the Tuskegee Airman, and leaked information to *Time* magazine on the invasion of Italy. He claimed that the 99th's low kill ratio was due to cowardice and lack of aggressiveness. In fact, their lack of kills had more to do with the types of missions they were given, which didn't present the 99th with opportunities to engage the enemy.[50]

The Tuskegee Airmen had reached a sort of crossroads following the invasion of Italy in 1943. The growing number of black enlistees accepted to the program as aspiring pilots, mechanics, and crew members was sufficient to develop more squadrons. Davis had been sent stateside to command an all-black fighter group, the 332nd. Simultaneously, senior military officials were lobbying Army Chief of Staff General George C. Marshall to end the experiment due to "poor performance" of the 99th in combat.[51] Davis was furious. He had never been told of any of the alleged problems with the 99th. Davis held a press conference at the Pentagon to defend his men by presenting evidence and testimony to a committee formed to study the use of black servicemen. The committee found that the performance of the 99th was on par with other units of its size using the same planes. The committee's findings were validated in January 1944 when the 99th shot down twelve German aircraft in two days while protecting troops on the beachhead in Anzio, Italy.[52]

Davis was promoted to full colonel and then assigned command of the 332nd Bomber Group. He returned to the states to command the all-black 477th Bombardment Group. Davis would go on to become the Air Force's first black general. He had numerous assignments of increased responsibility before retiring as a three-star general in 1970. President Bill Clinton brought him back on active duty for one day to promote him to four-star general, the highest peacetime rank in the US military. General Benjamin O. Davis Jr. was one of the many black war heroes of WW II who continued to serve through the Vietnam War.

Roscoe C. Brown, the last surviving "Jet Killer" from World War II and member of the famed Tuskegee Airmen, died on July 6, 2015. Roscoe, and two of his other black flying mates, won the title "Jet Killer" for squaring off against the foremost aircraft of its time and the world's first jet-powered fighter plane: the German Messerschmitt. They successfully destroyed that aircraft and survived the aerial "dog fight." To truly appreciate their skill and courage, consider that the P-51, the propeller-powered fighter plane that the Tuskegee Airman piloted, had a top speed of 437 miles per hour, and was armed with six .50 caliber browning machine guns with 380 rounds of ammunition each. The P-51 Mustang's maximum altitude was 12,800 meters with a rate of climb of 975 meters per minute. By contrast, the German engineered Messerschmitt Me 262, nicknamed the swallow because of its sleek design and speed, had a top speed of 559 miles per hour, and was armed with four 30mm cannons and twenty-four 55mm rockets. It could climb to a height of 11,450 meters at 1,200 meters per minute. Shooting down a German Me 262 was a rare feat, and the Me 262 is credited with a 4:1 kill ratio over allied aircraft in air to air combat.[53]

By war's end, the 99th and 100th Pursuit Squadrons participated in 1,578 combat missions in Africa, Italy, and Germany. They are credited with destroying 262 enemy aircraft and damaging another 148, destroying over 950 enemy rail cars and motorized vehicles, and destroying one enemy ship. They lost twenty-seven bombers while serving in escort duty, compared to the Army Air Corps average of forty-six among other P-51 bomber escort squadrons. They won ninety-six Distinguished Flying Crosses (ninety-five airmen, Captain William Campbell having won two). The Tuskegee Airman won fourteen Bronze Stars, 744 Air Medals, eight Purple Hearts, and one Silver Star.[54]

Minorities in World War II 107

Figure 4.1. P-51 Mustang, a propeller-driven fighter flown by the Tuskegee Airmen in 1944. *Photo courtesy of National Archives*

BLACK SAILORS IN WW II: FIGHTING FOR THE RIGHT TO FIGHT

The Navy had slightly more than 5,000 black sailors in its ranks when America entered World War II. All were serving as messman, stewards, or laborers, and there were no black officers in the active duty Navy. These black sailors belonged to the Stewards Branch, an all enlisted component of the Navy with different uniforms distinguishing them from the rest of the general Navy. They were generally recognized as inferior, and they were forbidden from giving orders to sailors in the Navy's general branches, even if a steward had been in the Navy for twenty plus years and out ranked a sailor right out of basic training. These black sailors comprised less than three percent of the Navy's total force structure in 1941.[55]

The Stewards Branch was essential to maintaining many of the customs and traditions that grew out of naval warfare. Because naval warfare is based upon projecting combat power from a ship armed with cannons—essentially a floating fortress—the ships are adorned with many of the creature comforts of buildings you could find on land in a military base. This is true as relatively modern advances to warfare and navy ships evolved. Officers in the Navy have historically enjoyed an elite status onboard ships that have included dining messes with china, tablecloths, silverware, and country club-like appointments. The Stewards Branch was essential to the maintenance of this lifestyle aboard

Figure 4.2. Messerschmitt Me 262, world's first jet fighter, was flown by the German Luftwaffe in 1944. *Photo courtesy of National Archives*

ships at sea. Only black sailors, and in some cases in the Pacific Filipinos, served in the Stewards Branch. They were trained cooks and butlers. The Stewards polished silver, set tables, did the dishes, and prepared meals, as well as laundry and shoeshining for everyone aboard the ships. Essentially, they performed the majority of tasks unrelated to direct combat or combat support (combat support included tasks such as communications, ship and weapons maintenance, firefighting, and navigation). In addition to overcoming the racist policies of segregation in the armed services, black inclusion in the Navy had another issue to overcome; if blacks were admitted to general service, who would do all the cooking, cleaning, and silver polishing aboard the ships?

The NAACP and black civic leaders pushed back against this status quo and appealed to the Navy and President Roosevelt for change. The Navy responded by stating they had no plans to change their policies regarding segregation or the employment of black draftees. The Navy's policy was not only detrimental to the morale of the black sailors currently serving in menial roles, but also on the black community whose money was counted on to fund the war effort. In March 1943, the Baltimore Afro-American published a photo of nearly one hundred Stewards from the Naval Academy, ranging in age from early twenties to late forties, on the steps of a mess hall. Three white men who ran the mess hall operation at Annapolis, two officers, and one civilian were in the center of the group. The caption read, "Here are 93 cooks in the US Naval Academy, all of whom are buying war bonds."[56]

Aside from the political misgivings of the Navy's segregation policy, there were the obvious operational inefficiencies. Navy recruiting ads blared over the radio and print media proclaiming they needed ablebodied young men to join the fight against imperialist Japan and Nazi Germany, then extolling in a muted tone or fine print that black men wishing to join the Navy could only serve as messmen. At recruiting stations across America, this played out as the Navy begging for manpower, yet turning away qualified, prospective black enlistees because quotas for cooks and dishwashers/messmen were already filled, and the Navy would not assign black enlistees to any other Military Occupational Skill (MOS). One Marine recruiter directly stated that they were in dire need of manpower, but that he was taking "no enlistments from black men."[57]

Dissatisfied with the Navy's official response, the black political movement appealed directly to President Roosevelt. The NAACP asked Roosevelt to end segregation in the Navy through Executive Order.[58] Roosevelt declined to do so but did write to his Secretary of the Navy Frank Knox. Knox was the Republican nominee for vice president in 1936, partial owner of the *Chicago Daily News*, and former Assistant Secretary of the Navy. FDR selected Knox partly to drum up bipartisan support for the defense and foreign policy measures he was proposing in the wake of France's fall to Nazi Germany.[59]

FDR overturned Knox's initial response to the NAACP by offering the following guidance to Knox: "I think that with all the Navy activities the Bureau of Navigation might invent something that colored enlistees could do in addition to the rating of messmen."[60] FDR also provided Knox with some political insight as to why the operational changes were necessary by stating, "Officers of the U.S. Navy are not officers only but are American citizens as well. They should therefore be expected to recognize social and economic problems which are related to national welfare . . . It is incumbent on all officers to recognize the fact that about 1/10th of the U.S. Population is composed of members of the Negro race who are American citizens."[61]

Three months later in April 1942, Secretary Knox announced that the Navy, Marine Corps, and Coast Guard would begin accepting and training black recruits for general service. The Navy planned to enlist 14,000 black sailors during the first year, and general service opened to blacks on June 1, 1942. The Navy trained black recruits in segregated facilities at Camp Robert Smalls—a base named after an African American Civil War hero who hijacked a Confederate vessel, and sailed it out of Charleston, delivering it to the US Navy.[62]

BLACKS' EARLY HISTORY IN THE US NAVAL ACADEMY: THE FIRST BLACK "MIDDIES"

The US Naval Academy at Annapolis was established in 1845. John H. Conyers was the first black Navy cadet, midshipman, admitted in September 1872. Robert Brown Elliot, a member of the US House of Representatives from South Carolina who also served as South Carolina's twenty-eighth Speaker of the House and State Attorney General, nominated Conyers. Elliot was forced out of office when the last Union troops withdrew from South Carolina following the end of Reconstruction in 1877. Midshipman Conyers experienced similar harassment, hazing, and beatings as the first black cadets did at West Point. His classmates even attempted to drown him. Three classmates were dismissed for the incident, but the abuse continued until Conyers withdrew in October of 1873.

Alonzo Clifton McClennon and Henry Edwin Baker were the next two black midshipmen admitted to the Naval Academy. Midshipman McClennon scored second highest on his entrance exam and was admitted by Richard H. Cain, a black congressman from South Carolina. McClennon resigned his appointment within a year, but went on to graduate from Howard Medical School and serve as a prominent doctor in Augusta, GA and Charleston, SC.[63]

Baker was admitted to Annapolis in 1873, a year after McClennon's withdrawal. Both men were aware of the mistreatment of Midshipman Conyers and still applied. Baker was dismissed from the academy for use of "opprobrious language" (cursing like a sailor). Baker's harassment and abuse is better documented than his two black predecessors. Baker was goaded into the altercation that lead to his suspension for use of foul language. After the Secretary of the Navy reinstated Baker, two freshmen midshipmen—John Hood from Alabama and Lawson Melton from South Carolina, attacked Baker. Ironically, Melton was endorsed for his appointment by the same black congressman who endorsed Baker. The two men were dismissed for their roles in the attack, and they boasted that they would repeat their offenses in the future if presented with the same circumstances. Hood, however, was reappointed by US Representative Goldsmith Hewitt of Alabama and graduated in 1879.[64]

Baker fell behind in his studies, and although he passed his end of year examinations, he was asked to repeat his freshman year along with twenty other freshmen. The attacks continued the next year and Baker resigned permanently. Baker went on to graduate from Howard Law School and joined the US Patent Office in 1877. Baker rose to the rank of Second Assistant Examiner by 1902. His area of expertise was black inventors. Baker penned three books on the subject before his death in 1928.[65] Baker described the harassment he endured at the Naval Academy:

> I was several times attacked with stones, and was forced finally to appeal to the officers ... My books were mutilated, my clothes were cut, and in some instances destroyed, and all the petty annoyances which ingenuity could devise were inflicted upon me daily, and during seamanship practice attempts were often made to do me personal injury ... No one ever addressed me by name. I was called the "Moke" usually, the "damn nigger," for variety. I was shunned as if I were a veritable leper, and received curses and blows as the only method my persecutors had of relieving the monotony ... [66]

This poignant testimony is but a pebble in the mountain of injustice black servicemen and women have endured to serve the country they love. There would not be another black midshipman at the US Naval Academy for sixty years.[67]

WESLEY A. BROWN

Wesley A. Brown became the first black graduate of the US Naval Academy at West Point in 1949, a year after Truman desegregated the armed services. Wesley initially attended Howard University and was appointed to the Naval Academy by Congressman Adam Clayton Powell Jr. in 1945. Brown graduated 370th out of nearly 800 graduates. He enjoyed a distinguished military career, retiring at the rank of lieutenant commander in 1969 after twenty years as a naval civil engineer and serving combat tours in Korea and Vietnam. The Navy dedicated a five million dollar indoor athletic facility at the Naval Academy in his name on May 1, 2008. Brown lived to see the dedication and passed away on May 22, 2012. He was an accomplished athlete at the Naval Academy where he ran cross country with President Jimmy Carter.[68]

THE NAVY'S GOLDEN 13

The Navy did not begin its officer training program for black sailors until January 1, 1944. Until then, the Navy had only commissioned a handful of black officers who served in the Navy reserves. Most of them were physicians, dentists, or ministers. There were only three means of becoming a Navy officer at that time: ROTC or the Naval Academy; the V-12 college training program; and direct commission appointments usually reserved for health care professionals or ministers. The Navy commissioned sixteen black sailors on March 17, 1944 following their completion of its V-12 college program, just eighteen months before the Japanese surrender.[69]

Although these men were hand-selected from thousands of applicants, the Navy was surprised when their composite final exam scores came back two-tenths of a point higher than any other class previously tested. The Navy was so surprised in fact that they ordered the men to retake the test. This time, the composite results were even higher! Of the sixteen who completed the course and passed the exam, inexplicably only thirteen were given their commission as officers: John W. Reagan, Jesse W. Arbor, Dalton L. Baugh, Frank E. Sublett, Graham E. Martin, Phillip G. Barnes, Reginald Goodwin, James E. Hair, Samuel E. Barnes, George C. Cooper, William S. White, Dennis D. Nelson, and Charles B. Lear.[70] These twelve, newly minted officers and one warrant officer were immediately labeled "Deck Officers," a designation that, up until that point, was limited to Navy officers who had a physical or mental impairment preventing them from serving in the full range of expected duties.

A few months after Knox's death, the Navy started a second V-12 Officer's Training Program of twenty black officer candidates. This time, they were not isolated on Camp Smalls, but trained in integrated classes with white candidates—a first for any armed service. By January 1945, the Navy had thirty-four black officers on active duty in civil engineering, medical and dental fields, supply, and the chaplain's corps. The Navy had also begun integrating some of its dining halls, dormitories, and recreational facilities on both US coasts.

These small but significant steps paved the way for the Navy's smoother transition to full integration once Executive Order 9981 was issued. Despite President Roosevelt's urging that the Navy expand roles for black sailors, the Navy's new policy met with mix results. On the one hand, the Navy was recruiting and training thousands of black inductees for expanded roles of service within the Navy—electrician's mate, communications and radio specialist, plumbing specialist, ammunition handler, etc. The problem came in how these newly trained, skilled sailors were being employed. Once sent to their bases for assignment, local commanders were assigning them to labor units that performed loading and unloading of ships, mess hall operations, stevedore, cook, and other mess hall duties that were not consistent with their primary Military Occupational Skill (MOS).

Consequently, black sailors trained for highly technical MOSs, some of whom came to the Navy with college degrees, were being assigned to manual labor roles and other shore duty at bases around America and the Pacific. The net effect was more blacks electing to be drafted into the Army or Army Air Force where they had a chance to serve as officers or in direct combat roles in segregated units. The Navy had no segregated war ships or units, so sea duty aboard combat ships was also not an option. Blacks in Northern and Midwestern urban communities were beginning to form the opinion that FDR was either insincere about increasing the roles in which black sailors served or he was ineffectual. Either way, FDR's political adversaries were playing up the glaring disconnect between FDR's words and what was happening in the Navy.

THE USS *MASON*

Adele Stevens, then a special advisor to the Secretary of the Navy Knox, and First Lady Roosevelt endorsed a plan to build a war ship for an all-black sea crew. This ship, USS *Mason*, carried the military designation DE529. It was built in the Boston Navy Yard, an elite Evarts-class destroyer, measuring 289 feet long, weighing 1,140 tons, and boasting an impressive array of armaments. It was clearly a ship designed for battle. The ship was commissioned on March 20, 1944, amid much fanfare. The governor of Massachusetts, the mayor of Boston, and the president of the Boston Chapter of the NAACP were all in attendance. This was to be the Navy's own version of the "Tuskegee Experiment."[71] The *Mason* is credited with aiding twelve smaller, civilian vessels during the storm of the century in October 1944. The ship's radio antenna and two main supporting beams below deck snapped during the storm. The ship's crew repaired the broken antenna and floor beams in the storm and rendered aid to the smaller vessels. Two British ships were ordered to accompany the *Mason* but returned to harbor upon seeing how violent the sea had become. Commodore Alfred Lind, Commander of the Convoy NY 119, recommended the commanding officer and its entire crew for individual commendation, but they were never awarded. After World War II, the ship itself became a training ship, and was decommissioned as scrap metal in 1947.

In 1998, Secretary of the Navy John H. Dalton decided to name a new Arleigh Burke Class Destroyer in honor of the USS *Mason* (DE529). President Clinton awarded sixty-seven surviving members of the *Mason* their long overdue presidential citation in 1994.[72] The *Mason* was one of two war ships comprised of primarily black crews that served during World War II. The other was the PC-1264 Submarine USS Chaser commissioned on April 25, 1944. PC-1264 was a smaller ship whose mission was to destroy German submarines operating off the Atlantic coast. It was commanded by Navy lieutenants. The Navy's first black admiral, Samuel Gravely had his first sea-fairing assignment aboard PC-1264. Eventually black sailors from the eight different specialties required to run the ship were promoted to petty officer once deemed proficient enough to train future crew members. They replaced the white petty officers who were assigned initially to train the black sailors, making PC-1264 the Navy's only all-black ship.

RACIAL TENSION IN THE NAVY PERSISTS

In 1943, the Navy was inducting an average of 12,000 black recruits each month, in part because the Army and Army Air Force had met their quotas for black inductees who preferred combat units and pilot training programs not offered by the Navy. By the end of 1943, there were 100,000 black enlisted sailors with projections for these numbers to increase. Despite concrete steps to improve the plight of black sailors, the Navy still lagged behind the other services in 1944.[73] With the 1944 election closing in, and the swelling of the ranks of black sailors, the Navy's use of black sailors exclusively in non-combat roles on shore and aboard ships became an ever-growing black eye for the War Department, Roosevelt, and members of Congress. Increasingly, constituents expressed concern that black men would not be given the opportunity to serve their country in the Navy with the same dignity and pride as white inductees. Editors of the Baltimore Afro-American wrote in a widely circulated editorial that:

> Colored people stand to suffer grievously from the Navy's indifference to national welfare in its defiance of President Roosevelt's oft-expressed pronouncements that there must be the fullest use of all our human and national resources to win the war . . . black recruits enter the service with the full knowledge that they are barred from fighting ships except as flunkies . . .[74]

In another editorial, the Baltimore Afro-American suggested that if either of the Republican nominees for president were elected, Dewey or Wilkie, "we would not have lily-white fighting ships."[75]

In response to this continued political pressure from the black community, FDR and members of Congress goaded Knox on numerous occasions to improve conditions for black sailors, which could best be described as steeped in Jim Crow subordination and subjugation. Knox's deference to Navy uniformed leaders who were entrenched in the status quo prevented the Navy from making significant strides in improving the use of black military manpower.

Under Secretary of the Navy Adele Stevens pointed out that the other services were getting the most educated and talented black recruits because their programs offered more promise to fight in combat and receive officer training. Roosevelt wrote Knox repeatedly, emphasizing that the sole use of "colored sailors" as custodial flunkies was politically untenable. Nonetheless, Roosevelt felt no need to integrate ship crews. Building a separate fleet of ships was also not an enduring solution as with the *Mason*. This presented a conundrum for Navy leaders, which they addressed by training black sailors for more combat support roles, and then allowing local commanders to use the sailors as they saw fit. The result was more black sailors cleaning up after white sailors.

When Secretary Knox died unexpectedly in 1944, James V. Forrestal was appointed as the new Secretary of the Navy. Forrestal was a wealthy banker whose family immigrated from Ireland shortly before the Civil War. Forrestal attended Princeton University but did not graduate due to financial difficulties.[76] Forrestal worked his way up the ranks of the banking industry, starting as a bond salesman and eventually became president of the bank. During his time as a Wall Street banker, Forrestal joined the local Urban League whose stated mission was to improve blacks' economic self-reliance, parity and civil rights.[77] In Forrestal, Under Secretary Stevens had a shrewd, pragmatic, and visionary leader who understood the business case for more efficient use of black manpower, as well as the moral imperative.

THE FIRST BLACK MARINES, "MONTFORD POINT MARINES"

The United States Marine Corps had the most racist, exclusionary policies of all branches of the military at the beginning of World War II. There were literally zero black men serving in the Marine Corps when America entered World War II on December 8, 1941. The thought of black men serving in the US Marine Corps was completely antithetical to the Marine Corps' values at the time. The Marines considered themselves to be an elite, all-male, all-white brotherhood of warriors. Inherent in their value system was the notion that this elite quality automatically excluded black men, in keeping with much of the nation's legally enforced segregation—an off-shoot of the belief that black Americans were inferior in every conceivable way, and therefore should be separated from the white majority population.

Forrestal knew it would be impossible to change the culture of the Marine Corps, which was and still is subordinate to the Department of the Navy, though it is its own distinct armed service. Forrestal began to recruit prominent Navy leaders who shared his vision and could be counted upon to carry out President Roosevelt's wishes to expand opportunities for blacks in the Navy and Marine Corps beyond the stewards' branch. One leader he recruited was Admiral Ernest J. King, Chief of Naval Operations and the US Fleet. As open as King was in embracing Forrestal's vision, then Commandant of the Marine Corps, Major General Thomas Holcomb was equally opposed.[78]

Holcomb was born in 1879, which made him sixty-two at the start of World War II. He served forty-four years as a Marine Commissioned Officer, serving as the Commandant of the Marine Corps from 1936 to 1943. Holcomb guided Marine Corps expansion from a pre-war population of 18,000 to 385,000 when he stepped down. Holcomb was legendary in the Marine Corps, and dedicated to using every fiber of his influence to bar blacks and other people of color from entering the Marine Corps.

In an April 1941 testimony to the Navy's General Board, Holcomb testified that blacks have no "right" to join the Marine Corps. He stated, "The Negro race has every opportunity now to satisfy its aspirations for combat by serving in the Army."[79] Holcombe eventually become the first Marine Corps officer ever promoted to the rank of four-star general. This quote best sums up Holcomb's feelings towards admitting blacks into service in the US Marine Corps: "If it were a question of having 5,000 whites or 250,000 Negroes, I would rather have the whites."[80] Holcombe believed that the Corps was too small to accommodate an integrated force and that integration would erode efficiency. For him, integration was never under consideration. Holcomb characterized blacks' desire to enter the Corps as an attempt to gain admittance into a "club that doesn't want them."[81]

In April 1942, Secretary Knox announced that the Marine Corps would begin taking black inductees on the order of President Roosevelt. The following month, the Navy ordered the Marine Corps to begin plans to accept 900 black men per month. Holcomb was a no-nonsense type of leader who was considered to be practical and a good follower. He did not want to repeat the same mistakes the Army made in World War I with the 92nd Division and, to his credit, he provided prudent instructions to his senior Marine generals to prepare for the inevitable, stating, "All Marines are entitled to the same rights and privileges under Navy Regulations."[82] Black Marines would not be coddled nor harassed; they were expected to "conduct themselves with propriety and become a credit to the Marine Corps."[83]

The Marine Corps prepared to train its new black inductees, all-volunteers, at Montford Point Marine training camp. Montford Point was the worst training camp in the Marine Corps inventory, located near Camp Lejeune, NC. These black Marines became known as "Montford Point Marines," and although seventy-five percent of these first black volunteers were college educated, nearly all the black Marines were trained to become stewards, messmen, or laborers. The Marines would not accept black men for officer training either. After their training, these Montford Point Marines were sent to the Pacific Theater to replace white labor units who were then thrust into combat.

Like the Tuskegee Airmen, the black Marine volunteers were a self-selecting group of high achievers, drawn by the appeal of being the first black Marines to complete training in what was considered a small, elite, group of perhaps the toughest American warriors. The Marine Corps probably fully understood the quality of trained black Marines within their ranks even if they didn't outwardly acknowledge it. The Corps became adept at extolling the accomplishments of its first black graduates. Pictures of Private First Class Edward Swann were plastered in the *Chicago Defender* with him in his dress uniform, ringing the doorbell of his parents' Brooklyn, NY, home. The *Baltimore Afro-American* ran a story on four black Marines promoted to sergeant in May 1943. This conspicuous display of black success was principally to achieve two ends: to demonstrate to the administration they were compliant, and to belay the political pressure of black community leaders.

BLACK MARINES IN COMBAT DURING WORLD WAR II

Two units amongst the Montford Point Marines were selected for combat defense battalions. They would continue their training as a primary fighting force as opposed to the service and support units the previous black Marines were trained for. Despite these conspicuous displays of success, the reality for black Marines was more of the same bait-and-switch embellishment of reality.

The Marine Corps began to pick from the ranks of its newly trained Marines those whom they believed to have leadership potential for the task of leading their contemporaries. Among this group of early black Marines were two that became legendary. Edgar R. Huff, born in Gadsden, Alabama, was the first black Marine promoted to the rank of sergeant (a non-commissioned officer), and went on to become the Marine Corps' first black sergeant major (the highest enlisted rank in the military). Equally famous was fellow Alabaman, Gilbert Johnson, nicknamed Hashmark because of the crisp service stripes he wore on his uniform. Johnson had sixteen years of combined service when he joined the Marine Corps in 1943 at thirty-seven years of age. Johnson had two years of college and had served in both the Army and Navy. He was a Navy officer's steward first class when he reported for Marine training.[84]

Johnson most likely would have been promoted to sergeant first, but was considered to be "outspoken" by his superior officers and not an ideal candidate. The two men eventually both became NCOs and were reassigned as, "acting Jacks," a slang term for Marine Drill Instructors. Black drill instructors oversaw all training for black Marines at Montford Point by May 1943. Both men were assigned to the only two black Marine units whose primary mission was combat: the 51st and 52nd Composite Defense Battalions. These battalions were comprised of seacoast artillery, antiaircraft artillery, infantry, and tank units designed to defend small overseas bases that housed supply lines, depots, and hospitals.

3RD MARINE AMMUNITION COMPANY, 18TH AND 20TH DEPOT COMPANIES

By many accounts the 51st and 52nd Defense Battalions achieved impressive training records. Partly motivated by fear of failure and the knowledge that the weight of their community and their loved ones was riding on their success, they likely pushed themselves harder than they otherwise would have. In September 1943, the 51st Defense Battalion was moved to an isolated portion of Montford Point to undergo specific, large unit combat training, and to field all of its equipment, howitzers, and anti-aircraft gun pieces in preparation for deployment into the Pacific Theater. They were the only Montford Point Marines engaged in this type of training, and wore their isolation as a badge of honor despite being housed in a run-down base camp—a camp formerly used for the Civilian Conservation Corps and as a war-dog training facility.[85]

After months of training, the men's morale sank. They were beginning to believe their organization as a combat unit was a public relations stunt to get more blacks to enlist in the Marines, only to make them stewards and stevedores. The men resolved to double down on their training until one day in November they put on a gunnery display for several Marine Corps top brass. They broke all previous coastal and antiaircraft firing records that day. The demonstration was not reported to the War Department, but the 51st did receive orders to deploy to the Pacific Theatre in January 1944. The men's elation would soon turn to disappointment when they arrived on the sleepy Ellice Islands to relieve the 7th Defense Battalion. They never saw actual combat during World War II.[86]

The only black Marines to see combat were the 3rd Marine Ammunition Company and the 18th and 20th Depot Companies. They participated in the Saipan Island Campaign, June 15 through July 10, 1944. Their mission was to transport ammunition from the amphibious Marine landing vehicles to the Marines on the beach head, fighting their way inland to take full control of the island. This island was the first, in the series of the US's island-hopping campaign, to gain a foothold close enough to Japan to begin an invasion.[87] Men from these units were credited with helping to repulse an enemy counter attack during the night, and with knocking out an enemy machine gun position during the attack. Following the engagements, the Marine commandant, General Alexander Vandegrift reported the "negro Marines are no longer on trial. They are Marines period."[88] The 3rd Ammunition and 18th, 19th, and 20th Depot companies were included in the 4th Marine Division Presidential Unit Citation for that campaign. Black Marine ammunition would go on to play significant roles in the recapture of Guam and the Battle for the Island of Peleiu, as well as Iwo Jima and Okinawa.

LESSONS LEARNED FROM THE SEGREGATED ARMED FORCES IN WWII

In the final push leading up to Victory in Europe Day (V-E Day), the War Department loosened its policies regarding the segregation of black soldiers significantly. The more immediate and pressing concern was to move into Germany as quickly as possible, and to secure a German surrender. Lieutenant General John C. H. Lee officially suggested that black service troops be allowed to volunteer for combat. Lee made the recommendation in response to some of the fiercest fighting in the European Theatre in the Ardennes Forest and the manpower shortage that followed. Generals George Patton and Omar Bradley endorsed Lee's suggestion.⁸⁹ During the last major counter offensive following the allies' break out of Normandy and France, German soldiers posing as Americans at key check points were inflicting serious damage on American forces. General Patton ordered black soldiers to serve as check point security to thwart these attacks.

Once the War Department approved the recommendation, Benjamin O. Davis Sr. wrote the directive that secured over 4,000 volunteers from all black service units to be reassigned to white combat units, plugging holes where men were killed or wounded.⁹⁰ The directive required that each volunteer have scored within the top four categories of the AGCT, and volunteers could not be above the rank of private. Numerous black NCOs agreed to take a reduction in rank in order to join front line combat units. After the Americans successfully defeated Hitler's last, major coordinated counter-offensive on the western front, America and the allies knew they were in a race to Berlin. They needed to secure as much German territory as possible to prevent ceding that territory to communist Russia. This race to Berlin was the major impetus for the Army allowing black combat support troops to fight in integrated, white combat units as replacements to fill critical shortages.

One soldier, Bruce M. Wright, a twenty-five-year-old medic who was drafted into the Army in 1942 during his second year at Fordham University Law School, joined because he was hoping "to prove something and to make things better." As soon as the Americans successfully pushed through Germany's last major coordinated attack, and dispersed the German army into pockets of scattered resistance amid full retreat, the US military sent black soldiers back to their segregated units to dig graves, load cargo, and in some cases, prepare to be shipped to the Pacific Theatre to continue the assault against Japan.⁹¹

In some cases, the racism towards these men was so great that black servicemen were supervised in their manual labor by German POWs who drove the trucks while they labored. Before the experiment, a poll showed that thirty-five percent of white enlisted men believed that integration could be effective, and thirty-three percent of officers believed that integration within the Army would be successful. Following the "Bulge Experiment," seventy-seven percent of both groups believed integration could be successful in combat. The seeds had been sown for the major policy shift that would lead the nation's own foray into integration.

The Navy made great strides from using black sailors solely as messmen to fully integrating black sailors into all MOSs for which they qualified, despite local commanders in many instances forcing them to work outside their MOSs as messmen and port handlers. The Navy had 5,000 black commissioned officers by the end of the war, and had launched two war vessels staffed solely with black sailors and white officers. By the end of WWII, the Navy's policy was one of full integration. The Navy declared itself to be integrated in 1947 under the leadership of James Forrestal, first Secretary of the Navy who went on to become the first Secretary of Defense. A Navy memo dated February 1947 stated, "Effective immediately all restrictions governing the types of assignments for which Negro naval personnel are eligible are hereby lifted."[92] This made the Navy the first of the armed services to end segregation as a policy, a year before Executive Order 9981.

The Marine Corps made for an odd assortment of ideologies. On the one hand they were the last and most reluctant service to accept black service members, yet in some instances, their reverence for the warrior ethos allowed black Marines to be recognized on the merits of their ability. For example, the first black Marine combatants were in Saipan where the 3rd, 18th, 19th and 20th Ammunition Depot Companies were included in the Presidential Unit Citation with the 4th Marine Division in June 1944.[93] This example is in stark contrast to the 761st Tank Battalion. The 761st spent more consecutive days in combat than any other battalion-sized unit or larger (183 days), but waited until 1978 before they were given the same Presidential Citation many of the units they were attached to and fought beside were bestowed when the action occurred. However, in the final assessment, deference to the status quo won the day as the Marine Corps unceremoniously discharged almost all 17,000 black Marines following the war.

The Tuskegee Airmen were so exemplary in their duties the Army Air Force couldn't deny their success. Black airmen had proven they were more than up for the challenge. The Tuskegee Airmen were credited with sinking an enemy war ship with machine-gun fire and only losing escorted bombers on seven of their seventy-nine bomber escort missions. They lost a total of twenty-seven friendly bombers in contrast to an average of forty-six friendly bombers lost among other 15th Army Air Force P-51 groups.

The Secretary of the Air Force, Stuart Symington of Baltimore, was also a progressive North-Easterner where segregation wasn't as prevalent. Symington often expressed the sentiment that segregation was wasteful and inefficient, which is why the Air Force made the transition to full integration much more quickly than the Army and Marine Corps. Prior to the end of WWII, Assistant Secretary of War John McCloy directed all theatre-level commanders to provide progress reports on black units and recommendations for postwar racial policy immediately following the surrender of German forces in the European Theater. Truman Gibson, a black civilian working in the War Department, convinced McCloy to expand the parameters of the report to include the performance of black units as well.

Most commanders submitted reports that were in keeping with the racist dogma of the 1920s Staff College memo, which essentially said that black soldiers were mentally inferior, superstitious, adversely affected by cold, and afraid of the dark. General Joseph T. McNarney, Commanding

General of the Mediterranean Theatre of Operations, where both the Tuskegee Airman and the 761st Tank Battalion initially served, disagreed with such reports. In his assessment, the "colored soldier individually could be made into a good combat man, but "segregated units were a failure."[94]

The Army convened a committee of three generals to examine the Army's racial policy and prepare a report on how the Army could make better use of black troops. General Alvan C. Gillem Jr. led the committee. The report was entitled, Utilization of Negro Manpower in the Postwar Army Policy. The report was filed in April 1946 and recommended the Army end any special consideration based on race at the earliest possible opportunity. Armed with this report, Truman directed a systematic study of the use of black troops in the armed services, and assessed the political impact of ending segregation in the military through executive order. A month prior to the President's Committee on Civil Rights report, To Secure These Rights, attorney James Rowe, a former Roosevelt "New Deal" aide, teamed with Truman's own advisor, Clark Clifford, to formulate a political strategy for Truman. The analysis covered from November 1947 to November 1948. The assessment was that black voters could sway the election since many blacks had migrated to northeastern and mid-western cities, and as a block this contingent of voters could swing the election to the Republicans. Black voters were only brought into the Democratic camp through Roosevelt's "New Deal," which provided financial and unemployment relief to blacks and whites alike.[95]

The assessment went on to say that the South was solidly in the camp of the Democrats, so changing national policy (integration of the armed services) in and of itself would not be significant enough to lose the South as a voting bloc, but failing to address the concerns of black Americans may drive the black voting bloc in New York, Philadelphia, Cleveland, Chicago, Detroit, and Kansas City back to the party of Lincoln. What the assessment did not anticipate was the splintering of the Democratic Party over Truman and the Democratic Party's civil rights platform. Had the Southern delegates not formed their own party and aligned with the Republican Party, Dewey may have won the 1948 presidential election after all.

The Dixicrat's racial hatred both drove them out of the Democratic Party and prevented them from forming a bloc with Republicans in 1948. Modern, "Gingrich," Southern Republicans have managed to put aside the more distant grievance—freeing the enslaved—and formed that elusive alliance that was untenable in 1948 to create the present day, "Solid South" GOP voting bloc. Jimmy Carter, himself a Southerner, was the last Democratic presidential candidate to win the Southern voting bloc in the 1976 presidential election.

The biggest problem with Executive Order 9981 is that it did not specify a timetable for when the units should be completely integrated. The status-quo, old guard leaders who initially did not want to embrace this change included some very powerful men: General Omar Bradley, the Army Chief of Staff; and General Dwight David Eisenhower, Commanding General, Supreme Allied Forces in Europe. General Bradley was verbally reprimanded for contradicting the intent of Executive Order 9981 in a Washington Post interview the day after the order was issued. In April 1948, General Eisenhower testified before a Senate Armed Services Committee, "There is race prejudice in this country ... when you pass a law to get somebody to like someone, you have trouble."[96] This was Eisenhower's way of suggesting that the military is not a laboratory for social experiment and shouldn't be asked to do things the nation at large is unwilling to do. This is a common refrain used by military brass to resist policies dealing with social change. This type of logic misses the basic premise that the right to serve the nation in uniform is one of America's most common, unifying aspects of citizenship, particularly in an all-volunteer force. The physical ability to perform the job should take precedence above all other considerations.

Newly confirmed Secretary of Defense, Louis Johnson, delivered the final coffin-nail for segregation in the armed forces when he issued a DoD directive on April 6, 1949, instructing all the services to accept and assign personnel "only on the basis of individual merit and ability" and "without regard to race."[97] Johnson was, by all accounts, a gifted Virginia lawyer who believed fervently in the Constitution and the rule of law. He had no patience for the Army and Marine Corps' foot-dragging. With the policy battles put to rest, the seeds were sown for integrating the military. Systematically removing barriers to integration, including subordinate commanders who did not comply, had begun. Major General Edward M. Almond was one such subordinate commander. Almond commanded the Army's lone black combat division during the Italian Campaign (1944–45) in WWII—the 92nd Division.

Almond was assigned command of the 92nd from the day it was conceived in July 1942. MG Almond led the training of the 92nd Division at Fort Huachuca, AZ. The 92nd Division's 'official' combat record was poor, but the veracity of many of the reports used to compile the official combat record of the unit have been called into question. Some historians characterize the 92nd's record as a self-fulfilling prophecy, as was the practice of the armed forces when they were segregated. Southern officers, many of whom held segregated beliefs were assigned to all-black units; "little was expected from them," and in many cases "little was provided."[98]

The US Army continued to delay if not outright resist the integration order mandated by Truman. In his signature work on the Korean War, *The Forgotten War*, famed historian and former Editor in Chief of the Saturday Evening Post, Clay Blair, described MG Almond as "a devout anti-black bigot."[99] In his own words, Almond was quoted as saying,

"No white man wants to be accused of leaving the battle field. The Negro doesn't care . . . people think being from the South we don't like Negroes [sic]. Not at all, but we understand his capabilities. And we don't want to sit at the table with them." In spite of these racist views, Almond remained in a position of authority over several thousand black troops heading into the Korean War.

KOREA, THE ARMED FORCES MOVES TO FULL INTEGRATION, REALLY

The nation was war-weary and ready to resume some semblance of normalcy in the face of an emerging cold war. The US sought to dismantle its war machinery and integrate over 12 million service members into the economy. Truman, sensitive to the Russian's push to expand their territory, put a great deal of energy into establishing the United Nations as a deterrent to Russian aggression. It was a delicate task of building allies, projecting a robust military presence, and refocusing the nation's resources on growing the economy.

When the North Koreans crossed the 38th parallel and attacked South Korea, a special assembly of the United Nations convened. The UN's first Secretary General, Trygve Lie of Norway, declared after US Secretary of State Acheson informed him of the attack, "This is a war against the United Nations."[100] An emergency session of the UN Security Council was called on June 25, 1950. The member nations approved a US resolution, calling the invasion a breach of world peace, to come to the aid of South Korea. Eighteen nations signed on to provide troops: Belgium, Colombia, Greece, the Netherlands, and the Philippines provided battalion sized elements. Turkey contributed a brigade, and the United Kingdom, comprised of Britain, Canada, Australia, and New Zealand, contributed one division. The US committed seven ground divisions, plus air and sea power to go along with South Korea's eight divisions.[101]

President Truman placed General Douglas McArthur in charge of the UN coalition on July 2, 1950. Truman approved air support for South Korean ground forces and directed the Seventh Fleet to be deployed to the Taiwan Strait as a show of force to deter Chinese intervention.[102] McArthur knew that he did not have enough military might to push the North Koreans back into North Korea without US or other new ground forces, even with US Air support.

Mao Tse-tung offered some of his Chinese divisions which had been exiled to Taiwan following the Chinese Civil War, but Truman rejected the offer, reasoning acceptance might provoke communist China into more overt and direct support of the North Koreans, expanding the war and going against Truman's "limited war" objective. Instead, Truman authorized two American divisions from the occupying force in Japan to provide immediate assistance while more troops from the US could be marshalled, trained, and equipped. This was the beginning of the historic rift between General McArthur and President Truman. President Truman was explicit in his instructions: US planes and vessels were not to cross the 38th parallel.

The principle military architects of the Korea strategy were Secretary of State Dean Acheson, and General Douglas McArthur, Commander of the Far East Command. McArthur had at his disposal four US Infantry Divisions on occupation duty, organized under the Eighth

US Army in Japan: the 1st and 7th Cavalry Divisions, the 24th and 25th Infantry Divisions, and the 29th Regimental Combat Team in Okinawa. The South Korean Army had another 95,000 troops organized into constabulary divisions whose mission was to defeat pro-communist opposition to South Korean leader Syngman Rhee. The North Koreans had a much more formidable force that consisted of 135,000 troops, many of whom were veterans of the Chinese Civil War.[103]

For North Korea, in addition to their eight divisions, they had a tank brigade equipped with 120 Soviet T-34 Tanks, an artillery regiment, two other divisions at half strength, and five constabulary divisions all supported by Russian aircraft. The US was looking for a "peace dividend" after four years of national mobilization that cost $341 billion in 1945 dollars—the equivalent of seventy-four percent of the US GDP or $4.5 trillion 2016 dollars.

Almond shared with colleagues that he thought the 92nd's poor combat record held him back from positions of higher command. Despite Almond's poor record in command he was favored by General George C. Marshall, a fellow Virginia Military Institute (VMI) graduate. MacArthur selected Almond to be his chief of staff of the Eighth Army, whose area of responsibility included the entire Pacific Region. One of Almond's first actions as chief of staff was to assign the 24th Infantry Regiment (Colored), to Gifu, Japan. Gifu was halfway between Tokyo and Korea. The 24th was part of the American Japanese occupying Army following World War II. The 24th was also the last remaining regiment of the old, all-black 93rd Division; the regiment had been reorganized under the 25th Infantry Division but it had not been integrated as a regiment. Blair stated Almond sent the 24th to Gifu because, "Ned Almond wanted the blacks out of sight and in one place."[104]

The soldiers of the 24th Infantry Regiment wore their segregation as a badge of courage. They were the big kahunas in the community, and local merchants and vendors catered to their every whim. They were respected as men because of the money they brought into the community and the victory they achieved over Imperial Japan. The 24th's status in Gifu was in stark contrast to the Jim Crow ways of the US. Enlistment rates were among the highest in the Eighth Army, and their Regimental Commander, "Screaming Mike Hollaren," promoted unit pride with athletic competitions and boxing matches where the 24th normally did very well.

US Army policy at that time was to downsize the World War II force from 89 combat divisions and eight million men to 10 combat divisions and 591,000 men. To round out 10 divisions, the army de-scoped each combat regiment so there were two fighting battalions per regiment instead of the customary three battalions, all except the 24th Infantry Regiment.[105]

There were enough black soldiers to form three full battalions. So MG Almond did just that, as opposed to sending the black soldiers from the 24th Regiment's third battalion to round out other units in the Eighth Army to 100 percent strength. The soldiers of the 24th were the only combat regiment in the Far East with three battalions. Blair wrote, "On paper, the 24th was the strongest and best-equipped American unit in the Far East Command."

In the early stages of the war, the fighting was desperate, and many of the hard-scrabbled veterans from the Pacific Theater had left the armed forces to return to their families and lives at home. They were replaced by young, green draftees who had not been trained in night fighting, guerilla tactics, or many of the other combat drills required of that war. In some instances, American World War II–era bazooka rounds (anti-tank weapons) bounced off Russian-made T-34 Tanks. The UN abandoned conventional military strategy of mass and economy of force. They traded space for time to form a substantial enough force on the peninsula that could both repulse the North Korean advance, and launch a counterattack to push the North Koreans back across the 38th parallel.

Two Task Forces were organized. The all-black 24th was responsible for the first "Sizable American ground victory of the Korean War," wrote AP War Correspondent, Tom Lambert. The 24th launched a successful 16-hour assault on the town of Yechon, north of Pusan on the Naktong River in South Korea. US congressional record also states, "First United States Victory in Korea Won by Negro GIs." Personally, I think the 24th's success at Naktong officially ended all doubt of any unbiased observers as to the credibility of the black fighting man.

THE LEGACY OF OUR EARLY INTEGRATORS

As our World War II– and Korean War–era veterans leave us for a better place, we must never forget the personal sacrifices they made for our country, many of whom made the ultimate sacrifice. Millions more carry the psychological and physical wounds of their commitment to America throughout their lives, the greatest of unsung heroes.

The March 11, 2018, *Washington Post* carried an obituary about such a veteran, Anthony Acevedo. Acevedo was a WWII veteran of Mexican ancestry. He was a twenty-year old Army medic during the war. Like the other eleven million WWII veterans, Acevedo's service has its own unique story of sacrifice. He was born July 31, 1924, in San Bernardino, CA, and attended segregated schools for blacks, Hispanics, and Asians in Pasadena, CA. His father was an engineer who worked on government projects. Acevedo and his family were deported in 1937 for not having proper immigration papers. While in Mexico at the age of thirteen, Anthony and a friend intercepted and decoded Morse code signals that two German men were sending to a German submarine off the coast of Mexico. The boys turned in what they found to authorities, and the Germans were arrested.

Necessity has a way of forcing pragmatism upon policy makers and it did so again in 1943 when the Army accepted Acevedo into service with open arms. In exchange for his services, he was given promises of citizenship following the war. In January 1945, Acevedo's entire attrited unit was captured at the Battle of the Bulge. Acevedo was taken to a German POW Camp where he was beaten and tortured. He was shocked to learn that the German officer leading his interrogation knew his entire life story, including his family's deportation and the incident involving his friend and the German espionage attempt. In an attempt to break Acevedo, the German officer shouted, "For all your trouble they kicked you out of the United States. That's what the Americans do."[106]

During one roll call, the camp commandant ordered all Jewish POWs at Stalag IX-B to step forward, and then selected other POWs who "looked" Jewish, including Acevedo. The men were told they were going to a "beautiful camp" as 350 of them were loaded onto box cars so densely packed they could not kneel or sit. They traveled for six days and six nights until they reached a German concentration camp known as Berga an der Elster, a sub-camp of the infamous Buchenwald Concentration Camp. The men were used as slave laborers and forced to dig tunnels for the Nazi war effort.[107]

Once the US-led allies broke out of Belgium, they and the Russians began closing in on the Germans. The Germans forced the men to travel 217 miles in seventeen days, trying to stay ahead of American advances. Acevedo kept a secret diary of the conditions, writing, "Two more of our men died today + one last night makes 3 + 16 makes 19."[108] The men were forced to carry their sick and wounded on two wooden carts during the retreat. The lack of proper sanitation increased the number of deaths through dysentery. The men had to boil their water before drinking it, and subsisted off bread made from sawdust, ground glass, and barley. They would get an occasional Red Cross food package. They made a broth of the bread they got and thickened it with meat from rats and stray cats they trapped. The men were forced to sleep naked, two to a bunk without blankets.[109]

Acevedo continued to treat the men who were beaten and tortured as best he could. American service members who tried to escape or faltered in their work were shot execution style in the head. Acevedo plugged their fatal wounds with candle wax. Acevedo's secret diary was so detailed that he made an entry on President Roosevelt's death, April 13: "We held a prayer service for the repose of [President Franklin D. Roosevelt's] soul."[110] On April 23, 1945, Acevedo and his comrades were liberated. Only 120 of the 350 men who started the journey were still alive. Acevedo was 5'10" and 149 lbs. at the time of his capture; he weighed only eighty-seven pounds when American forces liberated him.

The Army forced the survivors to sign non-disclosure statements because the information from the debriefing was deemed classified for many decades. Acevedo returned to Mexico after the war where he became a surgical technician. He then returned to the US, used the GI Bill to become an aerospace engineer, and worked for aerospace companies until he retired in 1987. Acevedo raised four children: Tony, Rebecca, Fernando, and Ernesto. Anthony Acevedo was a true patriot who volunteered for twenty years at the Veterans Hospital in Loma Linda, CA.

The Army declassified his case and revealed that, not only were he and his fellow soldiers POWs, but they were survivors of Germany's network of concentration labor camps, making Anthony Acevedo the only known non-Jewish, Mexican-American Holocaust survivor. Acevado donated his diary to the Holocaust Memorial Museum in Washington, D.C. His diary was the first the museum received written by an American in a concentration camp. Acevado's son Fernando came across paperwork from a psychological interview conducted for a military disability application that detailed a brutal gang rape of his father and his comrades. Fernando asked his father if it was true, to which Anthony replied, "Oh yeah. I want you to tell everybody what I went through."[111]

Anthony Acevedo's story and millions like this tell us that no one, or no one group, owns the American brand. It has been forged through the toil, blood, sweat, and tears of all Americans: black, white, Hispanic, Asian, Jewish and Gentile, men and women, transgender, heterosexual, and gay and lesbian. To deny this fundamental truth for the sake of exploiting differences dishonors their sacrifices in a most profound way. Their gracious and courageous contributions in the armed services were essential to securing our democracy—a fundamental truth that gives us all hope for a better country and a better world.

NOTES

1. Rawn James, Jr., *The Double V: How Wars, Protest, and Harry Truman Desegregated America's Military* (New York: Bloomsbury, 2013), 167–173.

2. Benjamin O. Davis Jr., *Benjamin O. Davis, Jr., American: An Autobiography* (Washington, D.C.: Smithsonian Books, 1991), 33.

3. James, *The Double V*, 87.
4. "Negro Revealed as 'Messman Hero' at Pearl Harbor," *Pittsburgh Courier*, March 12, 1942, http://www.newspapers.com/clip/7598595/oakland_tribune/ (accessed February 8, 2016).
5. James, *The Double V*, 84–97.
6. Morris J. MacGregor, *Integration of the Armed Forces, 1940–1965* (Washington, DC: U.S. Government Printing Office, 1981), 55.
7. Ibid.
8. James, *The Double V*, 146.
9. Ibid., 149.
10. Ibid., 146–151.
11. Ibid.
12. Howard Queen and Mary Penick-Motley, *The Invisible Soldier: The Experience of the Black Soldier, World War II* (Detroit: Wayne State University Press, 1987), 258–59.
13. Ibid., 259.
14. Gail Buckley, *American Patriots: The Story of Blacks in the Military from the Revolution to Desert Storm* (New York: Random House, 2001), 200, 483.
15. Douglas C. Sterner, *Go for Broke: The Nisei Warriors of World War II Who Conquered Germany* (Clearfield, UT: American Legacy Historical Press, 2007), 14.
16. Linda Lamura, *Nisei Soldiers Break Their Silence: Coming Home to Hood River* (Seattle: University of Washington Press, 2012), 126.
17. Douglas C. Sterner, *Go for Broke: The Nisei Warriors of World War II who Conquered Germany* (Clearfield, UT: American Legacy Historical Press, 2007), 79–89.
18. History.com Editors, "Japanese Internment Camps," *History.com*, October 29, 2009, https://www.history.com/topics/world-war-ii/japanese-american-relocation (accessed March 3, 2016).
19. Tetsuden Kashima, "Internment Camps," *Encyclopedia of American Studies*, edited by Simon J. Bronner (Baltimore, MD: Johns Hopkins University Press, 2016) https://eas-ref.press.jhu.edu/view?aid=390 (accessed March 29, 2017).
20. James, *The Double V*, 144–149.
21. Karem Jabar and Anthony Walton, *Brothers in Arms: The Epic Story of the 761st Tank Battalion, WWII's Forgotten Heroes* (New York: Broadway Books, 2004), 52.
22. Jabar, *Brothers in Arms: The Epic Story of the 761st Tank Battalion, WWII's Forgotten Heroes*, 54–61.
23. Henry L. Gates Jr., *100 Amazing Facts About the Negro* (New York: Pantheon Books, 2017), 86.
24. S. H. Kelly, "Seven WWII vets to receive Medals of Honor," *Army News Service*, January 13, 1997, https://history.army.mil/moh/7(AfrAm)WWIIVetsMOH.pdf (accessed January 11, 2016).
25. Buckley, *American Patriots*, 258.
26. Ibid., 332–333.
27. Ibid.
28. Jim Michaels, "Emerging from history: Massacre of 11 Black Soldiers," *USA Today*, November 8, 2013, https://www.usatoday.com/story/news/nation/2013/11/07/wereth-black-soldiers-battle-of-bulge-army-world-war-ii-history/3465059/ (accessed March 18, 2016).
29. Ibid.
30. Tina Langer, personal communication, May 21, 2004.
31. Ibid.
32. James, *The Double V*, 89–97.
33. "FDR Signs Public Law 18 that Mandates the Army Air Corps to Train Blacks," Smithsonian National Air and Space Museum, Smithsonian Institution, 2017, https://pioneersofflight.si.edu/content/fdr-signs-public-law-18-mandates-army-air-corps-train-blacks (accessed June 19, 2018).
34. James, *The Double V*, 88.
35. Buckley, *American Patriots*, 263.

36. James, *The Double V*, 91.
37. Richard M. Dalfiume, "The Fahy Committee and Desegregation of the Armed Forces," *The Historian* 31, no. 1 (1968): www.jstor.org/stable/24440952, 1–20.
38. William G. Jordan, *Black Newspapers and America's War for Democracy: 1914–1920* (Chapel Hill, NC: Chapel Hill Press, 2001), 92.
39. James, *The Double V*, 94–96.
40. Ibid., 94.
41. Phillip McGuire, *He, Too, Spoke for Democracy: Judge Hastie, World War II, and the Black Soldier* (Westport, CT: Greenwood Press, 1988), 10.
42. Ibid., 42.
43. Pat McKissack, and Frederick McKissack, *Red-tail Angels: The Story of the Tuskegee Airmen of World War II* (London: Walker Childrens, 1995), 34–35.
44. Ulysses Lee, *The United States Army in World War II: The Employment of Negro Troops*, United States Center of Military History (Washington, DC: Government Printing Office, 1963), 68.
45. Ibid., 64.
46. Lee, *The United States Army in World War II: The Employment of Negro Troops*, 51.
47. McKissack, *Red-tail Angels: The Story of the Tuskegee Airmen of World War II*, 61.
48. Barry M. Stentiford, *Landmarks of the American Mosaic: Tuskegee Airmen* (Santa Barbara, CA: Greenwood, 2012), 49.
49. James, *The Double V*, 165.
50. John Fleischman, *Black and White Airmen: Their True History* (New York: Houghton Mifflin, 2007), 86.
51. Ibid., 82–93.
52. Ibid., 89.
53. Karen Grigsby Bates, "Remembering Tuskegee Airman Roscoe Brown, Educator and Civil Rights Trailblazer," *NPR*, July 6, 2016, https://www.npr.org/sections/codeswitch/2016/07/06/484792854/honoring-tuskegee-airman-roscoe-brown (accessed July 6, 2016).
54. *Red Tails: The Real Story of the Tuskegee Airmen* (2012; Pittsburgh, PA: WQED, 2012), DVD.
55. James, *The Double V*, 167.
56. Ibid., 168.
57. Ibid., 169.
58. Ibid., 126–27.
59. "Frank Knox," *Naval History and Heritage Command*, June 9, 2015, https://www.history.navy.mil/our-collections/photography/us-people/k/knox-frank.html.
60. Historical Section Bureau of Naval Personnel, "The Negro in the Navy: United States Naval Administration History of World War II #84," *Naval History and Heritage Command*, April 24, 2020, https://www.history.navy.mil/research/library/online-reading-room/title-list-alphabetically/n/negro-navy-1947-adminhist84.html, 40.
61. Ibid., 305.
62. Ibid., 306.
63. Robert J. Schneller Jr., *Breaking the Color Barrier: The U.S. Navy Academy's First Black Midshipmen and the Struggle for Racial Equality* (New York: NYU Press, 2005), 37.
64. Ibid., 23.
65. Ibid., 23–27.
66. Ibid.
67. Ibid., 34.
68. Frederick Rasmussen, "Lt. Cmdr. Wesley A. Brown, Broke Color Barrier at Naval Academy," *Baltimore Sun*, May 24, 2012, http://www.baltimoresun.com/news/obituaries/bs-md-ob-wesley-brown-20120524-story.html (accessed June 11, 2016).
69. Paul Stillwell, *The Golden Thirteen: Recollections of the First Black Naval Officers* (Annapolis, MD: Naval Institute Press, 1993), 306.
70. James, *The Double V*, 181.
71. Ibid., 175.

72. Associated Press, "Black Crew of World War II Navy Ship Recognized for Heroism," *The New York Times*, February 19, 1995, https://www.nytimes.com/1995/02/19/us/black-crew-of-world-war-ii-navy-ship-recognized-for-heroism.html (accessed April 17, 2016).
73. James, *The Double V*, 170–82.
74. Ibid.
75. Ibid.
76. Ibid., 187.
77. Ibid.
78. Bernard C. Nalty, *The Right to Fight: African American Marines in World War II*, Marines, 2002. https://www.marines.mil/Portals/1/Publications/The%20Right%20to%20Fight%20African-American%20Marines%20in%20World%20War%20II%20PCN%2019000313200_1.pdf, 4.
79. Ibid.
80. Nalty, *The Right to Fight: African American Marines in World War II*, 1.
81. James, *The Double V*, 192.
82. Jonathon Southerland, *African Americans at War: An Encyclopedia*, Vol. 1 (Santa Barbra, CA: ABC-CLIO Press, 2004), 570.
83. Ibid.
84. Walter L. Hawkins, *Black American Military Leaders: A Biographical Dictionary* (Jefferson, NC: McFarland and Company, 2007), 235.
85. Nalty, *The Right to Fight: African American Marines in World War II*, 5.
86. Buckley, *American Patriots*, 319.
87. Nalty, *The Right to Fight: African American Marines in World War II*, 21.
88. Buckley, *American Patriots*, 322.
89. Ibid.
90. Ibid.
91. Ibid., 324.
92. Ibid., 340.
93. Nalty, *The Right to Fight: African American Marines in World War II*, 10.
94. Dalfiume, "The Fahy Committee and Desegregation of the Armed Forces," 149.
95. Clark, M. Clifford, "The Politics of 1948" (official memorandum to Harry S. Truman, Washington, DC: White House, November 19, 1947), https://www.trumanlibrary.gov/library/research-files/memo-clark-clifford-harry-s-truman (accessed April 9, 2016).
96. Buckley, *American Patriots*, 339.
97. James, *The Double V*, 235.
98. Ibid.
99. Clay Blair, *The Forgotten War: America in Korea 1950–1953* (New York: Times Books, 1987), 648.
100. Ibid.
101. Buckley, *American Patriots*, 347.
102. Richard W. Stewart, ed., "Peace Becomes Cold War," in *American Military History*, 2nd ed., Vol. 2, *The United States Army in a Global Era, 1917–2008*, 203–220 (Washington, D.C.: U.S. Army Center of Military History, 2010), 216.
103. Ibid., 223.
104. Blair, *The Forgotten War: America in Korea 1950–1953*, 151.
105. Stewart, "Peace Becomes Cold War," 216.
106. Matt Schudel, "Anthony Acevedo, U.S. Army Medic who Endured Prison-Camp Horrors During WWII, dies at 93," *The Washington Post*, March 11, 2018, https://www.washingtonpost.com/local/obituaries/anthony-acevedo-us-army-medic-who-endured-prison-camp-horrors-in-wwii-dies-at-93/2018/03/10/ac2273f0-23e2-11e8-86f6-54bfff693d2b_story.html.
107. Ibid.
108. Ibid.
109. Ibid.

110. Ibid.
111. Ibid.

FIVE

Women in the Armed Services

The struggle for equality is as old as the nation itself. Each minority demographic has fought to achieve the opportunity for self-determination as guaranteed in the Constitution since the US's inception. The struggle for women's equality dates to 1777 when the New York State Assembly made it illegal for women to vote, and then several states followed suit.[1] Like black Americans, women in uniformed service to America grew out of a need for labor.

It has been said that necessity is the mother of invention; I would add that necessity is also the mother of opportunity. Many minorities have gotten their first opportunities to excel in dire situations. It's interesting how "color-blind" our society can become when push comes to shove; see Branch Rickey, Doug Williams, and Tony Dungy. Even President Barack Obama may not have been elected if not for the dire economic outlook the nation faced in the days preceding the 2008 Presidential Election.

Sir Winston Churchill famously said, "Americans will always do the right thing—after exhausting all the alternatives."[2] Like many old adages, there is an element of truth here. Edith Nourse Rogers, Massachusetts's first woman elected to Congress, drafted a bill to establish a Women's Army Auxiliary Corps. The bill was held up by the Bureau of Budget and only resurrected after the United States entered WWII. It was signed into law May 14, 1942, authorizing the recruitment of 150,000 volunteers. President Roosevelt limited the initial Army women's auxiliary to 25,000 by executive order.[3]

Necessity also opened the door for the first women in military service in the United States. Many know the story of Molly Pitcher, the first woman credited with engaging in combat when she picked up for her husband who fell wounded on his cannon at the Battle of Monmouth during the American Revolution. Molly's primary duties were that of carrying pitchers of water to the troops and to cool the artillery pieces, thus earning the name, Molly Pitcher. Molly Pitcher is believed to be a figure of American folklore—an amalgamation of women who served during the Revolutionary War in support of their husbands and at the approval of the commander—but based on the actual Mary Ludwig Hays of Trenton, New Jersey. During the American Revolution, numerous women served as laundresses, seamstresses, water couriers, and medical attendants. These roles for women were born out of necessity, and in some instances, as in the tale of Molly Pitcher, women were thrust into combat support roles on the front lines.[4]

As warfare advanced and became more modernized, roles for women in the armed services became increasingly more detailed, and more central to the core functions of all armed services. During the Civil War, American women for the US and Confederacy served as cooks, nurses, administrators of hospitals (matrons), physicians, and spies. Some women fought in the infantry disguised as men. Dr. Mary Walker became the first and only woman to be awarded the Congressional Medal of Honor, one of only eight civilians to ever receive the nation's highest military honor. This trend continued into the Spanish American War when more than 1,500 women served in combat support roles.[5]

World War I provided the first real breakthrough moment for American women in the twentieth century. Beginning in 1914, over 33,000 women between the ages of twenty-one and sixty-nine served primarily as nurses, but also as support staff (secretaries, telephone operators and even architects). These women were so essential to the US effort that many of them continued to perform their support duties until 1923, five years after the US accepted the armistice! The efforts of these women were transformative on the US socio-political landscape, and they helped propel the passage of the 19th Amendment, which guaranteed women the right to vote.[6]

World War II was a complete national mobilization and required the country to pull together like it had never been compelled to before. Women were cast in large numbers into unfamiliar roles in the armed services and private industry. "Rosie the Riveter" is one of the iconic images of that timeframe that has become branded into American popular culture. Rosie the Riveter is an accurate portrayal of the role women played in the nationwide mobilization and industrialization in support of the US war effort. Women piloted combat aircraft from factories to military bases so that Navy and Air Force pilots could continue fighting and training. Combat pilot roles at that time were exclusively white males except for the Tuskegee Airmen. Thousands of women excelled in factory jobs and other skilled labor positions that were previously considered "male responsibilities." These women set a precedent for women workers outside of the house, and many never relinquished their newfound roles in the workforce.

THE ARMED SERVICES "AUXILIARY" SERVICES

The mantra that characterized US war policy regarding expanded roles for women was "to free a man to fight." Literally any position that didn't require heavy, manual labor was considered for women's service. In addition to the traditional supporting war roles women fulfilled (nurses, hospital administrators, and medical attendants) women during WWII also served as topographers, radio-telephone operators, communication specialists, military intelligence analysts, parachute riggers, mechanics, and supply clerks. Each armed service had a clever acronym for their women's auxiliary branches of service. The Army had the Women's Army Auxiliary Corps (WAAC), which was later changed to the Women's Army Corps (WAC), often pronounced "wax." The Navy and Marine Corps had the Women Accepted for Volunteer Emergency Service (WAVES), and the Air Force had the Women Air Force Service Pilots (WASP). The Coast Guard named their women's auxiliary service the Semper Paratus/Always Ready or (SPARs).

PIONEERS OF THE WOMEN'S ARMY CORPS (WAC)

The Women's Army Auxiliary Corps was molded after the British Army's Women's Auxiliary Territorial Service (ATS). Army Chief of Staff George C. Marshall was impressed by the organization and efficiency of the ATS, and directed the Army's first organizers to study the ATS once the WAC became public law. The Army dropped Auxiliary from the title in July 1943.[7]

The first group of eight hundred women started training at the Fort Des Moines Provisional Army Officer Training School, IA in 1942. This first group was trained in three major specialties: switchboard operators, mechanics, and bakers. WACs with the highest military aptitude scores were assigned to switchboard operations, followed by mechanics.[8] American society was not ready for women serving in large numbers in military roles. The WAC were trail blazers. The biggest challenges for women serving in uniform were dealing with inept civilian leadership that was prejudiced against women, and establishing a force from a group with no military traditions. Black WAC had to contend with the same racial barriers black servicemen had to overcome in addition to the challenges of being a woman in the military. Black WAC were assigned to janitorial or orderly roles, often well below their demonstrated aptitude on the GTE or their civilian schooling. Some black WACs were also sent to military camps where black soldiers trained to serve as "dates" for the black GIs. This was done out of fear that black servicemen would develop relationships with white women in those communities.

The Army disbanded the WAC in 1978, and fully integrated women into non-combat arms specialties, those that excluded direct combat as their primary mission. Women were first admitted into the service academies in 1976 after intense political debate in Congress and amongst military brass. Unsurprisingly, these milestone achievements advanced the way American society viewed women in the work force.[9]

Thousands of gifted women with strong, inherent leadership ability were drawn to the WAC once they were well established. The thought of being given the opportunity to lead a group of women in support of their country, with the same responsibilities and pay as men, was compelling. Oveta Culp Hobby was the first National Director of the WAC. Hobby was a self-taught socialite from Texas. She attended Mary Hardin Baylor College for Women in Waco, TX, as well as the South Texas College of Law and Commerce, and the University of Texas, Austin Law School. Hobby is credited with strengthening the image of the WAC, instituting higher admission standards, and implementing a code of conduct specific to the WAC. These policy changes influenced the military to make women part of the regular, active Army instead of an auxiliary, thereby transforming WAAC into WAC. At that point, women wore the US Army emblems and rank insignia for the first time. Hobby was later appointed as the first Secretary for the Department of Health, Education, and Welfare, which later became the Department of Health and Human Services. Hobby wore the rank of colonel while serving as the National Director of the WAC.[10]

Charity Adams was the first black woman to be commissioned as an officer in the WAC and the second to be promoted to the rank of major. She commanded the 6888th Central Postal Battalion (Colored) during World War II, stationed in Birmingham, England. The 6888th followed US troops into Europe after D-Day, and was later stationed in Rouen and Paris, France to keep up with advancing US forces. Adams eventually attained the rank of lieutenant colonel before the end of the war.[11]

Harriet West Waddy was the second of the only two black women to be promoted to field grade officer status during World War II. Waddy served with Mary McLeod Bethune on the Bureau of Negro Affairs prior to the war, and because of this experience Hobby selected her to serve as her aide on race relations in the WAC. Waddy also attained the rank of lieutenant colonel.

Florence K. Murray served at WAC headquarters during World War II. She graduated from Boston University Law School in 1942 and rose to the rank of lieutenant colonel. Murray became the first woman Rhode Island State Senator, and the first woman to sit on the Rhode Island Supreme Court.

THE NAVY MAKES WAVES

The Navy's WAVES are an example of inter-service rivalry at its best. Although the Army was the first service to include women in uniformed service (during WWII), the Navy was the first service to lobby for women to serve as part of an armed service and not as an auxiliary. The Navy's insistence on having women in uniform be part of the Navy caused a sea change in the Army's policy and instigated the Army dropping the auxiliary moniker from its title. Hence the Women's Army Auxiliary Corps became the Women's Army Corps. Equal pay then became a non-issue for the Army WAC who were also given the right to wear the same military rank insignia as their male counterparts, and afforded the same veteran benefits as their male service members.[12] The WAC however, were statutorily prohibited from serving in direct combat, or from serving in units whose primary mission was to engage in direct combat with the enemy, though many WAC served in high-level Army Headquarters in Britain.

The Army reluctantly accepted women serving as an auxiliary effort at the behest of Congresswoman Edith Nourse Rogers; she essentially wore the Army down into accepting women in uniform. Rogers was also essential to the Navy's establishment of the WAVES but demonstrated value added through a different technique. The Navy's Bureau of Aeronautics had already begun exploring how women could be used in shore duties to free men for sea duty. The Navy's original position was that any gains realized by women in uniform could be realized by the civilian work force. Persistent inquiries from Rogers' office caused Secretary of the Navy Knox to ask his bureau chiefs earnestly if the Navy had a use for women serving in uniform.[13] Most of the Navy's bureau chiefs replied no, but Rogers and other congressional leaders wouldn't relent. Seeing the writing on the wall, the Navy pivoted from resistance to identifying the best means of inclusion. The Bureau of Navy Personnel recommended to Secretary Knox that Congress be asked to authorize a women's service organization, but unlike the Army's WAC, the Navy wanted its women serving in uniform to be a part of the Navy Reserves. This was the Navy's way of one-upping the army.

The federal Bureau of the Budget said no to the Navy's proposal to include women as a part of the Navy by affixing them to the naval reserves. The two institutions became entrenched in a standoff over the characterization of women's service in uniform. The Navy's Bureau of Aeronautics turned to Dr. Margaret Chung, a San Francisco Surgeon and socialite, who helped push the legislation through the House of Representatives via contacts she made while serving as a Navy contract flight surgeon during WWI. Dr. Chung's confidants jovially called themselves, "Sons of Mom Chung."[14] Representative Melvin Maas from Minnesota was among Mom's disciples. Maas introduced a bill with Secretary of the

Navy Knox's concept of a women's naval reserve on March 18, 1942. The House Naval Affairs Subcommittee and the full House of Representatives approved the bill, but the Senate Naval Affairs Committee did not receive it favorably. The Navy knew they were in for a fight, and turned to the women of academia to work out the details of how the Navy would muster, train, and lead the program.[15]

The Navy reached out to Dr. Virginia C. Gildersleeve, Dean of Barnard College. She recommended that Secretary Knox's Chief of Naval Personnel take on Professor Elizabeth Reynard as a special assistant on women's issues. Reynard was well known for her academic work on women in the workplace.[16] Reynard and Gildersleeve organized the Women's Advisory Council to develop a framework for the Navy's new program. The committee consisted of eight prominent women from academia: Dr. Meta Glass, Sweet Briar College; Dr. Lillian Gilbreth, a prominent national figure on work place efficiency; Dr. Ada Comstock, President of Radcliffe College; Dean Alice Crocker Lloyd, University of Michigan; Mrs. Malbone Graham, noted lecturer; Marie Rogers Gates, wife of Thomas Sovereign Gates, President of the University of Pennsylvania; Harriet Elliott, Dean of Women, University of North Carolina; and Dr. Alice Baldwin, Dean of Women, Duke University.[17]

This committee's efficiency, professionalism, and high-quality work put to rest any fears the Navy may have had about women in uniform. Before the Senate could pass the proposal into law, the Women's Advisory Council had already tentatively selected a name, WAVES, and its first director, Mildred H. McAfee. Council members Gildersleeve and Elliott took the task of selling the legislation into their own hands. They used connections to present the ideas to Eleanor Roosevelt who sold the idea to her husband. President Roosevelt informed Senator Walsh, Chair of the Senate Naval Affairs Committee, that he preferred Secretary Knox's vision, and the WAVES were created on July 30, 1942, through Public Law 689.[18]

One hundred eight women were commissioned into the WAVES between August and September 1942. Mildred McAfee was brought on as director at the rank of lieutenant commander (O-4). She rose to the rank of captain (O-6) by the end of the war. McAfee, Reynard, and the committee worked tirelessly, outlining every detail of WAVES service from training, to uniform, to how they would be used, and to how the rest of the Navy would interact with the WAVES. Before war's end, the WAVES served in dozens of specialties. Like the WAC, the main mission of the WAVES was to free men for sea duty, something that some sailors loathed. WAVES served in 900 different shore locations in the US and Hawaii, yet they were prohibited from serving in combat or aboard war ships. At the end of 1942, there were 770 WAVE officers and 3,109 enlisted. By war's end there were 8,475 officers and 73,816 enlisted, which made up eighteen percent of all Navy shore personnel.[19]

The Navy set the standard with the rapid and efficient development of the WAVES. Even their uniforms were developed by a New York fashion house and were the envy of the services. Unfortunately, like the other services, the WAVES were negligent on their inclusion of black and minority women. They made little to no attempt to recruit black WAVES, and the first black WAVES were not admitted until October 1944 under pressure from black civic organizations. Harriet Ida Pickens and Frances Wills were the first black women accepted as WAVES officers. Seventy-two black women were accepted into the WAVES by September 1945, and they were fully integrated. The Marine Corps established the Marine Corps Women's Reserves in 1943, and by war's end, eighty-five percent of the Marines in the US Marine Corps Headquarters were women.[20]

The Navy took steps to make the WAVES component a permanent part of the Navy reserves, and asked Congress for permission to retain on active duty a reasonable number of WAVES to manage the reserve force. The Women's Armed Services Integration Act was signed on July 30, 1948, allowing women to serve in the regular Navy. The term WAVES continued to be popular until the 1970s even though the term no longer applied. The combat prohibition remained until 1991 when Congress passed a law authorizing women to fly in combat. Sixty-nine WAVES died during WWII of unspecified causes.

WOMEN AIR FORCE SERVICE PILOTS (WASP)

Women's Airforce Service Pilots were US federal civil service employees. Unlike the WAC and the WAVES, they were not part of the armed force they supported, in this case the US Army Air Force. The WASP were formed of two similar women pilots' organizations who performed the same mission for the US Air Force: deliver planes from the factory to military airfields for use in combat, and fly missions that supported military training. What the three organizations, WAC, WAVES, and WASP had in common was they were created with an eye towards performing non-combatant tasks that would free men for combat.[21]

The WASP were created from the Women's Flying Training Detachment (WFTD) and the Women's Auxiliary Ferrying Squadron (WAFS). Both were organized separately in 1942 under similar legislation that expanded flight opportunities for the feeder programs of the Tuskegee Airman. The proposals of the two women's flying organizations were advanced independently at the same time. Florida native, Jacqueline "Jackie" Cochran floated the idea by Army Air Force Chief of Staff Hap Arnold in 1940 who rejected it. Arnold promised Cochran she could be the commander of a women's flying organization should one be established. Cochran went to England to fly and train women pilots in the British Air Transport Auxiliary.[22]

Following the attack on Pearl Harbor on December 7, 1941, the US military grew exponentially. The manpower shortage of trained pilots was a conspicuous strategic barrier.[23] Colonel William H. Turner was the lead for the US Air Transport Command who was responsible for staging military aircraft where they were needed for shipment into combat zones. Turner turned to one of his staff officers, Major Robert Love, and his wife Nancy, who was a test pilot for a program to recruit and use women pilots. By the summer of 1942, Arnold was willing to implement the WAFS' plan devised by the Loves.

When Jackie Cochran learned of this arrangement with the Loves and WAFS, she returned from England and confronted Arnold. Being true to his word, Arnold gave Cochran permission to establish the WFTD in Houston, TX. The WAFS were stationed in New Castle, DE and performed the same mission as the WFTD until Arnold authorized combining the two programs on August 5, 1943. Over 25,000 women applied for the WASP, but only 1,074 were accepted. They flew over sixty million miles in every type of military aircraft in the US inventory. The WASP were granted retroactive veteran status in 1977 through an act of Congress, and they were awarded the Congressional Gold Medal in 2009.[24]

ETHNIC DIVERSITY IN THE WASP

Unlike their Navy colleagues, the WASP had a more difficult time with ethnic diversity than the WAC or the WAVES. There were two Mexican Americans, two Chinese Americans, and one Native American WASP. The only black WAF applicant was forced to withdraw her application. Again, the degree to which blacks were marginalized by the country cannot be overstated. This special contempt American society has historically had for black people is at the root of much of the racial animus that exists today, and until society acknowledges the history, we will never fully overcome it.[25]

ASSESSING THE IMPACT OF WOMEN IN SUPPORT OF THE US WWII EFFORT

To say World War II was pivotal for women in and out of the armed services would be an understatement. WWII's demand for labor provided unprecedented opportunities for women, and they came through with flying colors. An estimated 350,000 women served in uniform, and five million women entered the work force in support of the war effort.[26]

What all the women of the WAC, WAVES, WASPs, SPARs (Coast Guard), and Marine Reserve shared was an uphill battle against an intense slander campaign. In 1943, right-wing critics of Roosevelt's social programs, other reactionaries who opposed social change, and those who cited religious objections formed a formidable and demonstrative if informal campaign that slandered service women by casting them as sexually immoral.[27] Many servicemen ferociously opposed allowing women in uniform, and warned their sisters and female friends that they would be perceived as lesbians or women of ill repute if they joined the uniformed services.

Cowardly men were resentful that women were taking "safe" service jobs away from the combat zone, increasing the likelihood they would have to face the enemy in combat. Some civilian women resented the praise and adulation the services showered on women who volunteered in movie shorts shown before premiere pictures in theaters due to sheer jealousy. Other civilian women felt their jobs and relationships would be threatened by large numbers of outsider-women relocating to their geographical locations. Service women were often the butt of crude jokes and idle gossip. To make matters worse, some young women imitated servicewomen's uniforms to gain access to military bases or to make themselves feel important, stealing their glory, but not holding themselves to the same high ethical conduct of the women serving in uniform. Often, these women engaged in misconduct and were mistaken for actual Women's Auxillary members, further besmirching the reputation of the women's auxiliary.[28] However, the senior US military brass were full of accolades about the performance of women in uniform. General Douglas MacArthur called the WACs "my best soldiers; [they worked harder, complained less, and were better disciplined than the men]."[29]

Following the end of the war, women who served in uniform faced a similar backlash as black G.I.s—a culture clash that sought to restore societal norms back to pre-war conditions. Women were fired from factory jobs to make way for men returning home from the war, particularly black women, who had been forced to work almost exclusively as domestics outside the home prior to WWII. Despite the backlash, the way US society viewed women in the work force would forever be altered for the better. By 1950, thirty-two percent of adult aged women were working outside the home, fifty percent of whom were married. This represented a fundamental change from the previous model when women were expected to permanently leave the work force following the birth of their children.[30]

KOREA, VIETNAM, AND THE WOMEN'S RIGHTS MOVEMENT

Congress passed the Women's Armed Service Integration Act on June 12, 1948, primarily due to actions by influential women such as Congresswoman Edith Nourse Rogers, Eleanor Roosevelt, and others. The exceptional military and civilian service of the five million women who served during World War II was the overriding factor that made the legislation an easy sell. The bill enabled a permanent presence of women in the military, including WAC, WAVES, women in the Marine Corps, and women in the Air Force. It also created, for the first time, an organized reserve for each of these branches.[31]

The act was passed one month prior to the issuance of Executive Order 9981. These two policies were put into place at Camp Lee, VA for white and black WAC. The first training center for the permanent WAC was opened on Oct. 4, 1948. The WAC Training Center was commanded, staffed, and operated entirely by women. Over 30,000 women trained at Camp Lee before it was moved to a new location at Fort McClellan in 1954.[32] These fundamental policy changes laid the foundation for women to compete for positions of increased authority, beginning with the inclusion of women at America's storied military academies in the mid-1970s. This push for inclusion was part of the larger women's rights movement in America, and one of the significant culture clashes in modern US history.

Figure 5.1. New Women Auxiliary Commissionees, circa 1954. *Photo courtesy of the U.S. Army Women in Military History program*

THE US MILITARY ADVANCES IN WOMEN'S RIGHTS VS. CORPORATE AMERICA

Public Law 90-130, signed by President Lyndon B. Johnson on November 8, 1967, removed promotion and retirement restrictions on women officers in the armed forces.[33] Thereafter, it was possible for more than one woman in each service to hold the rank of colonel, and for women to achieve general (or flag) officer rank; this was a legacy policy of the World War II era WAC.

Two years later, President Nixon selected two women for promotion to brigadier general: Col. Anna Mae Hays, Chief of the Army Nurse Corps; and Col. Elizabeth P. Hoisington, Director of the Women's Army Corps. They were promoted simultaneously on June 11, 1970, in recognition of their equal importance. PL 90-130 also eliminated the two percent limitation on WAC numbers, permitting WACs to serve in the Army National Guard. At this point, only women who had a prior service record could join. Due to the war in Vietnam demanding so much money, the DoD would not make funds available to train women for enlistment into Guard service.

The Army began to transition to an all-volunteer force as the war in Vietnam ended. In the all-volunteer forces, women became an even more vital component of the military. The Army expanded opportunities for women to help fill vacancies before the draft ended in June 1973. In 1971, women with no prior-service experience were permitted to enlist in the National Guard. When estimates for male recruits revealed a looming shortfall in volunteers, Secretary of the Army Robert F. Froehlke approved a major expansion in WAC strength, and the opening of all military occupational specialties that did not require combat training or duty to women in August 1972.[34] That same year, the ban on women commanding units that included men was lifted. In September 1978, Congress passed Public Law 95-584, which disestablished all armed forces' Women's Auxiliaries as separate corps from their parent armed services, effective October 20, 1978. As a policy decision, women leading men systemically in large numbers was something unique to the military in American society. This was an astonishing achievement considering women needed a man to cosign for them to get a credit card prior to the Equal Credit Opportunity Act in 1974.[35]

This period also marked the beginning of other advancements for women. For the first time, Army regulations permitted women to request waivers for retention on active duty if married or pregnant, beginning April 9, 1971. In that same year, the Army Chief of Staff authorized WAC's entry into male drill sergeant schools and NCO academy programs.

WOMEN'S RIGHTS ADVANCES AT LARGE

During the 1960s and 1970s, Betty Friedan, Gloria Steinem, Shirley Chisolm, and countless women's rights leaders advocated for woman's reproductive rights; expanded career fields that had been dominated by men, such as medicine, engineering, architecture, mathematics, and science; and created more opportunities for women to lead full, autonomous lives, apart from the traditional caretaker duties prescribed to women by western society.[36]

The full autonomy of women apart from gendered roles remains a central and divisive political issue. Thirty-eight percent of American women who worked in 1960 were largely limited to jobs as teachers, nurses, secretaries, or domestic labor. Women were generally unwelcome in professional programs. As one medical school dean declared, "Hell yes, we have a quota.... We do keep women out, when we can. We don't want them here—and they don't want them elsewhere, either, whether or not they'll admit it."[37] As a result, in 1960, women accounted for only six percent of American doctors, three percent of lawyers, and less than one percent of engineers.[38] Working women were routinely paid lower salaries than men and denied opportunities to advance, as employers assumed they would soon become pregnant and quit their jobs, and that, unlike men, they were not the primary breadwinners.

WOMEN IN THE US MILITARY SERVICE ACADEMIES, A LONG ROAD TO COMMENCEMENT

The debate over the inclusion of women in the military academies was intense. Senator Jim Webb, Virginia, an Annapolis graduate and former Navy officer, wrote a piece for the *Washingtonian*, "Why Women Can't Fight," outlining how the academies were the domain of men to be molded into lethal combat leaders, and asserting that introducing women into that environment would fundamentally weaken the effectiveness of these institutions by fostering an environment less violent, and less lethal. He argued that lethality was essential to forge military leaders with the skill and fortitude to lead men into combat. The article remains controversial to this day, and some still point to it as a reason to keep Senator Webb from positions of prominence and notoriety.[39]

President Ford signed Public Law 94-106 on October 7, 1975. The law allowed women to enter the United States service academies for the first time. The United States Military Academy at West Point admitted 119 women in 1976, and the US Naval Academy's 1976 class included eighty-one women cadets, making up six percent of the freshman class. The Air Force Academy's class of 1980 included 157 female cadets (10 percent), who graduated on May 28, 1980.[40]

The prevailing sentiment of Marene (Nyberg) Allison and the first class of women at the US Military Academy (USMA) was that the Army didn't want them there, the academy leadership didn't want them there, and the school's faculty and male cadets didn't want them there. Yet, in July 1976, 119 young women stood at the gates to the USMA at West Point, NY, embarking on a course that would change their lives, the academy, and the Army forever.

Marene (Nyberg) Allison, a 1980 West Point graduate, recounted the early days when women first entered USMA, offering a snapshot of cadet life and training in the Army's first co-ed class. After the legislation was signed, West Point leaders reacted the way the military has typically reacted to social change—begrudgingly. The leadership failed to impress upon all its subordinate leaders that their mission was to make the transition successful without compromising mission effectiveness. By strictly interpreting the law and not giving enough deliberate thought to how they could facilitate change, they left the interpretation up to the rank and file, some of whom did not want to see women succeed at the academy. One small but prime example is captured in Allison's recollection on how she was to wear her hair:

> I had a platoon sergeant who decided that my hair should be as short as the guys and ... by August of 1976, I had hair less than one inch long all over my head. And the tactical officer had said to me, 'Cadet Nyberg, New Cadet Nyberg, don't get another haircut, and then the platoon sergeant would say, 'Cadet Nyberg, go get another haircut, so I just kept going to get haircuts.[41]

This lack of clear and unequivocal emphasis on mission success also meant that women were subjected to cruel treatment for the sake of equivalent training, even when the equivalency provided no value. The West Point leadership may have felt that they adequately prepared for their first co-ed class, but from Allison's experience they had not:

> From a change management perspective, [West Point] took the absolute worst way. You can do it the right way, the wrong way or the worst way. West Point decided to take the worst way ... it was very evident they had not prepared. Simple things like the bathrooms were not done. They had not decided how they were going to do some of the uniforms. They had not properly instructed some of the cadets on how to treat women. So, it was very evident going through it that these people didn't think we were supposed to be [t]here.[42]

As Marene mentioned, women's cadet uniforms were in transition in those early years. The first year, West Point women were issued men's white shirts, which didn't fit properly. They were issued full dress coats without tails, which looked out-of-place next to the male cadets in their full-dress coats with tails. It was originally thought that coats without tails would fit better on a woman's body, but a few years later, a better proportioned full dress coat with tails was designed and issued to the women. In 1976, the women were also issued modified gray pants:

> For the women . . . they took the gray pants with the black stripes and put a plastic zipper in it. So by the time–we hadn't even been at the Academy twelve hours–we had to go across the plain and do our oath of office, about half the women's zippers had already broken. So here we are 17-, 18-, 19-year-old women with 19-, 20-, 21-year old men in our [cadet] chain- of-command and you are in this kind of odd, unique situation.[43]

It's not surprising that she experienced sleep deficit at the Academy:

> You just jam so much in . . . you [are] trained that you can always do more and you can get more done . . . you never have time to fully plan everything out and do everything the way you want. Everything has to be spur of the moment where you finish that paper while you're studying for a math test while you're doing your physics lab. So you always learn to multitask and put more on the plate.[44]

The academic and military requirements were not, however, her most difficult challenge at West Point. She felt that her most difficult challenge was dealing with the fact that men really didn't want women there. While growing up, Allison had never had any limitations placed upon her as she pursued her goals, so it was difficult for her to arrive at West Point and have men say that she shouldn't be there because she was a woman. Nonetheless, she persevered. On May 28, 1980, Marene and sixty-one other women cadets became the first women graduates of West Point, and received commissions as second lieutenants in the US Army. Marene talks about how she felt on that historic day: "We were vindicated. I did it, against all odds, against a society that didn't know if it was ready for us, against a culture that didn't want us [t]here, and in a lot of ways, still doesn't want us [t]here."[45] So, what was the guiding thought or personal standard that helped Marene achieve success at West Point? She explains, "Survival. I am going to survive. I am not going to quit and I am going to make it through. Every day, you . . . woke up and said, 'I will make it until tonight and then I will start again tomorrow.'"[46]

After her graduation from West Point, Marene served six years on active duty as an Army military police officer, attaining the rank of captain. She left the Army to become a special agent for the Federal Bureau of Investigation (FBI). As of 2007, she was head of corporate security for a Fortune 500 company, one of only a few women to hold such a position, and her USMA experience was vital to her success. Marene is married with one son and resides in Pennsylvania.[47]

MODERN PIONEERS REAPING THE BENEFITS OF WOMEN'S INCLUSION

Because the services committed to changing policies that were barriers to gender equality back in the mid-1970s, they were able to reap the rewards of women with the courage, tenacity, and skill to negotiate the challenges to female inclusion in military leadership. The pioneers of the mid-'70s became the graduates of the early '80s, who became the first female four-star generals of the 21st century.

General Ann Dunwoody

General Dunwoody was credited with being the first female to crack the military's "brass ceiling" when she was promoted to lieutenant general in 2008 and became the Army's first woman Deputy Chief of Staff, G-4 (Logistics). Dunwoody, the daughter of a career Army officer, initially wanted to be a physical education teacher. She discovered her passion for soldiering in her junior year of college during a four-week Army introductory summer program, followed by an eleven-week Women's Officer Orientation Course. Dunwoody was commissioned as a second Lieutenant in 1975.[48]

Admiral Michelle Howard

Admiral Howard was the Navy's first woman to make the rank of four-star general in June 2016. She was the first African American woman to command a US Navy ship, and the first female Naval Academy graduate to make the rank of general. Admiral Howard graduated from the US Naval Academy in 1982, and was the first officer in her class to make the rank of admiral. She achieved numerous historic firsts, including the first African American and the first woman to serve as Vice Chief of Naval Operations, the second highest military position in the Navy.[49]

General Janet Wolfenbarger

General Wolfenbarger retired in 2015 after thirty-five years of military service. She was a member of the Air Force Academy's first co-ed class in 1976, and was commissioned a second lieutenant in 1980. Upon being confirmed as the Air Force's first woman four-star general, she was selected as only the eighth commander of the US Air Force's Materiel Command, responsible for research, development, testing, evaluation, acquisition management, and logistics support for Air Force weapon systems. After graduating from the academy, she earned multiple advanced degrees in engineering and aeronautics.[50]

Lieutenant General Patricia Horoho

Lieutenant General Horoho was the first Nurse Corps Officer, and the first woman to be selected as the Army Surgeon General, becoming the 43rd Army Surgeon General on December 7, 2011. Lieutenant General Horoho's career is replete with examples of preparedness in the midst of adversity. Lieutenant General Horoho was the head nurse of the Womack Army Medical Center Emergency Department, Fayetteville, North Carolina during the worst aeronautical accident in the history of Fort Bragg and perhaps the entire peace-time Army. One spring afternoon, a C-130 cargo plane and an F-16 fighter jet collided in midair. Lieutenant General Horoho helped lead the ER response team to that disaster. Twenty-four soldiers lost their lives that day out of the 134 that were seriously wounded.[51] General Horoho was also working in the Pentagon on September 11, 2001 when American Airlines Flight 77 crashed into the west side of the building, killing all sixty-four passengers and another 125 people in the Pentagon.[52] General Horoho's clinical training, leadership, and poise were put to the test again when she assumed command of Walter Reed Army Medical Center from her Nurse Executive/Deputy Commander position. She had a challenging role to fulfill when the acting commander became ill following the Washington Post scandal detailing inadequate infrastructure and administration.

Lieutenant General Nadja West

Lieutenant General West is the first black female to reach the rank of three-star general, as well as the first black general to serve as the US Army Surgeon General. Lieutenant General West is the highest ranking woman to have ever graduated from the USMA at West Point. General West was sworn in as the 44th Army Surgeon General on December 11, 2015. She was orphaned at birth and adopted by a Washington, DC family. West is a 1982 graduate of USMA, and holds a Bachelor of Engineering degree. West earned her Doctorate of Medicine from George Washington University School of Medicine in 1988.[53]

THE INTERSECTION BETWEEN WOMEN'S ADVANCES IN THE MILITARY AND SOCIETY AT LARGE

In 1962, Betty Friedan's book The Feminine Mystique captured the frustration of a generation of college-educated housewives who felt trapped and unfulfilled. Friedan stunned the nation by challenging the accepted wisdom that housewives were content to serve their families, and by calling on women to seek fulfillment in work outside the home. While Friedan's writing arguably spoke to an audience of educated, upper-middle-class white women, her work gained such notoriety that it was credited with sparking the "second wave" of the American feminist movement. The "first wave" pushed for women's suffrage during the turn of the 20th century, culminating with the passage of the 19th Amendment, which gave women the right to vote in 1920. The women who supported the war effort in Europe and women veterans made such significant contributions to women's suffrage that Congress recognized them for their achievements.[54]

Many fail to credit the military's progressive policies regarding pay equity and women in leadership positions, many of which placed women in direct supervisory roles over men at a time when such things were unthinkable in corporate America. Moreover, policy and public law meant that military women had access to funded training programs for doctors, surgeons, pilots, and scientists previously only open to men.

A 2017 RAND Corporation study found that in the US women still earn 20 percent less than men doing the same jobs. The study estimated that at the present rate of closure (income-gap), US women will approximate the earning of men performing the same job in 2059.[55] The same study found that women are still less likely to be promoted than men at most levels. A major study conducted by LeanIn.Org and McKinsey & Co. surveyed 34,000 men and women at 132 global US companies, and found women make up 46 percent of the work force, 33 percent of senior manager/director positions, and only 29 percent of vice president/executive level positions.[56] By contrast, women in the military make up 15 percent of the total work force, 25 percent of senior management/director level positions, and 17 percent of vice president/executive level positions.[57]

Women in the military make up roughly five percent of CEOs (generals) compared to about 6.4 percent of Fortune 500 CEOS.[58] This number is especially noteworthy when considering the military historically has been a very non-traditional career choice for women, and women make up only about 17 percent of the US Armed Forces officer corps. The big difference between women in the corporate sector and women in the military is that the policy gains made by women in the 1960s and '70s have laid the ground work for present day progression, and women in leadership roles is more a part of the culture than a novelty. The armed forces continue to explore novel policies to allow women to break from the service for the purposes of child birth and child rearing, and then return at the same level of pay and authority. The women's auxiliary corps disbanded in 1978, yet only three women have risen through the ranks to attain the military's highest rank, four-star general: Army General Ann Dunwoody, Air Force General Janet Wolfenbarger, and Navy Admiral Michelle Howard. The military leads corporate America with respect to women's inclusion, but the US armed forces could do even better.

This analysis also reveals it takes a very long time to grow a flag officer; work that began in the late 1970s—admitting women into service academies and including them in the armed forces, not as a separate auxiliary—has only recently produced the first four star generals in the twenty-first century. The military's system of advancement is very formal and stair-stepped, only allowing for modest, accelerated promotional opportunities. One might have perhaps five or six opportunities for accelerated promotion over a thirty-year career, with very low selection rates, typically less than two percent. Given these realities, the military has no time to delay in removing remaining barriers to full inclusion. The good news is that under the Obama Administration, significant strides were made to continue the march towards gender equality in career opportunities for women.

MODERN MILESTONES FOR WOMEN IN THE MILITARY

The division of labor within the household is a well-documented barrier to career advancement. A study by LeanIn.Org and McKinsey & Co. found that women in senior management positions are seven times more likely to bear the majority of household duties compared to men. The survey also noted that when there is a household responsibilities imbalance, only thirty-four percent of those executives' espoused aspirations to one day become a top executive.[59] Journalist and author Cokie Roberts, posited in her book, *We Are Our Mother's Daughters*, that women should consider a more strategic approach to career planning, and manage career goals in quantifiable chunks around the traditional expectations and roles women play in Western society.

Other corporations have taken novel approaches to promoting gender equality such as shadow mentor programs, and hiring dashboards that seek to provide transparency for corporations that want to hold managers accountable for considering and hiring women executives. Similarly, the military has recognized the unique role women play in our society, and has taken steps to develop policy that supports balancing professional and domestic requirements.

The defense department doubled its maternity leave from six to twelve weeks on January 28, 2016, in recognition of the challenges new parents have balancing the demands of family and career. The Department of the Navy increased its maternity leave to a full eighteen weeks. These moves were made to support military families, improve retention, and strengthen the future force. The Parental Leave, Support for New Parents Program is available to all service members on active duty for twelve months or more.[60]

By far and away the most novel program emerging from the DoD with promise as a model for the corporate sector is the Navy's Career

Intermission Pilot Program. This program was approved in 2009 as part of the 2009 National Defense Authorization Act. The plan is a nod towards Roberts' advice, and allows for up to twenty officers and twenty enlisted service members to take a one-time temporary transition from active duty into the Individual Ready Reserve (IRR). Participants receive full-time healthcare benefits, other military privileges, and a monthly basic pay stipend (one-fifteenth of their base salary) while taking a sabbatical from active duty. The selected members are allowed to return to active duty up to three years later at the same rank and time in service they held prior to taking the sabbatical. The Navy believes this program will allow leaders flexibility to reward top sailors who feel forced to choose between career and family demands.

ACHIEVEMENTS, CHALLENGES, AND OPPORTUNITIES

The Department of Defense rapidly removed barriers to women's full inclusion to the military in the 1990s. Congress authorized women to fly combat missions in 1991, and authorized women to serve aboard combat ships in 1992, with 41,000 women serving in the Persian Gulf War under President George H. W. Bush.[61] In 1998, women flew combat missions off of US aircraft carriers in the Persian Gulf, marking the first time women flew in combat. In 2000, Kathleen McGrath became the first woman to command a US Navy war ship assigned to a combatant zone, the USS McGrath.[62] In 2004, Colonel Linda McTague became the first woman commander of a fighter squadron in the history of the US Air Force.[63] In 2005, Army Sergeant Leigh Ann Hester became the first woman awarded the Silver Star for combat action against the enemy.[64]

The true watershed moment occurred on January 24, 2013 when outgoing Secretary of Defense Leon Panetta announced that the DoD had removed gender-based restrictions on women serving in combat. The recommendation was made by the Joint Chiefs of Staff based on women serving with valor in over ten years of persistent conflict in combat zones in Iraq and Afghanistan. Panetta announced that the next step was for each of the armed services to study how they would open the remaining positions for women to serve or ask for exemptions.[65]

On December 3, 2015, Secretary of Defense Ashton Carter announced that the military would be opening all "remaining occupations and positions to women. There will be no exceptions." Women would be allowed to "drive tanks, fire mortars and lead infantry soldiers into combat."[66] This step opened approximately 220,000 additional jobs to women. Carter announced women would also be allowed to compete for elite Special Operations units, such as the Army's Delta Force and the Navy SEALs. On August 21, 2015, Captain Kristen Griest and Lieutenant Shayne Haver became the first women to graduate from the Army's prestigious Ranger

School—the same school that former NFL legend Pat Tillman graduated from before being killed in Afghanistan. Sixty percent of male soldiers failed the course in 2014. Of the nineteen women who started with Giest and Haver, they were the only two who graduated. Both women are graduates of the USMA at West Point.[67]

The fact that women have had the legal authority to hold leadership positions at the highest levels, and that the combat exclusion barring women from serving in combat has been removed are huge credits to the armed forces. However, for all its gains, systemic bias remains. The military will not be able to move forward regarding gender equality until it gets a handle on sexual assault and sexual harassment.

During the air campaign of the Persian Gulf War in 1991, two women were taken as prisoners of war. The senior ranking woman of the two, Major Rhonda Cornum, testified before the Presidential Commission on the Assignment of Women in the Armed Services in June 1992 that she was "violated manually–vaginally and rectally."[68] Major Cornum, (now BG Retired) was a flight surgeon, and part of a crew shot down over enemy territory in Iraq during the air campaign of the war. She was one of three members who survived the crash. Specialist Melissa Coleman, the other female POW during the Gulf War, reported she was the victim of indecent assault. Fortunately, America has not yet had to contend with significant numbers of women being exposed to this type of risk in combat.

TWENTY-SIX YEARS BEFORE "ME TOO," THERE WAS TAILHOOK

The sad reality is that many women in the armed forces face sexual harassment and sexual assault from their fellow service members in staggering numbers. The Navy's Tailhook scandal broke the previous year in September 1991, and illustrated this point. When details of rampant and pervasive sexual abuse at the Navy's "Top Gun" Aviators Convention in Las Vegas, NV were publicized, it was portrayed as an embarrassment to the Navy.[69]

Seven months after Tailhook, the Navy released its findings in which over 1,500 people were interviewed, but only two were named as suspects. Ultimately, Secretary of the Navy H. Lawrence Garrett resigned under pressure for his mishandling of the scandal. Admiral Duvall "Mac" Williams led the Navy's investigation of Tailhook. The Navy's first woman Assistant Secretary of the Navy, Barbra Pope, pressed Williams on the inadequacy of the investigation. Williams replied that he encountered a wall of silence; the men refused to testify against one another. Pope continued to press Admiral Williams for details, and he attempted to white wash the incident as a "boys will be boys" phenomenon. Pope emphatically stated that when someone is "manhandled against their will, that is assault."[70] Williams lost his composure and implied that the women brought the incident upon themselves, and that women and men could not work together because it always comes down to sex.[71]

Navy Lieutenant Paula Coughlin took matters into her own hands following the Navy's attempted cover-up. Lieutenant Coughlin was a victim of sexual assault at the Tailhook Conference before she fought her way to freedom and informed her seniors. Unsatisfied with the Navy's handling of Tailhook, Coughlin held a national press conference in front of the Pentagon, demanding that all Tailhook assailants be brought to justice. The Department of Defense took over the investigation, and wrote a scathing report on the Navy, revealing eighty-three women and seven men had been assaulted during the melee. 140 assailants were named, but none were prosecuted.[72]

Tailhook was the military's first "Me Too" moment some twenty-six years before the US's broader moment of truth regarding sexual harassment and sexual assault. In many ways, sexual assault in the military is another example of the military's problem being America's problem: in 1996, a rape ring was uncovered at Aberdeen Proving Grounds, MD; in 2003 rampant sexual abuse was discovered at the Air Force Academy; and in May 2017 it was reported that the Marine Corps had had a systemic ring of online sexual harassment of women Marines (e.g. nude photos were circulated without permission), creating a culture of misogyny and sexual assault since 2013. [73]

Attempting to eliminate sexual harassment and sexual assault within its ranks, the DoD has created the Sexual Assault Prevention and Response Office (SAPRO). SAPRO's mission is to serve as the single point of authority for program accountability and oversight, in order to enable military readiness and reduce—with a goal to eliminate—sexual assault from the military. SAPRO is also responsible for overseeing the DoD's sexual assault policy. They collaborate with the armed services and the civilian community to develop and implement innovative programs for preventing and responding to sexual harassment and sexual assault, as well as monitoring incidents across the armed forces.[74]

SAPRO reported in May 2017 that FY16 reports were up by 1.5 percent to 6,172 reported cases, including 5,350 cases against US service members, and 822 victims who were civilians or foreign nationals. 910 of the reported cases were against men, and another 481 of reported cases occurred prior to the victims joining the armed services.[75] Although the armed forces has made tremendous strides to eliminate sexual harassment and assault from the ranks, this challenge remains formidable. Congress has asked numerous times over the past decade: "should cases involving sexual assault and sexual harassment be adjudicated outside the chain of command?"

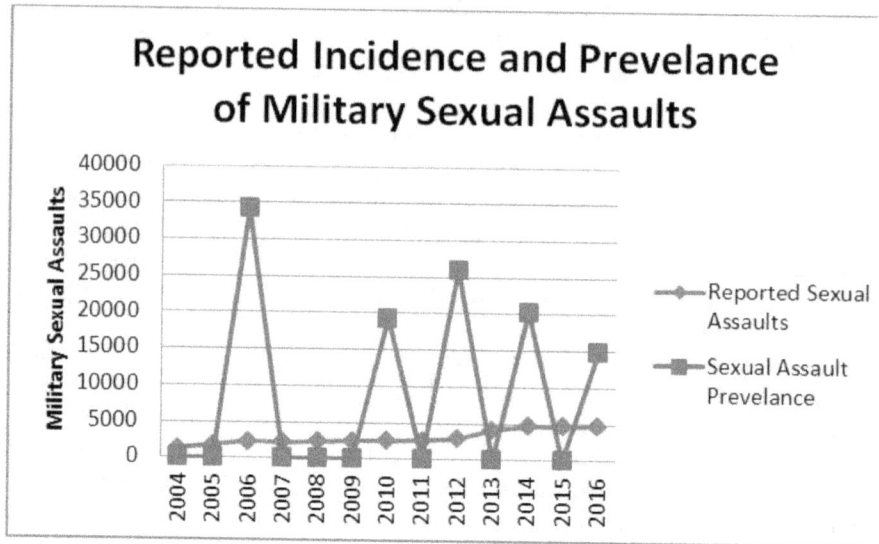

Figure 5.2. Department of Defense Sexual Assault and Prevention Response Office (SAPRO) Data. 2004–2016. *Source: Department of Defense SAPRO*

Sexual assault and sexual harassment pose an especially difficult challenge for military commanders, given the number of mishandled cases, and these issues remaining among the top threats to internal force protection. Like many of the military's problems relating to equality and social justice, their struggle with sexual harassment and sexual assault stems from American society's paternalism, including the tendency to subordinate justice for women survivors below protecting male offenders. One solution that could allow commanders continued adjudication of sexual harassment and sexual assault cases would be to have independent boards review commanders' decisions, with the identities of the victim and alleged assailant redacted so that only their ranks are known to the board. The board could be tasked with two responsibilities: 1) Review the case and determine appropriate punishment independent from the commander's decision, 2) Once the board's decision is made, they could be informed of what the commander decided, then the board could opine on the appropriateness of the commander's proposed decision. This information would then be returned to the commander before he or she decides how to handle each case. The commander's decision would then be reviewed by their superior. Commanders who render inappropriate decisions could themselves be subject to punishment. Sexual harassment and sexual assault are typically more about a power imbalance and exerting control over the victim. The military's traditional hierarchy makes it the ultimate power structure where commanders wield immense power over their subordinates. This structure can and has led to disastrous, unintended consequences. Sexual harassment and sexual assault present yet another opportunity for the armed forces to lead a formidable crusade against one of the most pervasive social ills of our time.

NOTES

1. "The Woman Suffrage Timeline," The Library of Congress, accessed January 8, 2014, http://www.thlizbrary.org/suffrage/.
2. Scott Horsely, "A Churchill 'Quote' That U.S. Politicians will Never Surrender," NPR, October 28, 2013, http://www.npr.org/sections/itsallpolitics/2013/10/28/241295755/a-churchill-quote-that-u-s-politicians-will-never-surrender
3. "Edith Nourse Rogers: 1881–1960," *History, Art & Archives: United States House of Representatives,* June 21, 2018, https://history.house.gov/People/Listing/R/ROGERS,-Edith-Nourse-(R000392)/
4. Emily J. Tiepe, "Will the Real Molly Pitcher Please Stand Up?," *Prologue Magazine* 31, no. 2 (Summer 1999), accessed June 21, 2018, https://www.archives.gov/publications/prologue/1999/summer/pitcher.html.
5. "Mary Edwards Walker: The Only Woman to Receive the Medal of Honor," *NBC News,* May 21, 2014, http://www.nbcnews.com/news/military/mary-edwards-walker-only-woman-receive-medal-honor-n111596 (accessed March 5, 2018).
6. "Women in the Army," *U.S. Army Heritage and Education Center,* U.S. Army, September 8, 2017, https://www.army.mil/women/history/.
7. Mattie E. Treadwell, *United States Army in World War II: Special Studies, The Women's Army Corps,* United States Army Center of Military History (Washington, DC: Government Printing Office, 1991), https://history.army.mil/books/wwii/Wac/index.htm.
8. Bernard A. Cook, *Women and War: A Historical Encyclopedia from Antiquity to the Present,* Vol. 1 (Santa Barbara, CA: ABC-CLIO, 2006), 242.
9. "History of the WAC and Army Women," *Women's Army Corps Veterans'-Army Women United (WACVA-AWU),* March 19, 2016, https://www.armywomen.org/wacHistory.shtml.
10. Judith Bellafaire, "The Women's Army Corps: A Commemoration of WWII Service," *U.S. Army Center for Military History,* February 17, 2005, https://history.army.mil/brochures/WAC/WAC.HTM (accessed June 21, 2018).
11. Richard Goldstein, "Charity Adams Earley, Black Pioneer in Wacs, Dies at 83," *NY Times,* January 22, 2002, http://www.nytimes.com/2002/01/22/us/charity-adams-earley-black-pioneer-in-wacs-dies-at-83.html (accessed March 9, 2018).
12. Darlene M. Iskra, *Women in the United States Armed Forces: A Guide to the Issues* (Santa Barbara, CA: Praeger, 2010), 151.
13. Jean Ebert and Marie-Beth Hall, *Crossed Currents: Navy Women from WWI to Tailhook* (Brassey's: Washington, D.C., 1993), 27–28.
14. Ibid.
15. Joy Bright Hancock, *Lady in the Navy* (Annapolis, MD: Naval Institute Press, 1972), 53.
16. Ebert, *Crossed Currents: Navy Women from WWI to Tailhook,* 32.
17. Ibid, 32.
18. Ibid.
19. Susan H. Goodson, *Serving Proudly* (Annapolis, MD: Naval Institute Press, 2001), 115.
20. Ibid.
21. Rebecca Maksel, "The Roald Dahl Aviation Story that Disney Refused to Film," *Air & Space Magazine,* May 22, 2014, https://www.airspacemag.com/daily-planet/fifinella-mischievous-gremlin-180951401/.

22. Kathleen Cornelsen, "Women Airforce Service Pilots of World War II: Exploring Military Aviation, Encountering Discrimination, and Exchanging Traditional Roles in Service to America," Journal of Women's History 17 (2005): 111–119, https://www.semanticscholar.org/paper/Women-Airforce-Service-Pilots-of-World-War-II%3A-and-Cornelsen/4b9fd1b4cf051b127c3dfff7c51f6d74928eefb9.

23. "Public Law 111–40—July 1, 2009: Women Airforce Service Pilots Congressional Gold Medal," *Congress.gov*, accessed January 25, 2018, https://www.congress.gov/111/plaws/publ40/PLAW-111publ40.pdf.

24. Shannon Collins, "WASPs Were Pioneers for Female Pilots of Today, Tomorrow," *U.S. DoD News*, March 2, 2016, https://www.defense.gov/Explore/News/Article/Article/684700/wasps-were-pioneers-for-female-pilots-of-today-tomorrow/ (accessed December 5, 2017).

25. Ellen Carol DuBois and Lynn Dumenil, *Through Women's Eyes: An American History with Documents* (Boston: Bedford St. Martins, 2015), 549.

26. "A History of Women in the U.S. Military," *Infoplease*, February 28, 2017, http://www.infoplease.com/us/military/women-history.html (accessed October 7, 2015).

27. Leisa D. Meyer, *Creating G.I. Jane: Sexuality and Power in the Women's Army Corps During World War II* (New York: Columbia University Press, 1998), 33–51.

28. Treadwell, *United States Army in World War II: Special Studies, The Women's Army Corps*, 184.

29. Ibid., 95–96.

30. "American Women and World War II," *Khan Academy*, accessed December 27, 2017, https://www.khanacademy.org/humanities/us-history/rise-to-world-power/us-wwii/a/american-women-and-world-war-ii.

31. Melissa K. Wilford, "Army Celebrates Service of Women Soldiers," *U.S. Army*, October 20, 2008, https://www.army.mil/article/13428/army_celebrates_service_of_women_soldiers (accessed June 21, 2018).

32. "Women in the Army."

33. Ibid.

34. Ibid.

35. Natasha Turner, "10 Things that American Women Could not do Before the 1970s," *Ms. Magazine*, May 28, 2018, https://msmagazine.com/2013/05/28/10-things-that-american-women-could-not-do-before-the-1970s/ (accessed February 9, 2016).

36. "The 1960s–70s, The American Feminist Movement: Breaking Down Barriers for Women," *Tavaana*, June 21, 2018, https://tavaana.org/en/case-studies/1960s-70s-american-feminist-movement-breaking-down-barriers-women.

37. Gail Collins, *When Everything Changed: The Amazing Journey of American Women from 1960 to the Present* (New York: Little, Brown & Company, 2009), 231–38.

38. "The 1960s–70s, The American Feminist Movement: Breaking Down Barriers for Women."

39. James Webb, "Women Can't Fight," *The Washingtonian*, November 1, 1979, https://www.washingtonian.com/1979/11/01/jim-webb-women-cant-fight/ (accessed January 12, 2018).

40. "A Story of Honor and Continuous Innovation," U.S. Air Force Academy, accessed June 21, 2018, https://www.usafa.edu/about/history/.

41. Marene Allison, "At the Gates of West Point," The Women's Memorial, Oct. 21, 2006, https://www.womensmemorial.org/oral-history/detail/?s=at-the-gates-of-west-point (accessed April 22, 2018).

42. Ibid.

43. Ibid.

44. Ibid.

45. Ibid.

46. Ibid.

47. Ibid.

48. Todd Lopez, "First Female Four-star General Retires from Army," US Army, August 16, 2012, https://www.army.mil/article/85606/First_female_four_star_general_retires_from_Army/ (accessed March 9, 2017).

49. "U.S. Navy Biography: Admiral Michelle Howard," *America's Navy: Forged by the Sea*, US Navy, December 1, 2017, http://www.navy.mil/navydata/bios/navybio_ret.asp?bioID=394 (accessed March 9, 2017).

50. "General Janet C. Wolfenbarger," *U.S. Air Force*, July 1, 2015, https://www.af.mil/About-Us/Biographies/Display/Article/107934/general-janet-c-/ (accessed March 9, 2017).

51. Henry Cuningham, "Obama Nominates E.E. Smith Grad for Army Surgeon General," *Fayetteville Observer*, May 5, 2011, http://www./#2/a477ecb2-6a43-5de7-97c3-9e87b8e9afee.html (accessed March 10, 2017).

52. Mary Ellen Condon-Rall, *Attack on the Pentagon: The Medical Response to 9/11* (Fort Detrick, MD: Borden Institute, 2011).

53. Maria Tolleson, "Maj. Gen. Nadja West Confirmed as 44th Army Surgeon General," *U.S. Army*, December 11, 2015, https://www.army.mil/article/159884/maj_gen_nadja_west_confirmed_as_44th_army_surgeon_general (accessed March 29, 2017).

54. "Milestones: Understanding the History of Women's Representation Helps to Inform our Work for Gender Parity," *Represent Women: Parity for Women in Politics, Represent Women*, March 17, 2017, https://www.representwomen.org/women_history.

55. Megan Hammons, "Is There a Gender Gap in the U.S. Military?" *Veteran Aid*, January 25, 2017, https://www.veteranaid.org/blog/2017/01/25/gender-gap-u-s-military/ (accessed Jan 27, 2018).

56. Rachel Thomas, Marianne Cooper, Ellen Konar, Magan Rooney, Ashley Finch, Lareina Yee, Alexis Krivkovich, et al., *Women in the Work Place Study 2017* (New York: McKinsey & Company, 2017).

57. US Department of Defense, Office of the Deputy Assistant Secretary of Defense for Military Community and Family Policy, *2015 Demographics: Profile of the Military Community* (Washington, DC: DoD, 2015), pdf, https://download.militaryonesource.mil/12038/MOS/Reports/2015-Demographics-Report.pdf (2016).

58. Valentina Zarya, "The 2017 Fortune 500 Includes a Record Number of Women CEOs," *Fortune Magazine*, June 7, 2017, https://fortune.com/2017/06/07/fortune-women-ceos/.

59. Nikki Waller, "How Men and Women See the Workplace Differently," *The Wall-street Journal*, September 27, 2016, http:// graphics/wsj.com/how-men-and-women-see-theworkplace-differently/ (accessed December 20, 2017).

60. Lisa Ferdinando, "Carter Announces 12 Weeks Paid Military Maternity Leave, Other Benefits," *U.S. DoD News*, January 28, 2016, https://www.defense.gov/Explore/News/Article/Article/645958/carter-announces-12-weeks-paid-military-maternity-leave-other-benefits/ (accessed January 18, 2018).

61. "Time Line: Women in the U.S. Military," *Colonial Williamsburg Foundation*, 2008, http://www.history.org/History/teaching/enewsletter/volume7/images/nov/women_military_timeline.pdf (accessed January 30, 2017).

62. John Lang, "Albuquerque Woman to Command Navy Fighting Ship," *Albuquerque Times* (Albuquerque, NM), March 25, 1998.

63. "Time Line: Women in the U.S. Military."

64. "Women in the Army."

65. Claudette Roulo, "Defense Department Expands Women's Combat Role," *U.S. DoD News*, January 24, 2013, https://archive.defense.gov/news/newsarticle.aspx?id=119098 (accessed February 01, 2016).

66. US Department of Defense, "Department of Defense Press Briefing by Secretary Carter," Transcript, Pentagon Briefing Room, Washington, DC, December 3, 2015, https://www.defense.gov/Newsroom/Transcripts/Transcript/Article/632578/department-of-defense-press-briefing-by-secretary-carter-in-the-pentagon-briefing/ (accessed July 7, 2016).

67. Elizabeth Chuck, "Kristen Griest and Shaye Haver, First Female Army Rangers, Graduate Grueling School," *NBC News.com*, August 21, 2015, https://www.nbcnews.com/news/military/history-making-first-female-army-rangers-graduate-n413766 (accessed August 22, 2015).

68. "Female POW in Gulf War was Sexually Assaulted," *Washington Post*, June 11, 1992, https://www.washingtonpost.com/archive/politics/1992/06/11/female-pow-in-gulf-war-was-sexually-assaulted/2bacbed7-5279-4126-a772-f1918c6598c2/ (accessed April 12, 2017).

69. Caitlin V. Muldoon, "Honor, Courage, Commitment: Understanding Sexual Assault in the United States Navy" (PhD diss., Old Dominion University, 2015).

70. Judy Mann, "The Woman Who Said 'No' to the Navy," *Washington Post*, February 5, 1993, https://www.washingtonpost.com/archive/local/1993/02/05/the-woman-who-said-no-to-the-navy/7a2f5549-ea8d-41e9-8862-be98ef660bbb/ (accessed April, 29, 2017).

71. Michael Winerip, "Revisiting the Military's Tailhook Scandal," *NY Times*, May 13, 2013, https://www.nytimes.com/2013/05/13/booming/revisiting-the-militarys-tailhook-scandal-video.html (accessed March 30, 2018).

72. Derek J. Vander Schaaf, "Report of Investigation: Tailhook 91-Part 2, Events of the 35th Annual Tailhook Symposium," Official memorandum for Secretary of Defense, Arlington, VA: Department of Defense, April 12, 1993, https://apps.dtic.mil/dtic/tr/fulltext/u2/a269008.pdf (accessed April 9, 2018).

73. US Department of Defense, *Annual Report on Sexual Assault in the Military: Fiscal Year 2017*, Washington, DC: DoD, May 4, 2018, https://sapr.mil/public/docs/reports/FY17_Annual/DoD_FY17_Annual_Report_on_Sexual_Assault_in_the_Military.pdf, 3.

74. US Department of Defense, "Mission and History," *Sexual Assault Prevention and Response*, accessed April 11, 2017, https://www.sapr.mil/mission-history.

75. US Department of Defense, *Annual Report on Sexual Assault in the Military: Fiscal Year 2017*, 3.

SIX
Lesbians, Gays, Bisexual, and Transgender Members in the Armed Services

The LGBTQ+ community's struggle for acceptance in the US shares many commonalities with that of other marginalized populations. Homosexuals have always been part of our society, yet their acknowledgement and the degree to which they have been accepted in mainstream society has ebbed and flowed over time with acceptance generally increasing over time. Like other minority groups, military service has played a pivotal role in homosexuals being more broadly accepted by the American public. There is significant evidence that homosexuals have played a vital role in America's defense throughout history, dating back to before the US was a sovereign nation. In the early days of the American Revolution, Benjamin Franklin summoned a German military protégé, Baron Von Stueben, to assist with organizing a poorly trained, poorly equipped, Continental Army. Von Stueben was a promising captain in the Prussian Army—considered the most advanced, well trained Army in the world at the time. He was reluctant upon first hearing Franklin's offer, but allegations about Von Stueben's involvement in a homosexual affair in the Prussian Army may have hastened him to come to America.[1] General George Washington met him with enthusiasm in 1778, and asked him to review the Continental Army at Valley Forge. Washington was so impressed with Von Stueben's assessment that he charged him with creating a cohesive Army from the US Continental Army and the thirteen state militias.[2] Von Stueben took to the task of infusing military order, discipline, drills, training, and tactics from his training as a Prussian Army Officer. Washington assigned two of his own aides, John Laurens and Alexander Hamilton, to Von Stueben who had to retrain each state militia into the newly adopted Continental military training methods. Hamilton and Laurens were known to have had a homosexual affair that lasted years, though both men were married.[3] Congress commissioned Von Steuben as a Major General who went on to become the first Army Inspector General. The drill manual that the three men played a part in delivering to the field became the official drill manual of the US Army until 1812.[4] Gay men quite literally played founding roles in establishing the US Military.

There are dozens of examples of highly decorated gay Navy captains who served with distinction in the 1800s. Gay soldiers fought on both sides during the Civil War, and in the US Cavalry during the westward expansion under General Custer. Their homosexuality was known, but they were permitted to continue serving because of their contributions. It wasn't until 1919 that a provision in the Uniformed Code of Military Justice (UCMJ), the Articles of War at that time, established sodomy (oral or anal sex between men) as a felony offense within the armed services. Under this provision, thousands of service members were discharged over the next two decades.[5]

During WWII, the emphasis from sexual contact began to shift to sexual orientation when psychiatrists deemed homosexuality a mental disorder that was detrimental to uniformed service. Psychiatrists began excluding potential draftees as medically unfit for service if they determined a potential recruit was not using homosexuality as a means of malingering, but was actually homosexual or even presented a proclivity toward homosexuality.[6]

Homosexual men knew concealment of their sexual identity was necessary if they wanted to maintain societal acceptance. The demand for military personnel during World War II imposed the continuation of this societal norm while the military grew by some sixteen million men and 350,000 women. There was no provision in the UCMJ for lesbian sexual behavior, so gay women generally got a pass. In fact, military chaplains and drill sergeants were instructed to be sympathetic to women far away from home for the first time who formed "intense friendships" with other women.[7] In essence "Don't ask, don't tell" (DADT) was the prevailing practice of the military during WWII even though it was not yet policy.

Many young men and women came to grips with their homosexuality during military service when thrust into close quarters with large numbers of strangers for the first time in their lives. We know through oral histories at the National Archives, journals, and surviving service members who have since come out that many service men and women were unaware they had romantic feelings for members of the same sex prior to joining the military at eighteen, nineteen, or twenty years of age.[8] These men and women not only learned about themselves, but learned there were others like them and how to recognize one another, successfully forming networks of friends, both in and out of the military.[9]

After WWII, the need for military personnel greatly diminished as the government sought to shrink the active force to pre-war levels by any means available. Scores of veterans were prosecuted for sodomy and forced to leave the service. Many of those discharged under such conditions were labeled "sexual psychopaths," and chose not to return home. These veterans, as well as others who served undetected, relocated in great numbers to cities such as San Francisco, New York, and Los Angeles, and formed the beginning of large gay communities in these areas.[10]

CHALLENGES OF THE '70S AND '80S

Many members of the gay and lesbian community believed that Truman's 1948 executive order desegregating the military should have served as a model for lifting the ban against openly gay service members. The success of US civil rights legislation in the 1960s that ended state-sanctioned discrimination based on race, religion, gender, creed, or national origin, spurred many gay rights advocates into lobbying to include sexual orientation as a protected status. As a political agenda, gay rights began to take shape in the 1970s.[11]

Gay rights advocates continued challenging the military's ban on homosexuals during the 1970s and 1980s. Though these challenges were unsuccessful, the Department of Defense did refine its policy on homosexuals in the armed forces in 1982. They essentially stated that homosexuality was incompatible with uniformed military service, asserting that it ran counter to the order, discipline, trust, and unit cohesion necessary to effectively muster an armed force. The directive implied that the close quarters that military forces sometimes maintain made the presence of homosexuals an infringement on heterosexuals' privacy. The policy also intimated that homosexuals posed a greater security risk than heterosexuals.[12]

Although the military continued to use homosexuality as grounds for discharge, they no longer characterized the nature of service as dishonorable. Honorable discharges for homosexuality became the norm when homosexuality was the sole purpose for separation.[13] Seventeen thousand gay and lesbian service members were discharged under the DoD's restated directive from 1983 to 2002.[14] Gay and lesbian advocates were dissatisfied with this very modest refinement of the DoD position and continued to push for change.

THE EVOLUTION OF DON'T ASK DON'T TELL (DADT)

As a campaign pledge, President Clinton took up the cause of eliminating homosexuality as a prohibition to military service. Once elected, Clinton and Secretary of Defense Les Aspin committed to lifting the ban on gays and lesbians serving openly in the military. They encountered mild opposition from the military brass and strong opposition from members of Congress, particularly the ultra-conservative wing of the Republican Party and Democrats from the Bible Belt. It is more than coincidental that these same two political factions formed the basis of resistance to Executive Order 9981, and gays in the military was one of a handful of social issues that caused Southern Democrats to switch party affiliation.

Senator Sam Nunn (D) of Georgia, Chairman of the Senate Armed Services Committee, was one of the most vocal critics of Clinton's cause. The opposition to homosexuals serving in the military argued that gays and lesbians would compromise the privacy of heterosexuals and erode trust among service members. In turn, this undermined trust would be detrimental to the good order and discipline necessary for unit cohesion. Clinton argued that the emphasis should be placed on conduct, not sexual orientation: "There is no study showing homosexuals to be less capable or more prone to misconduct than heterosexual soldiers," and "misconduct is already covered by the laws and rules" of the services.[15] Clinton and Aspen systematically poked holes in the historical arguments against homosexuals serving in the military, beginning with the notion that homosexuals were unfit for service. This argument was easily defeated by listing the long history of known gay men with exemplary and even heroic service records.

Gay rights opponents then referenced the psychiatric designation of homosexuality as a mental disorder from the 1920s through the 1970s (the American Psychiatric Association removed homosexuality from its list of diagnosable psychological conditions in 1973).[16] Gregory M. Herek, an Associate Research Psychologist at the University of California Davis, and an authority on public attitudes toward lesbians and gay men testified before the House Armed Services Committee on behalf of numerous professional associations. Herek stated that the research data shows there is nothing about lesbians and gay men that makes them inherently unfit for military service, and there is nothing in the data that makes heterosexuals inherently unable to work and live with gay people in close quarters: "The assumption that heterosexuals cannot overcome their prejudices toward gay people is a mistaken one."[17]

In the 1950s during McCarthyism, Senator Joe McCarthy and others claimed homosexuals posed a greater national security threat than heterosexuals. The Navy tested that theory and discredited it in the Crittenden Report, which stated alcoholics and adulterous heterosexuals were more of a security threat than homosexuals.[18] At that point, the last remaining premise for excluding homosexuals from military service was the illegality of sodomy. American society was not ready for that debate in public hearings, which became one of the driving forces behind DADT. The Clinton Administration had effectively dismantled all performance related challenges to gays serving in the military, and this lingering moral judgement would remain in this round of legislation.

The National Defense Research Institute prepared a landmark study for the Secretary of Defense in 1993 entitled, *Sexual Orientation and U.S. Military Personnel Policy: Options and Assessment*. The study found that the ban to homosexuals serving openly in the military could be removed with little to no impact on enlistment and retention, provided the restrictions were done thoughtfully, with an accompanying strategy for messaging.[19] Despite these findings, opposition to openly gay service members remained. Senator Sam Nunn (R) GA led this opposition with Chairman of the Joint Chiefs of Staff General Colin Powell and Powell's successor, General John Shailkashvili, in agreement.[20]

On the other side of the camp, stood figures like Barry Goldwater who was in favor of a reform that would allow homosexuals to serve in the military. Goldwater—a former presidential candidate, retired major general, and Republican senator—wrote an Op Ed in the *New York Times* entitled "You don't have to be straight to shoot straight."[21] The article prompted floods of phone calls from opposition groups who cited substantial public opposition to Clinton's open service proposal. The Clinton Administration compromised with the opposition; they would not remove the ban on gays and lesbians serving in the military, but they would prohibit military leaders from questioning or investigating a service member solely to determine their sexual orientation. The National Defense Authorization Act (NDAA) directed the services to continue following guidance contained in the 1982 DoD Directive—instructions were to be embedded in a funding bill for the armed services restricting commanders' authority to investigate or question homosexuality. President Clinton signed the provisions into law on November 30, 1993.[22]

DADT still barred openly gay and lesbian citizens from joining the military, but military leaders were not permitted to ask about one's sexual orientation, investigate to determine if a service member was homosexual, or harass service members suspected of being homosexual.[23] On December 21, 1993, Secretary of Defense Lee Aspen signed a new DoD Directive that gave the services a sixty-day implementation period that took effect on February 28, 1994. DADT did not remove the moral judgement on gay sex, which was still considered sodomy in the UCMJ, and was still permissible grounds for separation.[24] Under DADT, 10,000 servicemen and women were discharged for homosexuality over a nine-year period, 1994–2003.[25]

DADT was a compromise on one of Clinton's campaign promises. Gay rights advocates campaigned ardently to elect President Clinton, and he promised he would repeal the military ban against gays serving openly. They were understandably frustrated when he failed to deliver. But as cumbersome as DADT appeared on the surface, it is arguably a prime example of open debate, compromise, and effective democratic governance. Although awkward, DADT was a necessary evolution to gays and lesbians serving openly. It allowed gay members to serve with less fear of harassment, provided they did not make their sexual orientation a topic of discussion. COL Grethe Cammermeyer was one of thousands of gay service members reinstated to military service by a federal court based on the passage of DADT.[26]

For all its pragmatism, DADT was still lacking. It still restricted homosexuals' freedom of speech and conduct, while heterosexuals were allowed to live more freely. The ability to self-disclose and form normative relationships with colleagues is beneficial to one's social life and self-esteem. And the inability to engage honestly with professional colleagues in casual conversation has been linked to loneliness and social isolation.[27] Homosexuals in the military were trapped in a catch 22 under DADT. On the one hand, if they revealed their sexuality they jeopardized their professional careers; on the other, if they withheld information they were deceiving their colleagues. Biomedical researcher and communications expert, Mary Ann Fitzpatrick, noted that a certain degree of self-disclosure is an integral component in common social interaction, and an equal exchange of information is expected to form normal, balanced relationships.[28]

Moreover, as gay rights activist and researcher Margaret Cruikshank noted, the opposition was a moral opposition, and had nothing to do with unit cohesion, military readiness, or heterosexual privacy. She explained, "the military does not want to accept homosexuals because it would advance the idea that they are equal to heterosexuals . . . the exclusion of homosexuals from the military is inherently political and is about discrimination and second class status."[29] Cruikshank's assertion is in keeping with other counterarguments advanced by marginalized and underrepresented groups fighting for inclusion. Exclusion is never about the reasons advanced—the water fountain, the requisite amount of courage, or the "appropriate" bathroom; these arguments are a thinly veiled excuse for preserving the status quo to protect the majority's world view and dominance.

Despite the progress DADT represented, it was fraught with deficiencies and provided only very limited protection. PFC Barry Winchell, a twenty-one year old infantry soldier stationed at Fort Campbell, KY, was murdered in his sleep by a fellow platoon member in July 1999. Winchell was dating a transgender civilian, and his fellow soldiers spread rumors of his relationship, which lead to a fight between him and his murderer, Calvin Glover. Winchell bested Glover in a fair fight. After other soldiers ridiculed Glover for losing, he killed Winchell with a baseball bat in the barracks as Winchell slept.[30] The murder of PFC Winchell removed the final veneer concealing the oppositions' true rationale for opposing LGBTQ+ citizens' right to serve freely in uniform: a belief in hetero-superiority. Glover was so incensed that he lost a fair fight to someone he believed himself to be superior to, he murdered his fellow soldier in a fit of rage and shame. Glover's beliefs regarding homosexuals is a form of tribalism that has bifurcated American society, so much so that terms such as conservative and liberal go beyond describing one's political ideation. American society has expanded the definitions such that these terms influence how and if we associate with one another.

PFC Winchell's murder and other similar incidents prompted Defense Secretary William Cohen to order a review of the "don't harass" mandates under DADT, which found that anti-gay sentiments were pervasive throughout the DoD. The DoD adopted a new anti-harassment policy in July 2000. The Center for the Study of Sexual Minorities in the Military issued a report on the harassment provisions of DADT, titled *The Practical and Conceptual Problems with Regulating Harassment in a Discriminatory Institution*. This report stated that, despite the military's intention to curb harassment of personnel perceived to be gay or lesbian, policies prevented adequate and equal protection under the law.[31] Specifically, DADT precludes the military "from instituting certain measures that would give meaning to the harassment ban, such as allowing victims to report harassment without the fear of being discharged."[32] Secondly, the military failed to establish a broader structure to give teeth to the anti-harassment mandate, unlike its policies against gender and racial discrimination.[33] The military's ban on harassing gay and lesbian officers is not "codified" in "Don't Ask, Don't Tell," any executive order, or a federal statute. As Director of the Servicemembers Legal Defense Network (SLDN) Steve Ralls notes, DADT failed to provide an avenue for service members to report discrimination based on sexual orientation, and the DADT "policy is the nation's only law that authorizes the firing of a person for being gay or lesbian," effectively punishing "gays, lesbians, and bisexuals for coming out."[34]

Despite these shortcomings, DADT provided a platform for the gradual "mainstreaming" of homosexuals into the American collective, and survived five major court challenges. One of the first major litmus tests of DADT came in January 1998 when Navy Chief Petty Officer Timothy R. McVeigh, (not to be confused with convicted Oklahoma City bomber, Timothy J. McVeigh) won an injunction against the US Navy who was seeking to discharge him for homosexual conduct after seventeen years of service. District Judge David Sporkin ruled the Navy violated DADT when it used McVeigh's America Online email account and username to launch an investigation into his sexual orientation. Sporkin's ruling stated, "Suggestions of sexual orientation in a private, anonymous email account did not give the Navy a sufficient reason to investigate whether to commence discharge proceedings."[35] Sporkin called the Navy's investigation a "search and destroy mission" against McVeigh.[36] The *New York Times* called the decision a victory for gay rights, with implications for millions who use online services.[37]

DADT survived four other major court challenges to its constitutionality: *Richenberg v. Perry*, 1996; *Thomasson v. Perry*, 1996; *Able v. United States*, 1998; and *Holmes v. California National Guard*, 1998. In each case, the courts affirmed the government's interest in maintaining its ban against the supposedly destructive influence of homosexual conduct. The firestorm of debate surrounding DADT continued until 2010, forming the back drop for public policy debates waged by gay rights advocates, civil libertarian organizations, and American popular culture.

THE SHIFT OF US PUBLIC OPINION

A 1994 NBC/*Wall Street Journal* poll showed forty percent of people favored gays and lesbians serving in the military while fifty-two percent of Americans opposed the idea.[38] But gay rights advocates continued pushing for equal rights. Two major events exemplify how American policy and public opinion began to slowly shift, becoming more sympathetic to gay rights. On April 14, 1997, Ellen DeGeneres announced that she is a lesbian with the words "Yep, I'm Gay" on the cover of *Time* magazine. Ellen followed the *Time* article with an episode on her self-titled ABC sitcom when her fictional character also came out on the April 30, 1997, episode.[39] Then, in 2003, Massachusetts became the first state to allow gay marriage after its highest court ruled that the state's ban violated the constitutional rights of same-sex couples.

Popular opinion began to shift toward support for gay and lesbian service members to serve openly at the turn of the 21st century. The principal candidates for the Democratic presidential nomination in 2000, Al Gore and Bill Bradley, were both in favor of openly gay and lesbian service members being permitted to serve in uniform. Their support drew considerable criticism from some retired, high ranking officials, most notably, Marine Corps General Charles C. Krulak. He and others vociferously objected to Gore's statement that he would use the issue (support for ending DADT) as a litmus test when considering candidates for the Joint Chiefs of Staff.[40] That year, the Democratic Party platform was silent on the issue,[41] while the Republican Party Platform asserted "that homosexuality is incompatible with military service."[42]

Conservative critics of DADT were disappointed that President George W. Bush did not withdraw DADT and return the military to its earlier, complete ban on gays and lesbians serving in the military. But the fact that Bush did not withdraw DADT was further evidence of an overall shift in public opinion. By Bush's second term, a 2004 CNN/USA Today/Gallup Poll revealed that sixty-three percent of Americans favored gays and lesbians serving while thirty-two percent opposed such service—a significant change from the 1994 poll.[43]

In July 2004, the American Psychological Association (APA) issued a statement that DADT was discriminatory based on sexual orientation. The APA cited empirical evidence that failed to show that sexual orientation was germane to any aspect of military effectiveness, including unit cohesion, morale, recruitment, and retention.[44] In February 2005, the Government Accounting Office (GAO) issued a report that estimated the cost of DADT: at least $95.1 million was spent in training replacements for the 9,488 troops discharged from 1994 through 2003, noting that the true figures might be higher. These separations of gay and lesbian service members were especially detrimental to the services in shortages when the DoD lost fifty-nine Arabic and nine Persian linguists crucial to waging the war on terrorism.[45]

In February 2006, a University of California Blue Ribbon commission, which included former Reagan Administration Assistant Defense Secretary Lawrence Korb, estimated the true cost of DADT was closer to $363 million. The commission reported that the earlier GAO assessment failed to consider the lost value of the departed service members, $14.3million for relocation costs, and $79.3 million in recruiting costs.[46] In December 2006, Zogby International released the results of a poll of military personnel that found 26 percent favored allowing gays and lesbians to serve openly; 37 percent were opposed; and 37 percent expressed no preference or were unsure. Of those who had experience with gay people in their unit, 6 percent said their presence had a positive impact on their personnel morale; 66 percent said it had no impact, and 28 percent said it had a negative impact. Regarding overall morale, 3 percent said the presence of homosexuals had a positive impact and 64 percent said it had no impact.[47]

In January 2007, retired Chairman of the Joint Chiefs of Staff, General John Shalikasvili, who originally opposed DADT, announced he was now in favor of repealing the measure so that gay and lesbian service members could serve openly. Former senator and defense secretary William Cohen also joined Shalikasvili in favor of repealing DADT, and replacing that policy with one that allowed homosexuals to serve openly. Shalikasvili wrote that the military has been stretched thin by deployments in the Middle East, and we must welcome the service of any Americans who are willing and able to do the job.[48]

There were now at least four positions to the DADT debate: those who opposed DADT because they felt it was still discriminatory against the LGBTQ+ community, those who opposed DADT because they didn't want any gays serving at all, those who had little or no investment in LGBTQ+ rights but viewed prohibiting their service as a logistical and financial waste, and those who supported DADT. Massachusetts Governor Mitt Romney defended DADT during his first presidential run in 2008 saying, "When I first heard [the phrase], I thought it sounded silly and I just dismissed it and said, well, that can't possibly work. Well, I sure was wrong. It has worked. It's been in place now for over a decade. The military says it's working and they don't want to change it . . . and they're the people closest to the front. We're in the middle of a conflict right now. I would not change it."[49] Romney's initial reaction to DADT is an example of how many Americans viewed the policy, and then gained an appreciation for its pragmatism. At the end of the day, those who believed as Romney did when DADT was first introduced are now more closely aligned with those advocating for open service. In November 2007, twenty-eight retired generals and admirals urged Congress to repeal DADT, citing evidence that 65,000 homosexual people were serving in uniform, and that there were as many as one million gay veterans.[50] The delicate amity between those for and against gay service was imploding under the weight of both shifting public perception and LGBTQ+ advocates pointing out glaring holes in the DADT doctrine.

DON'T ASK DON'T TELL REVISITED AS PUBLIC LAW

During the 2008 presidential campaign, Senator Barack Obama advocated for a full repeal of the laws barring gays and lesbians from serving in the military. Eighteen days after the election, the Obama Administration walked his earlier campaign promise back somewhat by stating he wanted to confer "with the Joint Chiefs and his political appointees at the Pentagon to reach a consensus, and then present legislation to Congress."[51] Obama carefully avoided the mistakes of the Clinton Administration, which attempted to tackle both homosexuals serving in the military and healthcare reform as their first endeavors. Healthcare reform never gained any real traction, and many initially regarded DADT as a Clinton failure because his stated goal was to allow homosexuals to serve openly in the military—a policy change that didn't have enough political backing among Congress and military brass. Over time, people saw DADT as a pragmatic solution, and a necessary intermediate step before gays and lesbians could serve openly in the military.

In July 2009, Colin Powell stated on CNN that the policy was correct for the time. However, sixteen years later attitudes had changed, and he conceded it was time to review the law. As the sitting Chairman of the Joint Chiefs of Staff at the time of the DADT debate, Powell was one of the architects of DADT and an early opponent to gays and lesbians serving openly in the military. Admiral Mike Mullen, then current Chairman of the Joint Chiefs said in the same interview, "The policy would continue to be implemented until the law was repealed," and that his advice was to "move in a measured way."[52] Given his prominent role in DADT policy, Powell's admission that it was time to revisit the issue was a powerful development in the fight for gay rights.

Popular opinion for gays and lesbians serving openly in the military had been growing since the passage of DADT in 1999. Several factors shifted public opinion in favor of repealing DADT. De-stigmatizing homosexuals through military service increased public support for them; people who may not have been able to relate to homosexuals before, may have become more aware of them as a diverse group of individuals, sharing mainstream American values. In addition, there was a confluence of gay and lesbian rights activists, gays and lesbians in popular culture coming out, and growing evidence that homosexuality was not at odds with uniformed service. In Obama's first State of the Union Address, he firmly stated that he would repeal DADT within a year to allow gays and lesbians to serve openly in the military: "This year, I will work with Congress and our military to finally repeal the law that denies gay Americans the right to serve the country they love because of who they are. It's the right thing to do."[53] When Obama noted their love of country, he emphasized their patriotism, highlighting a commonality that homosexual service members could share with those who might oppose their sexual orientation. He also emphasized gay rights as a civil and human rights issue by using the phrase "because of who they are."[54] Here, Obama followed the example of Truman some sixty years before by framing openly gay and lesbian service as a civil rights issue.

The Center for American Progress, a left-leaning, independent, non-partisan policy institute released a report in March 2010, which stated that a smooth transition to homosexuals serving openly in the military could be achieved if eight specific changes to internal military regulations were implemented.[55] On March 25, 2010, Defense Secretary Gates tightened rules around DADT, limiting the authority to discharge military personnel from service on the grounds of DADT to flag officers, and increasing the burden of proof. Gates then directed a study on the impact of repealing DADT, which was conducted by the DoD's Comprehensive Review Working Group (CRWG) and released on November 11, 2010.

The CRWG's study considered the impact that lifting the ban would have on unit cohesion, effectiveness, good order and discipline, and military morale. A survey in the study revealed significant differences between service members who believed they had served with homosexual troops and those who believed they had not. Those who believed they had thought the impact of lifting the ban would be negligible, those who perceived they had not served with homosexuals believed repealing DADT would pose a significant disruption to unit cohesion and morale. The committee inferred that stereotypes about homosexual troops, rather than empirical evidence, led to the perceived unrest associated with repealing DADT.

The study also cited how other countries transitioned to open service, the US military's adjustment to ending racial segregation in 1948, and its inclusion of women in 1978 as evidence that the overall risk to military effectiveness would be low if the US repealed DADT.[56] The Obama Administration urged Congress to repeal DADT with the ardent support of Gates and Chairman of the Joint Chiefs Michael Mullen. The Senate conducted two days of hearings to review the CRWG Study.

Despite the sway of popular opinion, there were still opponents to repealing DADT. The Center for Military Readiness, a right-leaning, independent, nonpartisan policy institute gathered over a thousand signatures from retired flag officers. Senator John McCain read from the letter during a February 2, 2010 congressional hearing, "we firmly believe that this law[DADT], which Congress passed to protect good order, discipline and morale in the unique environment of the armed forces, deserves continued support."[57] Such a statement from the old-guard of conservative supporters illustrates the notion that the change itself was more objectionable than the reasons cited for opposition to gays and lesbians serving in the military.

As members of both houses debated the validity of DADT, the Log Cabin Republicans—a group of gay, lesbian, bisexual, and transgender republicans—brought forth a lawsuit against the United States, asserting that DADT violated constitutional guarantees of due process and free speech for gay and lesbian service members. Judge Virginia A. Phillips ruled on September 9, 2010, that DADT was an unconstitutional violation of the First and Fifth Amendments.[58] Judge Philips granted an immediate world-wide injunction, prohibiting the Department of Defense from enforcing DADT policy, and ordering the military to suspend and discontinue any investigation or discharge proceedings based on DADT. The DOJ requested a stay of the injunction, which was eventually granted on October 20, 2010. The Log Cabin Republicans appealed to the US Supreme Court who refused to hear the case or lift the stay, and sent the case back to the district court for Judge Phillips to rehear. They instructed Phillips to apply the legal rules of intermediate scrutiny to ensure DADT must significantly further an important governmental interest that can be advanced in no other way.[59] The district court vacated the stay on July 6, 2011, ruling that DADT was unconstitutional and ordered an end to the enforcement of DADT.

Meanwhile in Congress, the debate on repealing DADT continued simultaneous to the court proceeding. Democrats in both houses of Congress first attempted to end DADT by amending the National Defense Authorization Act (NDAA) for Fiscal Year (FY) 2011. Their amendment, which cited the DoD CRWG 2010 study, passed in the House, providing a process for repealing DADT policies. The amendment also included a process through which each of the services would have to certify that the new policy had no detrimental effect to military readiness. At that point, the law would be officially repealed sixty days post-certification. But the day after the House bill passed, John McCain led a successful filibuster in the Senate. DADT was not taken up for debate again until the Senate met after the 2010 summer recess. Again, the Republican Party filibustered the bill.

Senators Joe Lieberman and Susan Collins then introduced a standalone bill that passed in December 2010.[60] President Obama signed the repeal law on December 22, 2010. Along with Obama, Secretary of Defense Leon Panetta, and Admiral Mike Mullen, CJCS sent their certification, as required by the DADT repeal law, on July 22, 2011, setting the official repeal for DADT for September 20, 2011. A Pentagon spokesperson announced that service members discharged under DADT would be able to re-apply to rejoin the military.[61]

Many gay and lesbian service members came out all over the world, including Navy Lieutenant Josh Seefried, one of the founders of OutServe, a leading LGBTQ+ rights advocacy group. Seefried had been concealing his identity for over two years under a pseudonym. Senior Airman Randy Philips conducted a social media campaign seeking support for homosexual service members to come out. A video of Philips coming out to his parents on September 19, 2010 went viral; the Huffington Post proclaimed Philips the "poster boy for the DADT repeal."[62] Retired Rear Admiral Alan Steinman became the highest-ranking service member to come out immediately following the repeal of DADT.[63] On September 19, 2011, US Navy Lieutenant Gary C. Ross married his same-sex partner of eleven and a half years, making them the first same-sex military couple to be legally married in the United States. Petty Officer 2nd Class Marissa Gaeta of the USS Oak Hill won the right to the traditional "first kiss" upon returning from eighty days at sea, and shared it with her partner Petty Officer 3rd Class Citlalic Snell on December 23, 2011. Her ship's commanding officer stated that the crew's reaction upon learning who was selected to have the first kiss following the raffle was positive.[64]

In addition to many service members coming out, several other positive developments played out. HBO produced World of Wonder: The Strange History of Don't Ask, Don't Tell, which Variety hailed as an "unapologetic piece of liberal advocacy, and a testament to what formidable opponents ignorance and prejudice can be."[65] On September 30, 2011, Under Secretary of Defense for Personnel and Readiness, Clifford Stanley announced that the DoD would allow chaplains to perform same-sex marriages "on or off a military installation," where local law permits, and when chaplains willingly volunteer. Air Force Colonel Gary Packard, leader of the team who drafted the DoD's repeal implementation plan, stated in an address to cadets at the Air Force Academy, "The best quote I've heard so far is, 'Well some people's Facebook status changed,' but that was about it."[66] Even the Marine Corps, the service that opposed the repeal the most, reported that repealing DADT had been uneventful.

These events did not bode well with the conservative base that opposed the repeal. A service member was openly booed at a 2012 GOP presidential candidates' debate when he asked the candidates about their positions on the repeal of DADT; none of the candidates acknowledged or responded to the boos from the audience.[67] Candidates Michele Bachmann, Rick Perry, and Rick Santorum all called for the restoration of DADT. Ron Paul, who voted for the repeal as a sitting congressman, did not, nor did Herman Cain, who called the issue a "distraction." Mitt Romney, the eventual GOP presidential nominee, side-stepped the issue by suggesting that reinstating DADT might interfere with draw-down operations in Iraq and Afghanistan. In the midst of these conservative reactions, President Obama commented at a dinner hosted by the Human Rights Campaign: "You want to be Commander in Chief? You can start by standing up for the men and women who wear the uniform of the United States, even when its's not politically convenient."[68] Obama's sentiment reflected mainstream American views on the subject. By the end of 2010, a host of polls revealed that the vast majority of Americans were in favor of gays and lesbians serving openly in the military, including every ideological group from liberals to white evangelicals. Four key polls placed the number in opposition to homosexuals serving openly in the military between twenty-three and forty percent—a definite minority.

THE TRANSGENDER STRUGGLE

Transgender individuals remained the only group of citizens banned from uniformed service following the repeal of DADT. That ended on June 30, 2016 when Secretary of Defense Ashton Carter changed the DoD policy: "Effective immediately, transgender Americans may serve openly, and they can no longer be discharged or otherwise separated from the military just for being transgender."[69] The decision came following a year-long study ordered by Carter. The study considered eighteen foreign, allied militaries that had already lifted bans on transgender members. Based on the analysis of foreign militaries, the RAND Corporation (who conducted the study) determined that the rate at which transgender members would require medical treatment that could affect their fitness for duty and deployability would be negligible.[70]

Secretary Carter and other senior DoD leaders met with commanders, and some of the estimated 7,000 transgender service members who served in all armed services, aboard ships, submarines, aircraft, and forward operating bases worldwide. The study considered medical and legal implications before the DoD announced its phased approach to fully implementing the policy. Secretary Carter stated that—after discussing the prevalence of transgender personnel in the workforce with civilian employers, insurers, and doctors—it was obvious that views of transgender people are becoming common and normalized in public and private sectors of American society.[71]

Carter stated that ultimately the decision revolved around three things: the force of the future, the existing force, and matters of principle. During the press conference following the announcement of the decision, Carter noted:

> [We in] the Defense Department and the military need to avail ourselves of all talent possible ... to remain what we are now—the finest fighting force the world has ever known, ... Our mission is to defend this country ... we don't want barriers unrelated to a person's qualifications to serve preventing us from recruiting or retaining the soldier, sailor, airman, or Marine who can best accomplish the mission ... The Defense Department must have access to 100 percent of America's population for its all-volunteer force to be able to recruit from among the most highly qualified, and to retain them.[72]

The policy was to be implemented over twelve months in three phases: 1) an immediate end to separating transgender uniformed service members solely on the basis of their gender status; 2) publication of a commander's guide within the first ninety days following the announcement, and training of the entire force on transgender member inclusion; and 3) the armed services and military academies would begin accepting transgender members into the armed services. Secretary of Defense Jim Mattis issued a memo on July 1, 2017, to delay accessions of openly transgender citizens by six months to "evaluate more carefully the impact of such accessions on readiness and lethality."[73] Military leaders had asked for a delay on the start of accessions, ranging from one to two years.[74]

On July 26, 2017, President Trump tweeted, "After consultation with my Generals and military experts, please be advised that the United States Government will not accept or allow Transgender individuals to serve in any capacity in the U.S. military."[75] President Trump's tweet was a premature tipping of his intent to repeal the ban irrespective of any analysis. In fact, the tweet caught Pentagon officials by surprise who had to issue interim guidance to clarify the legal position of the DoD regarding transgender members.[76] The tweet was followed by a memo to the Secretaries of Defense and Homeland Security informing them that the Armed Services and Homeland Security would return to the policy that banned transgender members from serving openly, and end the plan to begin accepting transgender citizens for military service, including Coast Guard service. A return to pre-2016 policy meant that these agencies could no longer pay for reassignment surgeries for transgender members who had been diagnosed by a physician as having a medical need for the surgeries. The rationale Trump provided was, "In my judgement the previous Administration failed to identify a sufficient basis to conclude that terminating the Departments' longstanding policy and practice would not hinder military effectiveness and lethality, disrupt unit cohesion, or tax military resources, and there remain meaningful concerns that further study is needed to ensure that continued implementation of last year's policy change would not have those negative effects."[77]

Because the DoD had no warning before Trump's Twitter announcement, military officials scrambled to issue guidance to guarantee transgender troops would not be eliminated from the service, and that all medical care (including reassignment surgeries) would continue. Marine Gen. Joseph Dunford, Chairman of the Joint Chiefs of Staff, issued a statement that the Pentagon would not change its policy until officially notified by the White House. That notification came in the form of Trump's August 2017 memorandum.[78]

On October 30, 2017, Judge Colleen Kollar-Kotelly, presiding over the case of *Jane Doe v. Trump et al.*, granted a preliminary injunction in favor of the plaintiffs, which restored the policy on transgender service members back to the one established by the Obama Administration in June 2016, except for the provision to pay for ongoing medical care. Judge Colleen Kolar-Kotelly refused to reverse that portion of the Trump memo because none of the plaintiffs were affected by that provision. Judge Marvin K. Garbis reinstated the entire Obama Administration policy on November 21, 2017 in the Maryland District Court. Garbis ruled that Trump's memorandum violated First and Fifth Amendment rights of transgender service members, and issued a preliminary injunction on the entire Trump directive, including the prohibition to pay for transgender related medical treatment. He explained, "President Trump's tweets did not emerge from a policy review, nor did the Presidential Memorandum identify any policymaking process or evidence demonstrating that the revocation of transgender rights was necessary for any legitimate national interest . . . "[79] The armed services began accepting applications from openly transgender citizens on January 1, 2018.

On February 24, 2018, Mattis recommended to President Trump that the DoD disqualify transgender persons from service who had a history or diagnosis of gender dysphoria except under three conditions: 1) they have been stable for thirty-six consecutive months in their biological sex prior to accession; 2) they were diagnosed with gender dysphoria after entering the service, provided they do not require a change of gender and remain deployable within applicable retention standards; or 3) they are current service members who have been diagnosed with gender dysphoria since the previous administration's policy took effect and prior to the effective date of this new policy.[80] The Trump Administration adopted Mattis's policy on March 23, 2018, reminding us that elections have consequences.[81]

The transgender policy that Secretary Carter developed under the Obama Administration stated two things: there should be no barriers unrelated to a person's qualifications that prevent any soldier, sailor, airman, or Marine who can best accomplish the mission from doing so; and that this fundamental principal speaks to one hundred percent of America's pool of all-volunteer service members. The fact that President Trump tweeted his intent to reverse the Obama Administration policy was more than foreshadowing; it was a fait accompli. Secretary Mattis was placed in the difficult position of justifying a pre-ordained outcome. It is difficult to conceive of any significant risk that 7,000 personnel could create in a cast of 1.3 million. I would submit that a half percent of the total force would be hard pressed to pose a significant risk to the DoD even if they worked for the enemy and were hand-placed into the ranks. Trump was pandering to his base rather than leading them. The irony of a commander in chief who obtained five draft deferments setting policy on who can serve in an all-volunteer force is rich.

NOTES

1. Randy Shilts, *Conduct Unbecoming: Lesbians and Gays in the Military* (New York: St. Martin's Press, 1993), 17.
2. Ibid, 23.
3. Johnathan Katz, "Alexander Hamilton and John Laurens: 1777–1783," *Out History*, http://outhistory.org/exhibits/show/hamilton-laurens/hamilton-laurens-letters (accessed January 29, 2018).
4. G. Dean Sinclair, "Homosexuality and the Military: A Review of the Literature," *Journal of Homosexuality* 56, no. 6 (2009): 701–718, https://www.tandfonline.com/doi/full/10.1080/00918360903054137, 703.
5. Shilts, *Conduct Unbecoming: Lesbians and Gays in the Military*, 32–41.
6. Allan Berube, *Coming Out Under Fire: The History of Gay Men and Women in World War Two* (New York: The Free Press, 1990), 149–153.
7. Leisa D. Meyer, *Creating G.I. Jane: Sexuality and Power in the Women's Army Corps During World War II* (New York: Columbia University Press, 1998), 33–51.
8. Berube, *Coming Out Under Fire: The History of Gay Men and Women in World War Two*, 67–74.
9. Margaret Cruikshank, "Gay and Lesbian Liberation: An Overview," in *Gays and Lesbians in the Military: Issues, Concerns, and Contrasts*, ed. Wilbur Scott and Sandra Carson Stanley (New York: Aldine De Gruyter, 1994), 3–16.
10. Barry D. Adam, "Anatomy of a Panic: State Voyeurism, Gender, Politics, and the Cult of Americanism," in *Gays and Lesbians in the Military: Issues, Concerns, and Contrasts*, ed. Wilbur Scott and Sandra Carson Stanley (New York: Aldine De Gruyter, 1994), 103–118.
11. Andrew Gumbel, "The Great Undoing?" *The Advocate*, Pride Publishing, June 20, 2009, https://www.advocate.com/news/2009/06/20/great-undoing (accessed July 9, 2012).
12. US Department of Defense, *Department of Defense Instruction 1332.14: Enlisted Administrative Separations* (Washington, DC: DoD, 1993), Pdf, https://archive.defense.gov/news/DoDI%201332%2014%20-%20REVISIONS%20032510.pdf.
13. Sinclair, "Homosexuality and the Military: A Review of the Literature," 705.
14. US General Accounting Office, *Homosexuality in the Military: Policies and Practices of Foreign Countries* (Washington, DC: GAO, June 1993), Pdf, http://archive.gao.gov/t2pbat5/149440.pdf.
15. Janet E. Halley, *Don't: A Reader's Guide to the Military's Anti-gay Policy* (London: Duke University Press, 1999), 68–70.
16. Jack Drescher, "Out of DSM: Depathologizing Homosexuality," *Behavioral Sciences* 5, no. 4 (December 2005): 565–75, https://www.ncbi.nlm.nih.gov/pmc/articles/PMC4695779/.

17. Gregory M. Herek, "Oral Statement to the House Armed Services Committee," Washington, DC, May 5, 1993, *Sexual Orientation: Science, Education, and Policy*, http://www.lgbpsychology.org/html/miltest2.html (accessed November 11, 2017).

18. Gregory M. Herek and Aaron Belkin, "Sexual Orientation and Military Service: Prospects for Organizational and Individual Change in the United States," *Palm Center: Blueprints for Sound Public Policy*, December 1, 2005, https://www.palmcenter.org/publication/sexual-orientation-military-service-prospects-organizational-individual-change-united-states/ (accessed May 11, 2007).

19. Bernard D. Rostker, Scott A. Harris, James P. Kahan, Erik J. Frinking, C. Neil Fulcher, Lawrence M. Hanser, Paul Koegel, et al., *Sexual Orientation and U.S. Military Personnel Policy: Options and Assessment* (Santa Monica, CA: RAND Corporation, 1993) https://www.rand.org/pubs/monograph_reports/MR323.html, 406.

20. "Timeline: A history of don't ask, don't tell," *Washington Post*, November 30, 2010, https://www.washingtonpost.com/wp-srv/special/politics/dont-ask-dont-tell-timeline/ (accessed Jan 26, 2018).

21. Associated Press, "Goldwater Backs Gay Troops," *New York Times*, June 11, 1993, https://www.nytimes.com/1993/06/11/us/goldwater-backs-gay-troops.html (accessed October 15, 2017).

22. US Department of Defense, *Department of Defense Instruction 1332.14: Enlisted Administrative Separations*.

23. Kirby L. Bowling, Juanita M. Firestone, and Richard J. Harris, "Analyzing Questions that Cannot be Asked of Respondents who Cannot Respond," *Armed Forces & Society* 31, no. 3 (April 2005): 411–37, https://journals.sagepub.com/doi/10.1177/0095327X0503100305.

24. Policy Concerning Homosexuality in the Armed Forces, 10 U.S.C. § 654 (2011), https://www.govinfo.gov/app/details/USCODE-2010-title10/USCODE-2010-title10-subtitleA-partII-chap37-sec654/summary.

25. Frank Barrett, Coit D. Blacker, Ralph Carney, Donald Campbell, Kathleen Campbell, Mark Eitelberg, John D. Hutson, et al., "Financial analysis of Don't ask don't tell: How much does the gay ban cost?" *Palm Center: Blueprints for Sound Public Policy*, February 2006, https://www.palmcenter.org/wp-content/uploads/2018/11/Blue-Ribbon-Report.pdf (accessed March 22, 2007).

26. "Timeline: A history of don't ask, don't tell," *Washington Post*.

27. Mark H. Davis, and Stephen L. Franzoi, "Adolescent Loneliness, Self-disclosure, and Private Self-consciousness: A Longitudinal Investigation," *Journal of Personality and Social Psychology* 51, no. 3 (1986): 595–608, https://doi.org/10.1037/0022-3514.51.3.595, 51.

28. Mary Anne Fitzpatrick, "Marriage and Verbal Intimacy," in *Self-disclosure: Theory, Research, and Therapy*, edited by Valerian J. Derlega and John H. Berg (New York: Springer Science and Business Media, 1987), 131–154.

29. Sinclair, "Homosexuality and the Military: A Review of the Literature," 707.

30. Thomas Hackett, "The Execution of Private Barry Winchell: The Real Story Behind the 'Don't Ask, Don't Tell' Murder," *Rolling Stone*, March 2, 2000, http://www.davidclemens.com/gaymilitary/rolstobarry.htm (accessed February 13, 2016).

31. Jeremy Johnson, "'Don't Pursue, Don't Harass' the Other Half of 'Don't Ask, Don't Tell,'" *Palm Center: Blueprints for Sound Public Policy*, May 8, 2010, http://archive.palmcenter.org/press/dadt/in_print/dont_pursue_dont_harass_the_other_half_of_dont_ask_dont_tell (accessed March 28, 2018).

32. Ibid.

33. Sharon Terman, *The Practical and Conceptual Problems with Regulating Harassment in a Discriminatory Institution* (Santa Barbara, CA: UC Santa Barbara Center for the Study of Sexual Minorities in the Military, May 2004) https://escholarship.org/uc/item/5n9649fm#main.

34. Johnson, "'Don't Pursue, Don't Harass' the Other Half of 'Don't Ask, Don't Tell.'"

35. Stanley Sporkin, "*McVeigh v. Cohen*, 983 F. Supp. 215 (D.D.C. 1998)," Memorandum Opinion, Justia US Law, January 26, 1998, https://law.justia.com/cases/federal/district-courts/FSupp/983/215/1989052/ (accessed October 13, 2017).

36. Ibid.

37. Philip Shenon, "Sailor Victorious in Gay Case of On-Line Privacy," *New York Times*, June 12, 1998, https://www.nytimes.com/1998/06/12/us/sailor-victorious-in-gay-case-of-on-line-privacy.html (accessed October 5, 2017).

38. Paul A. Gade, "Repealing Don't Ask, Don't' Tell: A Brief History," *The Military Psychologist* 27, no. 2 (2012): 21–25, https://www.militarypsych.org/uploads/8/5/4/5/85456500/military_psychologist_27-2.pdf. 21–2.

39. Robert Bianco, "20-year flashback: Ellen DeGeneres came out, and paved the way for more gay TV roles," *USA Today*, April 26, 2017, https://www.usatoday.com/story/life/tv/2017/04/26/ellen-degeneres-gay-coming-out-tv-20-year-anniversary/100888584/.

40. Steven Lee Myers, "Officers Riled by Policy on Gays Proposed in Gore–Bradley Debate," *New York Times*, January 7, 2000, https://www.nytimes.com/2000/01/07/us/officers-riled-by-policy-on-gays-proposed-in-gore-bradley-debate.html.

41. "2000 Democratic Party Platform," The American Presidency Project, August 14, 2000, http://www. presidency.ucsb.edu/ws/index.php?pid=29612 (accessed October 9, 2017).

42. "2000 Republican Party Platform," The American Presidency Project, July 31, 2000, https://www.presidency.ucsb.edu/documents/2000-republican-party-platform (accessed October 9, 2017).

43. Gade, "Repealing Don't Ask, Don't' Tell: A Brief History," 22.

44. Ibid., 23–24.

45. Associated Press, "Don't Ask Don't Tell Costs $363M," *USA Today*, February 14, 2006, https://usatoday30.usatoday.com/news/washington/2006-02-14-dont-ask-report_x.htm (accessed July 19, 2017).

46. Ibid.

47. John Zogby, John Bruce, Rebecca Wittman, Sam Rodgers, Zogby International, "Opinions of Military Personnel on Sexual Minorities in the Military," *Palm Center: Blueprints for Sound Public Policy*, December 1, 2006, https://www.palmcenter.org/publication/opinions-military-personnel-sexual-minorities-military/.

48. John M. Shalikashvili, "Second Thoughts on Gays in the Military," *New York Times*, January 2, 2007, https://www.nytimes.com/2007/01/02/opinion/02shalikashvili.html.

49. Carla Marinucci, "Romney defends general, don't ask, don't tell policy," *SF Gate*, March 17, 2007, https://www.sfgate.com/politics/article/CAMPAIGN-TRAIL-Romney-defends-general-don-t-2569666.php.

50. Tom Shanker and Patrick Healy, "A New Push to Roll Back Don't Ask, Don't Tell." November 30, 2007, *New York Times*, https://www.nytimes.com/2007/11/30/us/30military.html.

51. Rowan Scarborough, "Obama to Delay Repeal of Don't Ask Don't Tell," *Washington Times*, November 21, 2008, https://www.washingtontimes.com/news/2008/nov/21/obama-to-delay-repeal-of-dont-ask-dont-tell/ (accessed March 28, 2017).

52. Lesley Wroughton and Sandra Maler, "Time to Review Policy on Gays in the U.S. Military: Powell," *Reuters*, July 5, 2009, https://www.reuters.com/article/us-usa-military-gays/time-to-review-policy-on-gays-in-u-s-military-powell-idUSTRE5641A920090705.

53. Barack Obama, "State of the Union Address," Speech, January 27, 2010, *New York Times*, 2010. https://www.nytimes.com/2010/01/28/us/politics/28obama.text.html (accessed March 3, 2016).

54. Ibid.

55. Lawrence J. Korb, Sean Duggan, and Laura Conley, "Implementing the Repeal of Don't Ask, Don't Tell in the U. S. Armed Forces," *Center for American Progress*, March 23, 2010, https://www.americanprogress.org/issues/security/reports/2010/03/

23/7502/implementing-the-repeal-of-dont-ask-dont-tell-in-the-u-s-armed-forces/ (accessed March 23, 2018).

56. Carla Crandell, "The Effects of Repealing Don't Ask, Don't Tell: Is the Combat Exclusion the Next Casualty in the March Toward Integration?" *Georgetown Journal of Law and Public Policy* 10, no. 1 (2012) http://www.law.georgetown.edu/academics/law-journals/gjlpp/upload/zs800112000015.pdf (accessed March 23, 2018).

57. Chris Johnson, "New Report Undermines Officers' Letter Supporting Don't Ask," *Washington Blade*, March 3 2010, https://www.washingtonblade.com/2010/03/03/new-report-undermines-officers%E2%80%99-letter-supporting-%E2%80%98don%E2%80%99t-ask%E2%80%99/ (accessed March 23, 2018).

58. Phil Willon, "Judge Declares U.S. Military's Don't Ask, Don't Tell Police Openly Banning Gay Service Members Unconstitutional," *LA Times*, September 10, 2010, https://latimesblogs.latimes.com/lanow/2010/09/federal-judge-declares-us-military-ban-on-openly-gay-service-members-unconstitutional-.html (accessed March 3, 2018).

59. Ibid.

60. Carl Hulse, "Senate Repeals Ban Against Openly Gay Military Personnel," *New York Times*, December 18, 2010, https://www.nytimes.com/2010/12/19/us/politics/19cong.html (accessed January 11, 2018).

61. Clifford Stanley, "Repeal of Don't Ask Don't Tell and Future Impact on Policy," Memorandum for Secretaries of the Military Departments (Washington, DC: DoD, January 28, 2011) https://archive.defense.gov/home/features/2010/0610_dadt/USD-PR-DADT_28Jan11.pdf.

62. "Randy Philips, Gay Airman, Comes Out to Mom on YouTube," *Huffington Post*, September 29, 2011, https://www.huffpost.com/entry/airman-comes-out-to-mother_n_988047 (accessed February 7, 2017).

63. Thomas Francis, "On Base, Don't Ask, Don't Tell' Demise is Cause for Celebration," *NBC News*, September 21, 2011, http://www.nbcnews.com/id/44607673/ns/us_news-life/t/base-dont-ask-dont-tell-demise-cause-celebration/#.Xry6MBNKjOQ (accessed October 9, 2016).

64. Tim Dickinson, "It Got Better: Lesbian Couple Share Navy's 'First Kiss,'" *Rolling Stone*, December 22, 2011, https://www.rollingstone.com/politics/politics-news/it-got-better-lesbian-couple-share-navys-first-kiss-244688/ (accessed January 2, 2018).

65. Brian Lowry, "The Strange History of Don't Ask, Don't Tell," *Variety*, September 18, 2011, http://www.variety.com/review/VE1117946143 (accessed January 3, 2016).

66. Don Branum, "Academy Experts Discuss Effects of DADT Repeal," US Air Force Academy, October 28, 2011, https://www.usafa.af.mil/News/News-Display/Article/428632/academy-experts-discuss-effects-of-dadt-repeal/ (accessed November 9, 2015).

67. Mark Memmott, "Boos Heard at GOP Debate After Gay Soldier Asks about 'Don't Ask,'" *NPR*, September 23, 2011, https://www.npr.org/sections/thetwo-way/2011/09/23/140732553/boos-heard-at-gop-debate-after-gay-soldier-asks-about-dont-ask.

68. An ABC-Washington Post poll showed that in December of 2010, 77 percent of Americans felt gays and lesbians who publicly disclose their sexual orientation should be allowed to serve in the military. The numbers cut across partisan ideological lines, including the majority of: Democrats (86 percent), Republicans (74 percent), independents (74 percent), liberals (92 percent), conservatives (67 percent), and white evangelicals (70 percent). People claiming no religious affiliation were 84 percent in favor of homosexuals serving openly. A November 2010 poll conducted by the Pew Research Center found that 58 percent of Americans favored gays and lesbians serving openly while only 27 percent were opposed. A CNN poll conducted in November reported that 72 percent of adult Americans were in favor of homosexuals serving openly while 23 percent opposed it. A February 2010 Quinnipiac University Polling Institute's national poll put the numbers at 57 percent in favor of un-closeted service members and 36 percent opposed. "Don't Stand Silent When Soldier is Booed," October 1, 2011,

MSNBC, http://www.msnbc.msn.com/id/4474458/ns/politics-white_house/t/obama-dont-stand-silent-when-soldier-booed/.

69. Terry Cronk, "Transgender Service Members Can Now Serve Openly, Carter Announces," *U.S. DoD News*, June 30, 2016, https://www.defense.gov/Explore/News/Article/Article/822235/transgender-service-members-can-now-serve-openly-carter-announces/ (accessed February 1, 2016).

70. Agnes Gereben Shaefer, Radha Iyengar Plumb, Srikanth Kadiyala, Jennifer Kavanagh, Charles C. Engel, Kayla M. Williams, and Amii M. Kress, *Assessing the Implications of Allowing Transgender Personnel to Serve Openly* (Santa Monica, CA: RAND Corporation, 2016) https://www.rand.org/pubs/research_reports/RR1530.html.

71. Cronk, "Transgender Service Members Can Now Serve Openly, Carter Announces."

72. Ibid.

73. Jim Mattis, "Accession of Transgender Individuals into the Military Services," Memorandum for Secretaries of the Military Departments Chairman of the Joint Chiefs of Staff (Washington, DC: DoD, June 30, 2017) http://lc.org/070517TGDODmemo30JUNE2017.pdf, (accessed Jun 19, 2016).

74. Associated Press, "Pentagon Delays Decision on Transgender Enlistments by 6 Months," *Los Angeles Times*, June 30, 2017, https://www.latimes.com/nation/la-na-transgender-enlistment-delay-20170630-story.html.

75. Zeke J. Miller, "President Trump has Taken a Key Step to Implement his Transgender Military Ban," *Time*, August 25, 2017, https://time.com/4916871/donald-trump-transgender-military-ban/ (accessed May 2, 2018).

76. "Tweets on Transgender Military Servicemembers," *Harvard Law Review* 131, no. 3 (2018): 934–943, https://harvardlawreview.org/2018/01/tweets-on-transgender-military-servicemembers/.

77. Donald Trump, "Military Service by Transgender Individuals," Memorandum for the Secretary of Defense and the Secretary of Homeland Defense (Washington, DC: White House, August 25, 2017) https://www.whitehouse.gov/presidential-actions/presidential-memorandum-secretary-defense-secretary-homeland-security/ (accessed May 23, 2017).

78. Tom V. Brook, "Defense Secretary Jim Mattis' New Policy on Transgender Troops Expected by Wednesday," *USA Today*, February 19, 2018, https://www.usatoday.com/story/news/politics/2018/02/19/defense-secretary-jim-mattis-new-policy-transgender-troops-expected-wednesday/352918002/ (accessed November 5, 2016).

79. Andrea Noble, "Federal Judge Defies Trump Admin, Removes Pentagon Block on Funds for Gender Reassignment," *Washington Times*, November 21, 2017, https://www.washingtontimes.com/news/2017/nov/21/judge-removes-block-funds-gender-reassignment/ (accessed December 1, 2017).

80. Jim Mattis, "Military Service by Transgender Individuals," Memorandum for the President (Washington, DC: DoD, February 22, 2018) https://media.defense.gov/2018/Mar/23/2001894037/-1/-1/0/MILITARY-SERVICE-BY-TRANSGENDER-INDIVIDUALS.PDF.

81. Donald Trump, "Military Service by Transgender Individuals," Memorandum for the Secretary of Defense and the Secretary of Homeland Security (Washington, DC: White House, March 23, 2018) https://www.whitehouse.gov/presidential-actions/presidential-memorandum-secretary-defense-secretary-homeland-security-regarding-military-service-transgender-individuals/.

SEVEN
Remaining Challenges and Implications for the US and the Armed Forces

THE MILITARY'S PROBLEM IS AMERICA'S PROBLEM

The events of Charlottesville, Virginia, in August 2017 reminded the nation of the deep-seated hatred that still exists toward minorities and women. The tide of this culture war has ebbed and flowed over time and is now pushing those who advocate for inclusion further up the moral high ground. The Trump administration struggled to unequivocally and vociferously denounce the racist ideology displayed by white supremacists during the Charlottesville march, and fringe white supremacist groups appear to be emboldened by the administration's tepid rebukes. Two months later, Second Lieutenant Richard W. Collins III was brutally stabbed to death by a University of Maryland student who was linked to a white supremacist group through social media. Collins was a 23-year-old black man, a newly commissioned Second Lieutenant in the Army, who was set to graduate from Bowie State University the following week. His murderer, Sean Urbanski, stabbed Collins for refusing to vacate the sidewalk as Urbanski approached him shouting, "Step left, step left if you know what's best for you." These incidents are not mere coincidence. The Southern Poverty Law Center reported that the number of hate groups espousing racial animus in the US has increased by 20 percent during Trump's first year in office.[1]

Nonetheless, the US armed forces have come a long way from segregation as bedrock policy to recognizing diversity as a strategic imperative. The DoD's progress is evident in the numerous, transformative figures produced from its ranks, such as Colin Powell, Chappie James, Ann

Dunwoody, Eric Shinseki, John Shalilkashvilli, Ricardo Sanchez, and Nadia West. Most recently, General Charles Q. Brown Jr., commander of Pacific Air Forces, was nominated to be the 22nd Chief of Staff of the Air Force in March 2020.

The amicus curiae briefing filed on behalf of the University of Michigan in the university's bid to continue using race as a criterion in college admissions also suggests progress. Several retired generals, including Norman Swarzkopf Jr., Commanding General of America's 1991 Gulf War Campaign, filed the brief before the Supreme Court. Their brief detailed how diversity has served a greater public interest, how the armed services have benefited from inclusion, and that the military needs continued diversity and inclusion from ROTC programs.

But the progress left to be made in America and the DoD is also evident in data. Ethnic minority officers make up about 8 percent of all general officers, the highest military rank, despite making up 27 percent of the military population and 18 percent of all DoD officers. Black officers make up only 9 percent of the DoD officer corps despite comprising roughly 17 percent of the total armed forces population. Women account for 5 percent of general officers compared to 14 percent of all service members, 17 percent of the officer corps, and 51 percent of the general population. That is not to say these percentages should be exactly proportional, but the differences in the percentages have remained more or less consistent over time—an indication that some form of systemic bias is at play. The 2008 National Defense Authorization Act mandated a top-down review of diversity in the armed forces to improve these indices of diversity for women and ethnic minorities. The Military Leadership Diversity Commission (MLDC) developed 20 recommendations over 16 topic areas it was asked to review. Their recommendations addressed recruiting, retention, assignment, as well as promotion opportunities and disparities. These recommendations were intended to inform policy development that sets the conditions for a diverse armed forces that is representative of the public it serves. Such conditions then create fertile ground for policy that allows the services to establish a broader approach to cultivating diversity and enhancing military performance.[2]

A LOOK AT THE NUMBERS

The US armed services promotion systems are very structured, which allows for detailed comparisons. Military personnel are organized into more or less two main categories: enlisted service (that which begins with basic training upon entry into the armed services), or commissioned service (after completion of a four-year degree at one of the service academies, the completion of an ROTC program with a four year degree, or Officer Candidate School. The enlisted ranks range from E-1 to E-9, and it takes about 25 years or more to make it to the rank of E-9. Officer ranks range from O-1 to O-10 (four star general). The DoD has career progression models for officers and enlisted that show how long each service member should spend in each rank before being considered for promotion. Manuals and other regulations outline what types of professional schools and civilian education must be completed prior to promotion to the next grade, and what types of assignments each service member should obtain to be competitive for promotion. The DoD even sets target percentage rates for promotions to each rank/pay grade.

In 2001, the RAND Corporation conducted a study entitled Minority and Gender Differences in Officer Career Progression. The study examined promotion rates of officers from 1967 to 1991 using regression analysis. The surveyors compared the promotion rates of minority officers and women with those of white males, and found that all ethnic minority officers were promoted to the grades of O-4 (civilian equivalent of Director level), O-5 (civilian equivalent of Junior VP level), and O-6 (civilian equivalent of Sr. VP level) at lower rates than those of white males. White females were promoted to O-4 four percentage points higher than white males.[3] As a group, black males and white females had a higher promotion rate to O-6 than white males, though these findings were not statistically significant due to the small numbers selected to promotion to O-6. In my opinion the higher promotion rates of black males and white females to O-6 (again, very small numbers and statistically insignificant) is an indication that only the most outstanding black males and white females made the selection to O-5, and were therefore highly competitive for promotion to the next rank. The authors of the study did not offer an explanation for the statistically significant higher promotion rates of white females to O-4. I believe these higher promotion rates are a result of gender biases that happen to work in the favor of white females in certain contexts. I believe disproportionate access to high-profile assignments for white women at junior officer ranks has manifested itself in part as higher promotion rates.

In the armed services, general officers are kingmakers. Good evaluations from general officers get people promoted, and exceptional ones get people promoted early. Typically, an officer will not be evaluated by a general until he or she reaches the rank of O-5 (roughly 15 or more years of service), unless he or she serves as a military aide or executive assistant to a general. For the most part, generals personally select their aides and executive assistants, usually relying on the HR system to produce a list of candidates based on criteria the generals provide. Other times, these junior officers are recommended by other senior officers who work in support of the general. The Pentagon and other military headquarters are filled with women aides and executive assistants at the O-2, O-3, and O-4 (2–12 years of service) levels who dutifully go about their tasks of managing calendars, travel, speaking engagements, taking notes, preparing slides, generally ensuring the general's in and out boxes run efficiently, and that their principal stays on schedule. This is not to say that these young women aren't incredibly talented, eminently qualified, well-organized, multitaskers; however, it is an example of how mentorship and opportunity converge to result in professional success; talent can be found everywhere, opportunity cannot.[4]

In 2011, the MLDC conducted a similar study to the 2001 RAND study. They examined promotion rates by gender, ethnicity, and service as part of their 140-page report to Congress. The commission obtained promotion data from the services over a 4-year period, FY 2007 through FY 2010. Unlike the RAND study, the MLDC compared promotion rates of certain demographics against the average promotion rate, rather than using the promotion rate of white males as the benchmark. The MLDC findings revealed similar results to the regression analysis performed by RAND in 2001. Minority officers had promotion rates below average for promotion to O-4 through O-6 across all armed services and the Coast Guard. Black male officers in all armed services and the Coast Guard had significantly lower promotion rates than the average for O-4 through O-6.

The findings of the MLDC study validated those of the 2001 RAND study in many regards. Women's promotion rates in most instances were within a couple percentage points below or above the average promotion rate across all armed services. This maybe because all women were grouped by gender and not ethnicity, so white female promotion rates may be masking lower promotion rates of black, Hispanic, and other minority women. Future studies need to breakout female officers' promotion rates by race. Such an analysis would provide greater granularity on institutional bias that may affect promotion rates for women. The FY 2007–2010 data show the net effect of institutional and perhaps individual bias in officer promotion rates across all armed services and the Coast Guard, particularly for black officers.[5]

The promotion rates for more senior enlisted ranks reveal a picture of inclusion and equality of opportunity, except for in the Marine Corps, in which case black NCOs were promoted to the ranks of E-7 through E-9 at

Regression-Adjusted Promotion Outcomes for Officers Commissioned between 1967 and 1991

Race/Gender	Differences in Promotion Rates for Row Group vs. White Male Officers		
	O-3 to O-4	O-4 to O-5	O-5 to O-6
Black male	-4*	-6*	+5
Other minority male	-8*		
White female	+5*	0	+3
Black female	-4	-6	
Other minority female	-6	-3	

Figure 7.1. Regression Analysis of DoD Officer Promotion Rates from 1967–1991. Source: Military Leadership Diversity Commission (MLDC) Issue Paper #45

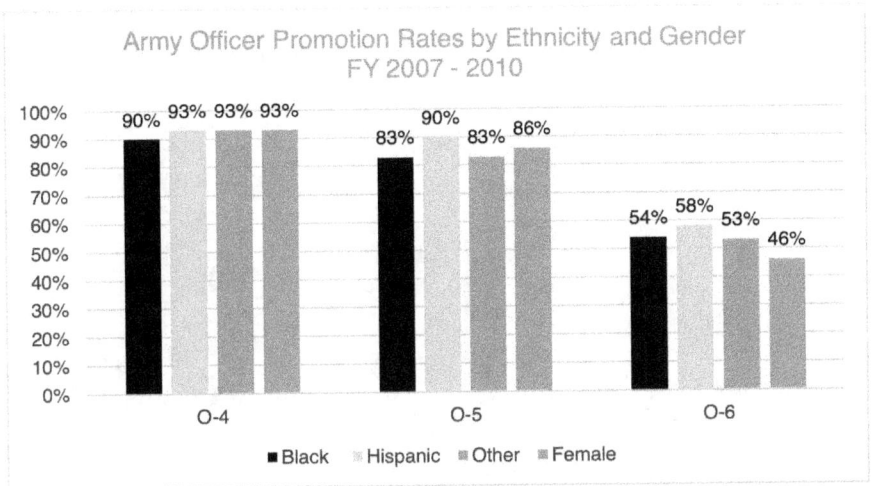

Figure 7.2. Army Officer Promotion Rates by Ethnicity and Gender 2007–2010. Military Leadership Diversity Commission Recent Officer Promotion Rates by Race, Ethnicity and Gender (Army). *Source: Military Leadership Diversity Commission (MLDC) Issue Paper #45*

significantly lower rates than the average. Women in the Marine Corps were also promoted to the rank of E-9 at significantly lower rates. These data indicate systemic bias, and implore further examination for the Marine Corps.[6]

The DoD's inability to achieve leadership that reflects the nation it serves is emblematic of America's problem within corporate industry. While both organizations are far from their respective goals, the DoD's floor is much higher. Once again, the DoD's problem is America's problem. In 2019, corporate America had three black CEOs of Fortune 500 companies, following Kenneth Chenault's departure from American Express. Chenault's retirement after 16 years as CEO is part of a downward trend of black CEOs who hit a high-water mark at seven in 2007, still representing only 2 percent.[7] For the entire existence of the Fortune 500, there have only been a total of 15 black CEOs. From 2005-2011, black CEOs weren't the only ones gaining traction to lead Fortune 500 companies; women, Latino, and American business leaders of Asian ancestry were also growing in number during this period, in which 12 Latinos and 13 people of Asian ancestry were appointed as Fortune 500 CEOs. The number of CEOs of Asian descent peaked in 2011 at 14.[8]

Unfortunately, this trend towards diversity in corporate leadership has stalled and reversed. The pace at which big businesses appointed CEOs of color has slowed dramatically. CEOs who broke racial glass ceilings have retired or were removed, and their ranks have been replen-

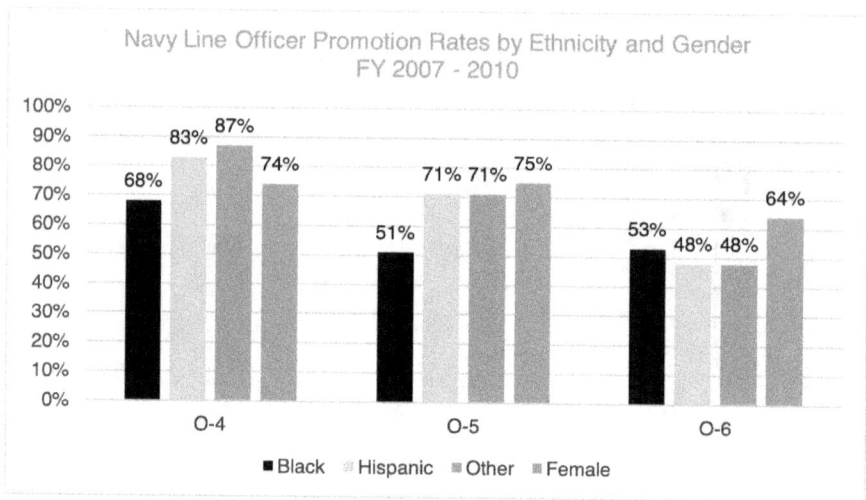

Figure 7.3. Navy Officer Promotion Rates by Ethnicity and Gender 2007–2010. Military Leadership Diversity Commission Recent Officer Promotion Rates by Race, Ethnicity and Gender (Army). *Source: Military Leadership Diversity Commission (MLDC) Issue Paper #45*

ished primarily with the former status quo: white men. Meanwhile, "women of color remain virtually nonexistent in the highest ranks of large business."[9] There is nothing wrong with white male CEOs; however, there is something wrong when all CEOs are predominately heterosexual, white males. Such homogeneity doesn't reflect the racial, gender, and ethnic diversity of the nation we live in, and our prospects of engaging global markets that are increasingly diverse are hindered when the senior management is homogeneous.

The bad news is that the outlook for increased diversity in corporate America is bleak. Renowned University of Minnesota Sociologist Ricard Zweigenhaft described the current pace of diversification in the highest ranks of corporations as "glacial" in a 2015 analysis.[10] What keeps the DoD's floor higher than corporate America's is the DoD's 70-year commitment to diversity and inclusion. For the most part, corporate America's diversity and inclusion efforts began in the 1970s, and were subject to the ebb and flow of popular opinion.

Presently, America seems to be suffering from what I call "Diversity Fatigue"—a weariness from discussions of past injustices and the subsequent guilt associated with them. One can infer from the history of social change in America and its opponents that much of Trump's "populism" has come from those who have grown weary of discussions about inclusion. He is also popular among those who outright oppose social change, but until now, have been silenced by the popular opinion that racism is

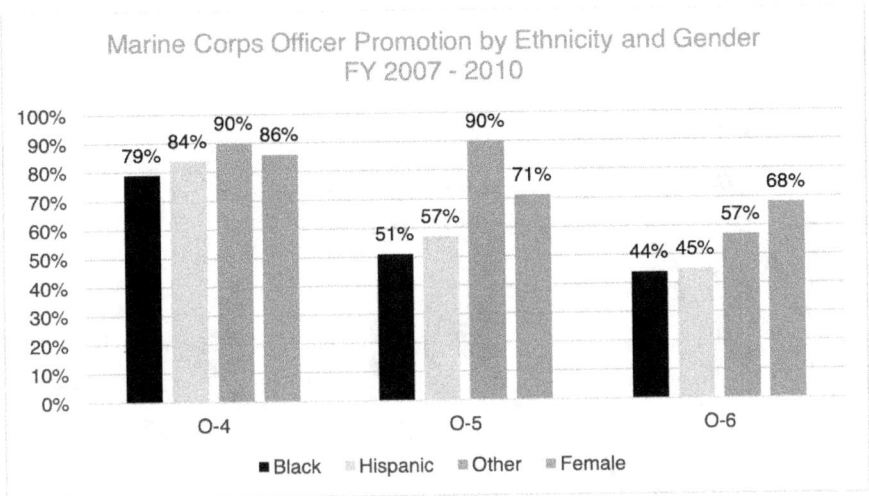

Figure 7.4. Air Force Officer Promotion Rates by Ethnicity and Gender 2007–2010. Military Leadership Diversity Commission Recent Officer Promotion Rates by Race, Ethnicity and Gender (Army). *Source: Military Leadership Diversity Commission (MLDC) Issue Paper #45*

publicly unacceptable. Trump seized upon this sentiment of diversity fatigue and appealed to both constituencies by stoking the fears of vulnerable, white, Middle Americans in the rust-belt, bible-belt, and heartland—those who are more likely to think their sensibilities and pocketbooks have been adversely affected by increased inclusivity. Wages have been flat for over a decade in these areas, and those who believe their way of life is threatened by closing factories, immigration, and shifting societal norms have become strange bed-fellows with those who are unabashed racists, bigots, sexists, and homophobes. Trump has given voice to the deepest, darkest thoughts and unfounded beliefs of frightened Americans. It is no wonder that many of his supporters espouse the same racial hatred and vitriol America waged two world wars against. It is no wonder that similar propaganda used to blindly incite the Germans in the 1930s is blindly inciting Americans in the twenty-first century, right down to the swastika.

An October 2017 study done by the Robert Wood Johnson Foundation in conjunction with the Harvard T.H. Chan School of Public Health found that most ethnic groups of Americans believe their own group faces discrimination, including 55 percent of white Americans.[11] If you grew up in an America where homosexuals were closeted, blacks lived exclusively in poor neighborhoods, and women stayed at home (e.g., instead of working, serving in the military, holding public office, or running for president, etc.), it might appear as though the rest of society is

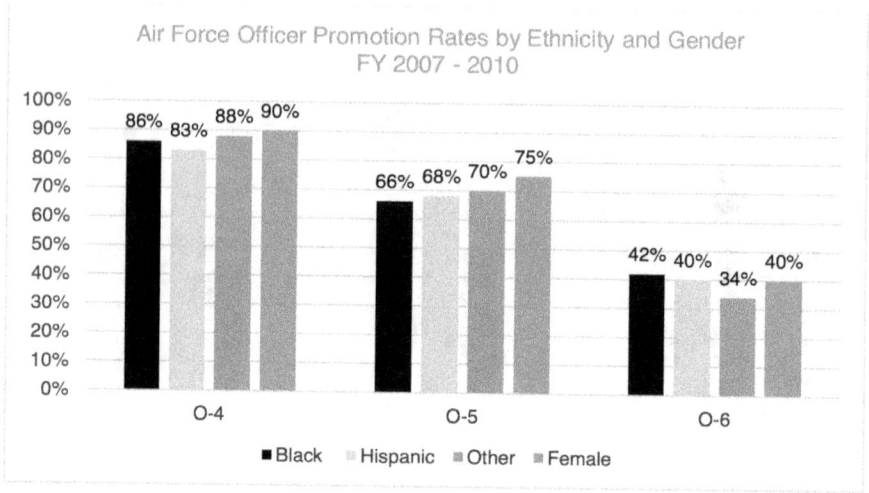

Figure 7.5. Marine Corps Officer Promotion Rates by Ethnicity and Gender 2007–2010. Military Leadership Diversity Commission Recent Officer Promotion Rates by Race, Ethnicity and Gender (Army). *Source: Military Leadership Diversity Commission (MLDC) Issue Paper #45*

now bypassing whites, especially white males. And that reveals the fundamental problem with discrimination: it directly victimizes those discriminated against, while affording privilege to those not discriminated against. The victims are prohibited from self-determination, and those not discriminated against never really understand how much of their self-determination was due to self. In the end, both groups are harmed. Rather than deal with this formidable truth, Trump stoked the fears of those who felt aggrieved, and exploited their vulnerability for personal and political gain. These aggrieved groups are desperate for a champion who will speak their truth and defend their worldview.

As the civil rights struggle reached its zenith in the 1960s, many Americans were forced to choose sides. Idling on the sidelines was no longer an option once Walter Cronkite reported on peaceful protestors being set upon with attack dogs and firehoses, and these images were piped into the living rooms of virtually every American household. The majority of Americans did not want to align themselves with those who would demean, debase, kill, and blow up churches to preserve segregation. Such sentinel events in American history were the beginning of racism becoming socially unacceptable. Those who were not in favor of integration were forced to choose between being aligned with hateful, maniacal racists, or becoming silent non-consenters, using passive aggressive measures to resist integration, while clinging to the notion that they were rational, non-racist beings.

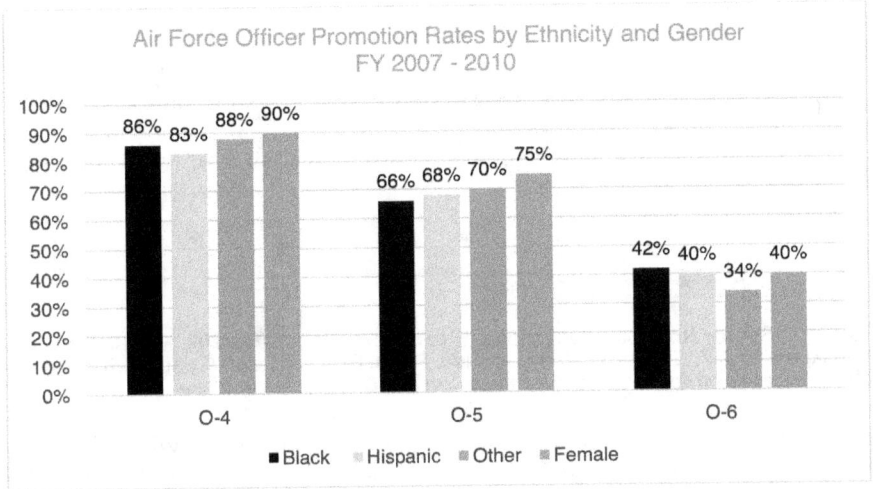

Figure 7.6. Coast Guard Officer Promotion Rates by Ethnicity and Gender 2007–2010. Military Leadership Diversity Commission Recent Officer Promotion Rates by Race, Ethnicity and Gender (Army). *Source: Military Leadership Diversity Commission (MLDC) Issue Paper #45*

As civil rights legislation opened America's promise to blacks, Jews, women, and other minorities, America's economy began shifting from a manufacturing one to an electronic and service-based economy (from blue collar to white collar). American manufacturers enjoyed huge profits during the '50s and '60s because the rest of the world's manufacturing infrastructure had been destroyed during WWII. This American manufacturing boom was doomed to come to an end once Japan, Germany, Great Britain, and China redeveloped their capabilities and began producing cheaper goods. At the same time, around the 1970s, women and minorities were freed from the legal discrimination they endured for centuries. These near simultaneous events made it seem as though women and minorities were succeeding at the expense of others. It was then that the seeds for today's white-victimization narrative were fertilized.

In the '40s, '50s, and '60s, white males enjoyed almost exclusive access to high paying jobs that required little formal education and provided on-site training. Women and minorities entered the workforce in larger numbers in the early 1970s. Armed with college degrees due to civil rights legislation passed in the 1960s, they provided additional competition for what had been an almost exclusively white male world. For many white men without college degrees, this social change seemed to victimize them, though they remained largely silent. That is, until right-of-center talk radio and, later, right wing television seized upon the growing frustration of this privileged group—a group that felt growing

Pay Grade	Navy		Air Force		Army		Marine Corps	
	Black	Overall	Black	Overall	Black	Overall	Black	Overall
E-7	21	21	23	23	26	28	26*	35
E-8	10	11	10~	9	18~	14	42*	48
E-9	11	11	17	19	19	22	38*	43
	Hispanic	Overall	Hispanic	Overall	Hispanic	Overall	Hispanic	Overall
E-7	21	21	22	23	32~	28	33	35
E-8	12~	11	11~	9	16~	14	44	48
E-9	13~	11	17	19	21	22	45~	43
	Other	Overall	Other	Overall	Other	Overall	Other	Overall
E-7	21~	21	24~	23	31~	28	31	35
E-8	8	11	8	9	17~	14	49~	48
E-9	10	11	11*	19	21	22	40	43
	Female	Overall	Female	Overall	Female	Overall	Female	Overall
E-7	20	21	22	23	30~	28	41~	35
E-8	11	11	11~	9	11	14	45	48
E-9	11	11	19	19	18	22	31*	43

* Indicates ≥ or > 5% difference of minority group from the overall average
~ Indicates minority group with greater promotion rate than the overall average

Table 7.1 Senior Noncommissioned Officer Promotion Rates 2007–2010. Promotion Rates to E-7, E-8, and E-9 by Service, Race, Ethnicity and Gender. *Source Military Leadership Diversity Commission (MLDC) Decision Paper #4*

diversity in America was threatening or denying them what they believed to be an unspoken birth right. These media outlets became the voice of a growing number of white Americans whose world had changed from their fathers' and grand fathers' experiences. Many of these Americans have been more or less silent since the late 1970s, afraid to speak out on what they perceived as threats for fear of being castigated. Their fear and anger have come to a head, and many of them are desperate for someone who will protect their sensibilities. Paradoxically, this segment of Americans is now aligned with a smaller segment of Americans who express outwardly racist, sexist, homophobic, and xenophobic ideologies—ideologies similar to those their great grandfathers fought against in Nazi Germany.

Equality can feel like oppression for those who have become accustomed to privilege. It is not surprising that privileged groups continue to resist equality, both in the private sector and within the military. Such resistance ranges from unconscious bias to blatant unfairness. This phenomenon is supported by America's history of gains in rights for women and minorities followed by a retraction or backlash against that progress.

THE MILITARY'S UCMJ DISPARITIES

The findings published in a 2017 study by Protect Our Defenders are even more troubling than the gender and racial promotion disparities in the armed forces. This study found that black and Hispanic service members are several times more likely to be prosecuted under the Uniformed Code of Military Justice (UCMJ) for the same offenses for which white service members are given non-judicial punishment. Commanders are given a great deal of authority in determining who should be preferred for UCMJ charges and who should be given non-judicial punishment, such as extra duty or confinement to the barracks; unfortunately, these

Race/Ethnicity/Gender	Average Officer Promotion to General (O-7) By Race/Ethnicity/Gender				
	Average Promotion Rate to O-7 (%)				
	Navy	Air Force	Army	Marine Corps	Coast Guard
Overall	2	3	2	7	3
Black	5~	2	2	0*	0*
Hispanic	2	1	1	16*	15~
Asian/PI	5~	4~	2	0*	0*
Female	4~	3	1	0*	1

* indicates = or > 5% difference of minority group from the overall average
~ indicates minority group with greater promotion rate than the overall average

Table 7.2 One-Star General Promotion Rates 2007–2010. FY 2007 to FY 2010 Promotion Rates to One-Star General by Service, Race, Ethnicity and Gender. Source Military Leadership Diversity Commission (MLDC) Decision Paper #4

decisions can be very subjective. Nonjudicial punishment is not part of a service member's permanent record, and is much less likely to adversely impact one's career. Because of the decentralized execution of the UCMJ, it is highly unlikely that some grand conspiracy is at work. It is more plausible that commanders are being influenced by factors such as implicit bias, leading them to criminalize blacks and other people of color at higher rates than whites. Even black generals accused of misconduct are dealt with more severely than their white counterparts for similar infractions and breeches of contract. These findings within the armed services come as no surprise given that the same racial bias is also prevalent in the greater US criminal justice system.

The UCMJ study found that black Service members in the Air Force, Marine Corps, Navy, and Army were: 71 percent, 32 percent, 40 percent, and 61 percent more likely, respectively, to face court martial or nonjudicial punishment than white service members. It also found that the Marine Corps, "had some of the most significant issues with race particularly in instances where the harshest penalties were possible. In an average year, black Marines were 2.61 times more likely than whites to receive a guilty finding at a general court-martial."[12]

There is a saying in military circles, "Rank has its privileges," which simply means the higher you advance the cushier the assignments become. This mantra plays out across most aspects of military service, even in military justice. For example, a private may be given extra duty for a DUI or even spend a short time in jail, whereas a senior NCO or officer would not be given extra duty or jail time in most instances. They would more likely be given a letter of reprimand that has the effect of ending their career, or they would be separated from service under a UCMJ chapter. That said, in theory equals are to be treated equally, all privates get similar sentencing, all NCOs get similar sentencing, all officers get similar sentencing, and likewise, in the rare instance where a general violates the UCMJ, all generals are to be treated similarly. This is a long-standing military custom that is generally respected for all ranks, by all services, but has not necessarily held true for all races.

Race/Ethnicity/Gender	Average Officer Promotion to Two Star General (O-8) By Race/Ethnicity/Gender		
	Average Promotion Rate to O-8 (%)		
	Air Force	Army	Marine Corps
Overall	38	41	88
Black	45~	31*	33*
Hispanic	25*	0*	0*
Asian/PI	50~	50~	33*
Female	39	37	0*

* indicates = or > 5% difference of minority group from the overall average
~ indicates minority group with greater promotion rate than the overall average
Note: The Navy did not present promotion rates to O-8 at the time data was collected.

Table 7.3 One-Star General Promotion Rates 2007–2010. FY 2007 to FY 2010 Promotion Rates to One-Star General by Service, Race, Ethnicity and Gender. Source Military Leadership Diversity Commission (MLDC) Decision Paper #4

To illustrate how such disparities manifest as reported in the Protect Our Defenders.org study, I offer four cases regarding punishment within the military. These high-profile cases gained public notoriety in 2012 when an epidemic of alleged misconduct occurred involving one-, two-, three-, and four-star generals and admirals, all of which occurred within the span of fourteen or fewer months. These cases were splashed all over mainstream news outlets and persisted in the media for roughly eighteen months. The situation was so bad that Secretary of Defense Leon Panetta ordered a top down review of how the military was teaching ethics. Of the four cases, one of the generals was a black four-star general and the other three were white four-star generals—all men, all engaged in alleged misconduct. Only the black four-star was reduced in rank and forced to retire. The other three white generals were given lesser forms of punishment or simply allowed to retire without a reduction in rank.

These four incidents were the cases of: General Stanley McChrystal, General David Petraeus, General John Allen, and General William Ward. On November 12, 2013, General William Ward, former Commander of Africa Command (AFRICOM) was reduced from four-stars to three after an eighteen-month investigation into allegations of excessive spending on travel-related business. The investigation found that Ward improperly charged the government for flight and hotel accommodation upgrades, and stays at expensive hotels for him, his wife, and his staff, and that Ward was improperly given tickets to a Broadway show. General Ward was the only general of the four to be reduced in rank, despite having committed arguably lesser offenses that did not pose significant national security concerns.

General Stanley McChrystal was famously removed from his duties for making disparaging remarks about President Obama, Vice President Biden, and other Obama Administration members in 2013 during a *Rolling Stone* magazine interview. As a US military officer one of the first things you learn is that the military is subordinate to civilian rule, and that it is expressly forbidden to speak ill of the President and his administration, or other elected officials. Doing so is a violation of Article 88 of the UCMJ, which states, "Any commissioned officer who uses contemptuous words against the President, the Vice President, Congress, the Secretary of Defense, the Secretary of a military department . . . shall be punished as a court-martial may direct."[13]

The constitutional founders were concerned that a powerful military that didn't respect elected civilian authority could easily become a military dictatorship. Article 88 guards against that.

Because of his disparaging remarks in the *Rolling Stone* article entitled, "Run Away General," McChrsytal was relieved of his duties as Commander of International Security Forces Iraq on June 23, 2010. A DoD Investigation was ordered in General McChystal's case after he was already removed from command and his resignation had been accepted. The investigation found no wrong doing despite McChrystal never denying making the remarks, and McChrystal was not interviewed as part of the investigation. It appears as though McChrystal's deeds were swept under the rug.

In General David Petraeus' case, he was found to have had an extra marital affair with his biographer, Paula Broadwell. The affair was uncovered in the wake of an FBI investigation initiated when Broadwell sent an anonymous, threatening email to Jill Kelley, a Tampa socialite who supported US Central Command social events from her Tampa home. Broadwell believed Kelley was getting too chummy with her lover, General David Petraeus. At the time of the FBI investigation, Petraeus was retired from active service, and had been sworn in as the CIA Director. Kelley reported the email to the FBI who initiated the investigation. The FBI interviewed Broadwell on October 21, 2012, and seized computers from her home. Broadwell admitted to starting the affair with Petraeus after he became CIA director in November 2011. However, Petraeus first met Broadwell at Harvard in 2006, and she had made several extended trips to Afghanistan when Petraeus was on active duty as the International Security Commander Afghanistan, the top US general in charge of all coalition forces in Afghanistan. Petraeus selected Broadwell to be his biographer after she expanded her PhD research into a book on him in late 2010.[14]

Had it been established that the affair began when Petraeus was in the active army, both he and Broadwell—who was also a Major in the Army Reserves—would have been subject to UCMJ punishable offenses. The UCMJ prohibits adultery or "improper" personal relationships, and officers can be disciplined or prosecuted for such offenses. Secretary of Defense Leon Pennetta chose not to investigate when the affair actually began, unlike McChrystal's case in which an investigation was done after McChrystal retired, presumably to clear McChrystal's name.[15] The FBI concluded its investigation on Petraeus, and prosecutors recommended that Petraeus be given two years' probation and a $40,000 fine for mishandling classified information. Patraeus denied mishandling the information, but it was found in his Arlington, VA home when the FBI conducted a search in April 2013.[16] Petraeus also could have been charged with providing a false statement and obstruction of an investigation, but he was not.

The plea deal was so lenient that Judge David Kessler ordered Petraeus to pay more than double the amount agreed to by prosecutors to "reflect the seriousness of the offense."[17] Broadwell, a West Point graduate and Military Intelligence Officer, was not charged with commission of a federal crime, despite being in possession of classified material without authorization because she had press credentials. Attorney General Eric Holder stated he would not "prosecute a journalist for doing their job."[18] Broadwell was, however, retroactively removed from an Army reserve promotion list; she had been previously selected for promotion to Lieutenant Colonel. Broadwell also had her security clearance revoked, had to withdraw from her PhD program, and has had difficulty finding work. Most companies see her as eminently qualified, but admit hiring her would be a "public relations nightmare."[19]

General John Allen was found to have been engaged in an embarrassing, "flirtatious" string of emails between 2010 and 2012 with Jill Kelley—the same woman involved in the Patraeus case. Their correspondence totaled "20,000–30,000 pages." Both Allen and Kelley were married at the time. The email exchange was discovered during the FBI's investigation of Petraeus and Broadwell. Other officials stated the 20,000–30,000 pages of email messages included duplicate messages, and that the actual total was closer to 300 emails.[20] The exact content of the exchanges was not made public, but they were so questionable that the DoD suspended Allen's nomination as the NATO Supreme Allied Commander pending the DoD Inspector General (IG) Investigation, and notified Congress of the investigation.[21] The DoD IG Investigation cleared Allen of wrongdoing on Friday, January 18, 2013, but the investigation was not made public. It has also remained unclear whether they investigated his use of his work email and computer to communicate with Kelley, or if Allen disclosed classified information—both of which are punishable UCMJ offenses. A senior Pentagon official who spoke under the condition of anonymity stated to the Washington Post that General Allen had not violated military prohibitions against conduct unbecoming of an officer.[22] Though General Allen disputes that he "engaged in any wrongdoing in this matter," it is inconceivable that a four-star general could have maintained a lengthy correspondence so salacious that it prompted an investigation, and that behavior not be characterized as inappropriate or unbecoming of an officer on its face. The sheer volume of the exchanges and the likelihood that he used government furnished equipment for it could also be characterized as fraud, waste, and abuse.

Regarding Allen's case, one anonymous Pentagon official stated, "Some of the messages are not the sort of things you would print in a family newspaper," "but that doesn't mean he violated military regulations by sending and receiving them." Those statements from the same senior official are emblematic of the problem the Pentagon has with investigating itself. Commanders have the authority to appoint whomever they want to conduct the investigation, provided the appointed officer is of equal or higher rank.

Commanders and senior military officials also have great latitude in limiting the scope of the investigation and the line of questioning. This type of absolute power in investigating and sentencing lends itself to unjust verdicts, and has prompted Congress to explore limiting commanders' authority in investigating allegations of sexual assault and sexual abuse. The degree to which the cases of Generals McChrystal, Petraeus, Ward, and Allen are similar or dissimilar may seem anecdotal. But when these individual cases are taken in aggregate, their adjudication shows undeniable disparities of punishment under the military's UCMJ. These discrepancies have persisted dating back to before the services were integrated. In the four cases at hand, the two uniformed minorities, Lieutenant General Ward and MAJ Broadwell, paid the largest prices for their misconduct. Broadwell now faces a very steep climb to resume her military and civilian career. Ward was reduced one rank from General to Lieutenant General and forced to pay $82,000 in restitution. The reduction in rank will cost him an estimated $30,000 per year for the rest of his life.[23] In my twenty-year professional military career, the only instances I can recall involving a general being reduced a rank involved the grounding of a ship and loss of life, or adultery involving the wives of multiple subordinates.

Too often, when levying punishment, people of color do not get the benefit of their humanity; there is a lack of empathy when deciding punishment. This trend is replicated in virtually every segment of American society. Research shows that black students, especially boys, are disciplined more often and receive more out-of-school suspensions and expulsions than white students for the same offenses.[24] A GAO Study released April 5, 2018, entitled "K–12 Education: Discipline Disparities for Black Students, Boys and Students with Disabilities," confirmed earlier school discipline disparities documented in 2012 findings.[25] Research from the US Sentencing Commission released in November 2017 shows that black men received federal prison sentences almost 20 percent longer on average that white men for the same offenses.[26] Even societal responses to illicit drug use differ vastly when contrasting responses to the crack epidemic of the '90s to today's opioid crisis. Of all institutions, the military is perhaps best positioned to blaze a path forward for equitable punishment for like offenses.

WHAT THE ARMED FORCES GOT RIGHT

The DoD was the first US institution to fully integrate, the first to achieve pay-equity, and the first in which women could hold leadership positions alongside and in command of men. The DoD's removal of the Combat Exclusion Policy casts wide dispersions against every glass ceiling in America. Though awkward, Don't Ask Don't Tell (DADT) was a precursor to gays serving openly in the military, which allowed the DoD to become one of the first large organizations in the country to accept openly homosexual members into service as a specified policy. The debate that DADT facilitated inspired gay and lesbian citizens to come out; openly gay and lesbian men and women serving in the military was then instrumental in swaying public opinion toward accepting gays and lesbians in mainstream American society. This acceptance led to 36 out of 50 states legalizing same-sex marriage, which, in turn, impelled the Supreme Court to legalize same-sex marriage nationwide in 2015.

DIVERSITY AS A STRATEGIC IMPERATIVE

While the DoD has fallen short of achieving its goal of representative populations amongst military leaders, its commitment to diversity has become bedrock policy. Such policy allows the DoD's diversity efforts to weather the ebbs and flow of popular opinion that have undermined diversity initiatives in corporate America. The DoD has had four major bodies examine ways in which the armed services can become more inclusive: the Fahy Committee, the Gessell Committee, the Defense Race Relations Institute (DRRI), and the Military Leadership Diversity Commission (MLDC).[27] The Fahy Committee (1949–1950)—instituted by President Truman—was responsible for assessing the possibility of integrating the armed services, and allowing for the "equality of treatment and opportunity for all persons in the armed services." The Gessell Committee (1962), commissioned by President John F. Kennedy, examined the effectiveness of policies and procedures in the armed forces regarding equal treatment on and off military bases, and suggested revitalizing efforts to expand opportunities for racial and ethnic minorities.[28]

Nonetheless, the late '60s and early '70s were tough years for America and the Armed Services. My father, a Vietnam Era War Veteran, left active service in the 1970s for one of many emerging opportunities in corporate America. Yet he remained in the Army Reserves. Once while at weekend drill, a group of his soldiers vandalized his car. They removed the hub caps, bent them irreparably, and left them on his desk with a note decrying their racial hatred. This type of racial animus was still prevalent in the US military as late as the mid to late '70s. The DoD is a learning organization. Although it repeated the successful strategy of the Fahy Commission, the DoD did not implement the recommendations of the Gessell Committee, which many believe would have prevented the racial strife the military suffered during the Vietnam Era, and perhaps saved my father's hub caps![29]

The DoD established the DRRI in 1971 out of lessons learned from the struggles of the 1960s post-Civil Rights Era. Military leaders acknowledged the need to overcome racial tensions that arose out of the political strife of the 1960s and '70s, both as a moral imperative and as a matter of military readiness. Since then, the DoD has embraced diversity as one of its core values. The DRRI began as an inter-service task force, convened to study the underlying causes of racial tension and conflict within the military, and was initially chaired by Air Force Major General Lucius Theus. The task force became permanently established at Patrick Air Force Base, Florida and started the Race Relations Education Board. The DRRI, eventually renamed the Defense Equal Opportunity Management Institute, became a think tank and leadership development school on diversity and inclusion for the DoD. Its new name reflects the growing array of issues covered in its courses, including sexual harassment, sexism, extremism, religious discrimination, and anti-Semitism.

The fourth body was the MLDC, established in 2009. The MLDC was tasked with conducting a comprehensive evaluation of policies and practices that shape diversity among military leaders. The commission consisted of thirty members, including veterans of various foreign wars, retired general officers, members from academia and industry, and leading subject matter experts on diversity. They held 13 public hearings, heard from senior military brass (active and retired), and conducted interviews of the active force before rendering their 140-page final report to the 112th Congress, President Obama, and senior officials within the DoD.

Until the Trump Administration, the DoD included diversity imperatives in its strategic plan, produced once every five years as part of the Quadrennial Defense Review (QDR). The 2012–2017 Diversity and Inclusion portion of the QDR outlined the implementation strategy of Executive Order 13583 (EO 13583), which directed executive departments and agencies to develop and implement a more comprehensive, integrated, and strategic focus on diversity and inclusion as a key component of their human resources strategies.[30] The 2015 National Security Strategy articulated these imperatives best when it asserted, "Our military might is unrivaled. Yet, American exceptionalism is not rooted solely in the strength of our arms or economy. Above all, it is the product of our founding values, including the rule of law and universal rights, as well as the grit, talent, and diversity of the American people."[31] That statement encompasses why the DoD is vested in diversity, not just for the sake of diversity but as a strategic advantage. The overarching direction of this inclusion strategy encourages direct leadership involvement and commitment. It also creates alignment, allowing the DoD to approach diversity and inclusion efforts in a coordinated, collaborative, and integrated manner with measurable outcomes.

This strategy advances three main goals: "1) Ensure Leadership Commitment to an accountable and sustained diversity effort. 2) Employ an aligned strategic outreach effort to identify, attract and recruit from a broad talent pool reflective of the best of the nation we serve, and 3) Develop, mentor, and retain top talent from across the total force."[32] This type of well-conceived, vetted, and sustained commitment to diversity and inclusion has brought America some of its most promising uniformed leaders, such as: General (Ret) Lloyd Austin, the 33rd Vice Chief of the Army Staff and first black CENTCOM Commander; General (Ret) Erik Shinseki, the Army's first Chief of Staff of Asian ancestry (34th) and the 7th Secretary of the VA; and General (Ret) Ricardo Sanchez, former Commander of Coalition Ground Forces in Iraq, who led the capture of Saddam Hussein. The DoD's culture of inclusion created space for the Colin Powells, Ann Dunwoodys, and Nadja Wests of the world. These diverse leaders were able to ascend to the heights of their abilities because the DoD fostered an environment mindful of the institutional bias that exists in our world, and developed strategies to mitigate its effects.

Despite the DoD's commitment to diversity and inclusion, it is still subject to the rise of "populism" in this country. To further guard itself against social regression regarding diversity and inclusion, the DoD must address the remnants of systemic bias in its policies and practices. The MLDC made 20 recommendations to DoD leadership, President Obama, and the 210th Congress. Congress called upon the MLDC to study: 1) how the armed forces could develop a demographically diverse leadership reflective of the public it serves; and 2) how the armed services can pursue a broader approach to diversity that includes the range of backgrounds, skills, and personal attributes necessary for enhancing military performance. Congress gave the MLDC sixteen specific tasks.[33]

In 2015, the DoD also authorized each of the services to pilot programs designed to ease the challenges of work-life balance. For many, these challenges can become career crossroads, especially for women due to societal norms and expectations placed on them as caregivers. The Department of the Navy is leading the way by expanding its maternity leave to 18 weeks of fully paid maternity leave, upping the ante on the DoD's 12 weeks of fully paid parental leave for either parent, male or female. These policies stand in stark contrast to much of the civilian workforce; the Center for Human Resource Research estimated that only 47.5 percent of women in the US received any type of compensated maternity leave in 2015.[34] Indeed, the DoD should be applauded for its sincere commitment to inclusion.

DOD'S REMAINING WORK

The MLDC does an outstanding job at developing comprehensive assessments of the barriers that prevent the DoD from achieving its diversity goals. Their report discusses branching and assignments, concluding that structural and perceptual barriers are the biggest impediments to building a force as diverse as the nation it defends. The DoD has already implemented one of their major recommendations from a 2011 report—the removal of the combat exclusion for women. The US military will be led by flag officers whose primary skill set is war-fighting, as it should be. Combat exclusion policies prevent women from serving in combat roles if they desire. A female combat exclusion policy systemically denies women the opportunity to become war-fighting leaders, and all but kills any opportunity for them to serve in the armed services at the very highest levels. Congratulations to the Obama Administration and the DoD for recognizing this problem, examining it in detail, and addressing it.

The MLDC examined key assignments: those recognized to be especially demanding, to have high visibility, and to provide competitive advantage for advancement. The services have all done a good job of developing notional career paths, encompassing work and educational assignments that will make a due-course officer effective, credible, and competitive for promotion.[35] But the services fall short of having professional checklists of minimum requirements that must be completed prior to each promotion window. The topic of assignments is very broad but an important one that deserves its own special task force to look specifically at where women and minority officers are being assigned. One only has to walk the halls of the various military headquarters across the world to see pictures of the lineage of commanders, going back to the 1800s in some instances. These photos tell the story of who is being assigned where and who isn't. In the Army, you will find black and other minority commanders well represented in Korea and other places deemed to be less desirable. You won't find many photos of former minority commanding generals lining the halls of Fort Bragg, NC, and Fort Campbell, KY; and chances are you won't find too many photos of prior lower tier commanders at those places either. For example, General (Ret.) Dunwoody was the first woman to command a battalion at Fort Bragg in 1992, and the first woman general to serve at Fort Bragg in 2000.

There really is no secret to having a long and successful military career; one must be technically sound and tactically proficient (hone your craft), follow the rules, and establish a network of mentors. If you want to be a general, work with one, get a copy of their bio and seek out the assignments that they held on their way to the top. The military is full of intelligent, ambitious professionals. Left solely to our own devices we tend to surround ourselves with younger versions of ourselves, or people we feel connected to. Because the military is a very structured organization that places a premium on regulations, it is organized to provide greater equity of opportunity, and therefore must leverage its structure to achieve this goal.

Although all of the services have laid out notional assignments that will set any officer up for a successful career, these career paths tend to be lacking in important details. For instance, a young officer may seek and obtain a company command as a captain, but not all company commands are created equal; the devil is in the details. Take for example two company commanders. The first is assigned to a training company tasked with converting young people off the street into soldiers. His position is technically the same as that of the second who commands Alpha Company, 3rd Battalion, 1st Brigade, 82nd Airborne Division. But here is where these two opportunities differ, despite what the career path manual says. The first commander will get an evaluation from an O-5 commander who has been selected for that position primarily because he was not as competitive as the O-5 who commands a battalion in the 82nd Airborne Division. The 82nd Airborne Division O-5 Commander is much more likely to make O-6 and O-7. A good evaluation from him carries more weight than a good evaluation from the O-5 commander of the training battalion.

Of course, everyone cannot command in the 82nd Airborne, but everyone can be given at least one high-profile assignment in the first nine years of their career before their O-4 promotion board. Most of the services tend to heap favor upon a cadre of "chosen ones" in such a manner that the favor they gleaned early in their careers yields dividends that compound. Over time, these "chosen ones" acquire much more exposure to leaders who are on track for accelerated promotion, and other high-profile jobs such as Military Aide to the Secretary of State or Congressional Fellowships. By the time the two officers in this example reach 15 years of service, the second commander's records will stand head-and-shoulders above his contemporary's.

Once these two officers come up for promotion to O-5, the officer who commanded in the training battalion has little chance of being selected ahead of the former, despite the two having been comparable in ability as young captains. By making structured provisions to give more officers the opportunity to take high profile assignments, the armed services would strengthen its officer corps, in part because there would be a greater diversity of officers with experience in high-profile assignments. And with greater diversity comes a wider range of valuable insights. The current system chooses haves- and have-nots too early in the careers of most officers through an inequitable distribution of opportunity. A task force should be created that uses computer modeling and other approaches to provide more equitable access to high profile opportunities early in an officer's career.

BETTER STRATIFICATION OF DATA

MLDC masks the true, relative comparison by lumping all women into one category, and by not breaking white males into their own separate category. When black, Hispanic, and Asian women are lumped into the same category with white women, we lose the ability to identify any impact race may have on their promotion rates. We also cannot detect how much higher the promotion rates are for white males when we compare all other groups to the average, but don't identify white males as a distinct group. This is not to say that the promotion rates should be exactly the same for each group, but significant differences between groups would be a fair indication that systemic bias may be influencing promotion rates. At that point, further analysis would be warranted, particularly if these differences persist over long periods of time.

GREATER SOCIOECONOMIC DIVERSITY

The first objective given to the MLDC was to develop a uniform definition of diversity for the entire DoD. This recommendation centered on identifying essential expertise in linguistics and cultures that could be used to enhance DoD capabilities. But even this new definition fails to capture another critical component of US diversity: socioeconomic diversity. When the US ended the draft in 1973, military leaders were fearful that low-income individuals would be overly represented within the ranks. One concern was that service members from poorer families would be less educated and less effective in an increasingly technical and complex military. Another concern was that children of poorer families would disproportionately bear the risks and sacrifices of uniformed service that benefits all Americans.

Part of the fallout of Vietnam was a rift between the American people and the military over the unpopularity of that war. American society appears to have recovered from that fallout. The DoD is again revered by the overwhelming majority of Americans regardless of political ideology. During this rift however, many of America's top colleges and universities removed ROTC programs from their campuses. Several administrations have been successful in reestablishing ROTC programs at many of America's top academic institutions through engaging with them, and through removing the prohibition against openly gay and lesbian service in the armed forces.[36]

On May 23, 2016, then Secretary of Defense Aston Carter was present for the graduation of Yale's first ROTC class since the program was removed from campus in 1972. Carter stated in his remarks, "For some of your classmates, you may be the first member of the military they've ever gotten to know."[37] Carter's insight is a reflection of the reality that the all-volunteer force has been increasingly drawing from a similar pool of people, many of whom are from families who have served in the military for generations. Navy Captain Vernon Kemper, the Yale Navy ROTC Commandant commented, "We need that diversity of thought."[38]

Today, all of the Ivy League schools and many of America's other leading academic institutions have ROTC programs on their campuses, or their students have access to these programs through adjacent campuses. These steps are significant and must be applauded. America is better and our institutions are stronger when we build bridges and identify shared values that benefit both organizations. Even with these steps, the DoD has not sufficiently addressed issues surrounding socioeconomic diversity. Particularly when you consider that the emerging warfare of the future will be information based, and will require different types of soldiers. The DoD must examine its assessment models critically, and devise service windows that are appealing to the new breed of service members required to advance American interests in cyberspace.

Amy Lutz, Associate Professor of Sociology at Syracuse University examined individuals who join the military by race, class, and immigration status.[39] The likelihood of a person serving in uniform based on race, ethnicity, or immigration status showed no differences. Socioeconomic status was the only descriptor with significant differences between those who had and had not served.[40]

These trends could be problematic for the all-volunteer armed services if they hold true over time. Children from affluent families who are more likely to hold positions of power and influence in corporations and politics are systemically excluded from the experience of serving in uniform. The very socioeconomic class that is underrepresented in the military, retains a disproportionate amount of power in civilian society to influence a range of decisions that affect the military. They are often the very people investing money and wielding influence to determine what benefits service members will receive, as well as the size and level of funding allocated to the armed services and the Veterans Administration. People who have served are more likely to understand the nuances of military service, and to have greater insights regarding military issues. Those who have served are also better positioned to act as ambassadors for veterans transitioning to civilian companies.

None of this is to say uniformed service is a prerequisite for positively advocating for the military and veterans. Rather, greater socioeconomic diversity in the armed services would benefit both the military and those privileged factions of society that hope to have a positive and informed influence on the military. I would submit that Prince William and Prince Harry of Great Britain are better positioned to advise Parliament, and to advocate on behalf of the British armed services due to their service in uniform. By contrast, the Bill Gateses, Mark Zuckerbergs, and other leaders from affluent American families are missing this opportunity; this segment of our society could be better business leaders, citizens, parents, and spouses with the benefit of military training. And our nation's military would be better for their service.

One possible solution for the armed forces is to change its career development models and make it more enticing for young people from affluent families (besides those whose parents were high-ranking brass). The military could create Training with Industry partnerships that are only designed for a limited time frame, say two to five years, in addition to the current twenty-year career model. This would aid the armed services in a couple of ways: 1) by creating advocates in corporate America who would be more likely to hire veterans and lobby their companies for veterans' programs, and 2) give the armed forces access to talented professionals from socioeconomically diverse backgrounds.

RENAMING CONFEDERATE BASES

The US Army, the last service to fully integrate, still has military installations named after Confederate leaders, countering the Army's core values—loyalty, duty, respect, selfless service, honor, integrity, and personal courage—and giving hubris to those espousing white supremacy. In turn, this degrades the descendants of former slaves who serve, as well as the uniform service members whose ancestors fought to defeat the Confederacy. Although it should have happened sooner, the 2021 National Defense Authorization Act is requiring the Army to rename these bases. It is important that the commission assigned to this project chooses new names that honor figures who better reflect the diversity of our nation.

We only need to look back a few years for an example of a white supremacist validating his bigotry with Confederate paraphernalia. On June 17, 2015, Dylann Roof entered the historic Mother Emanuel African Methodist Episcopal Church in Charleston, SC, and murdered nine black parishioners during their Bible study. Numerous press outlets linked Roof to white supremacist groups. Photos of Roof taken from his social media pages depicted him brandishing the Confederate Flag and burning the American Flag. Discovering those photos was a water-shed moment for many communities around America who reflected on the prominence of Confederate symbols in mainstream society. Many communities began removing statues and other artifacts glorifying the Confederacy and Confederate leaders. After activist Bree Newsome gained national attention for scaling a flag pole to remove the Confederate flag from the state capital, Governor Nikki Haley and the South Carolina state legislature permanently removed the Confederate flag, which had been there since April 11, 1961.[41] Haley, the first woman governor of South Carolina, and the first member of an ethnic minority to serve as governor made a stirring unifying statement in the days following the Mother Emanuel AME

Massacre, when she called for the South Carolina assembly to vote to remove the flag from the state capital. "The events of this week call upon us to look at this in a different way . . . " She argued that a symbol long revered by many Southerners was for some a "deeply offensive symbol of a brutally offensive past." Haley, who is Indian American, concluded her statement by saying, "it's time to move the flag from the capitol grounds."[42]

In December 2019, Haley back tracked from her original position in an interview with a conservative talk radio host. During that interview, Haley stated that the Confederate flag symbolized "service, sacrifice and heritage" for some people in her state until Dylann S. Roof "hijacked" it.[43] Haley's reversal is emblematic of America's historical contractions following gains for minorities. Renaming military bases named in honor of Confederates will leave white supremacists even fewer symbols of legitimacy. Confederate leaders' motivations for fighting may have been noble from a very narrow perspective, and they may have believed they were doing what was right for their communities. However, there were a significant number of Americans who owned slaves, but chose to remain loyal to the US. Why not honor their loyalty instead? Or perhaps we should honor those who remained loyal to a country that enslaved them because they still saw potential in our young nation. Not everyone gets to have their name prominently displayed on the front gate of a military base. Why, of all people, should veritable traitors receive such an honor?

In many cases, confederate monuments were erected in the spirit of reconciliation, not division. But if the bases were named in the spirit of reconciliation 100 years ago, they will be renamed in the spirit of reconciliation today. The irony that we named American Army bases after people who literally took up arms against the US to preserve an immoral institution that contradicted the Army's values is staggering. We can't even give these men the "that's how it was back in the day" pass, because their fellow slave owners in Kentucky, Maryland, West Virginia, and Missouri did not secede. Another dubious aspect of the argument that these bases were named after confederates as a gesture of peace and unity following the Civil War is that some weren't named until the 1940s.

[INSERT TABLE 7.4 HERE][44]

As stated earlier, the DoD's conflicts are America's conflicts. Despite the progress made, both the DoD and America lack the ability to step outside their respective bubbles and look at themselves earnestly. Only then can we all come to the obvious realization that inclusion and honoring confederate leaders are mutually exclusive. The DoD missed the mark when Brigadier General Malcolm Frost, the Army's Chief of Public Affairs, issued the following statement after the mass killings at Mother Emanuel: "There is no discussion under way [about renaming posts.] Every Army installation is named for a soldier who holds a place in our military history. . . . Accordingly, these historic names represent individuals, not causes or ideologies."⁴⁵ The attempt to strip such clearly political decisions of their political implications failed. The Army will now join the ranks of civilian leaders such as Mayor Mitch Landrieu and the City of New Orleans who removed their Confederate monuments from prominence. By removing the remaining vestiges of the Confederacy from prominent public spaces, the US military is becoming truer to its core values and its rich history of inclusion and equality. Choosing names that better reflect our national diversity would demonstrate the Army's recently renewed commitment to inclusion.

PROTECT THE INCLUSION OF TRANSGENDER PERSONS

Secretary of Defense Mattis delivered his recommendations for transgender persons serving in the military on February 24, 2018. He cited a review by a panel of experts, which stated that allowing the accession and retention of individuals with a history or diagnosis of gender dysphoria presents "substantial risks" to military effectiveness and lethality.⁴⁶ The Trump Era policy casts dispersions upon the DoD's efforts in "matters of principle" to remove barriers unrelated to a person's qualifications to serve. President Joe Biden reversed the Trump Era Policy on January 25, 2021, just five days after being sworn into office. The White House issued the following statement on the Executive Order: "America is stronger, at home and around the world, when it is inclusive, the military is no exception."⁴⁷ The Biden Administration Executive order is keeping with the DoD's own strategic aims to establish a military reflective of the people it defends.

Herein lies one of many fundamental differences between the Trump, Obama, and Biden Administrations. As a matter of principle, the Obama and Biden Administrations valued diversity and inclusion as a part of its core strategies for advancing the notion of American exceptionalism. The 2018 National Defense Strategy published by the Trump Administration does not mention the words diversity or inclusion anywhere in the fourteen page, unclassified version.⁴⁸ That is not to say the Trump Administration didn't place some value on diversity, but it is to say they didn't prioritize diversity as a national strategic imperative. Their exclusionary policy on transgender persons makes this clear. The Trump administration advanced the argument that the mere existence of transgender personnel within the ranks 'threatens the lethality' of the force. In contrast, the Obama and Biden Administrations advanced the notion that the exclusion of transgender personnel is an artificial barrier, not predicated on performance, that precludes the American armed forces from acquiring and retaining the most talented personnel for the mission regardless of race, religion, gender, or sexual orientation.

EQUITABLE SENTENCING FOR UCMJ VIOLATIONS

The DoD's failure to equitably administer justice within its ranks is a stain on one of America's finest institutions, revered nationwide for the sacrifice, excellence, and integrity it embodies. When the Pentagon brass fails to treat equals equitably, it is not only harmful to the individuals involved, but it is harmful to the morale of the rank and file. It causes the men and women in uniform to question the sincerity of the DoD's moral ethos. It is painful for all Americans to watch any of our uniformed heroes and heroines fall from grace. It is especially painful when it happens to minority leaders because there are so few. It is like a collective gut-punch to minority communities to learn how their heroes, heroines, and role-models are dispensed with unfairly, while their white, male contemporaries who also engaged in misconduct are allowed to retire with mere admonishments. The armed services often considers the selfless manner in which these leaders have previously served, and the uncharacteristic actions that caused their demise. In these instances, leaders convicted of misconduct are rightfully afforded some mitigation. Too often this same consideration is not offered to its minority leaders who arguably work harder to attain the same rank.

Congress has questioned the DoD's ability to administer justice within its ranks numerous times. The DoD must fix this shortcoming before their authority is taken away completely. There are several approaches the DoD should consider. They could convene a panel of higher-ranking officials to review cases with identifying information removed, and make recommendations to the sentencing commander for consideration. The DoD could also develop a table of penalties for specific violations that require a justification to the next highest commander if punishment departs from what is prescribed. Whatever method used, commanders should be held accountable for any racial disparities in sentencing; such accountability would improve performance.

AMERICA'S REMAINING WORK

For all of the progress the United States has made, significant work remains before we can declare ourselves a post-racial society.[49] More than fifty-five years ago in his famous "I Have a Dream Speech," Dr. Martin Luther King Jr. stood on the steps of the Lincoln Memorial and said, "In a sense we've come to our nation's capital to cash a check."[50] What King was referring to was the promise articulated in the 13th, 14th, and 15th Amendments: a promise made to former slaves and their children that they would be fully incorporated into the American experience with all the rights and privileges thereof. King went on to say, "Instead of honoring this sacred obligation, America has given the Negro people a bad check, a check which has come back marked 'insufficient funds.'"[51] King's metaphor illustrated a reality in America for black people and how starkly that reality contrasted with America's promise. This promise was hijacked by an unwritten truce, a side-deal made between politicians and endorsed by a large segment of Americans who were unwilling to change. If black America were to collectively re-present that check Dr. King spoke of today, I'm afraid it would still be returned, marked insufficient funds.

There is a direct and continuous link between the status of black people in America today and the subjugation that followed slavery. We can easily understand why literacy rates were low within the black community following the Civil War because educating blacks was illegal for the first 249 years in America. It is unsurprising that literacy rates still lagged behind the national averages in 1968 because even when legally permitted to have compulsory formal education, the education was segregated and proven in the Supreme Court to be inferior. While an inferior education is better than none, it does not fulfill the promise of equality of opportunity. The achievement gap which exists today is directly related to this history. These two lines of academic achievement, that of blacks and that of whites, have never come close to intersecting; they are directly tied to the legacy of slavery, legal subjugation, and unequal protection under the law. The legal machinery that once preserved the status quo, constraining black Americans and other minorities, has been replaced by a self-sustaining apparatus that is more complex than simply racism; it is based on race, socioeconomic status, geography and environment. For all of the unseemliness of this machinery, it is progress when compared to state-sanctioned discrimination, but America can and must do better.

The American military has invested a great deal of equity in making good on that promissory note—investments in individuals who have gone on to become not only military leaders, but civic leaders and captains of industry. Nationally, we still acknowledge and celebrate historic firsts, such as the first black commanding general in Fort Benning, GA's 100-year history. Major General Gary Brito achieved that distinction on March 15, 2018. Fort Benning, Georgia, is not Fort Bragg, North Carolina, but it is progress. Another recent first was West Point faculty selecting Simone Askew as their first black female First Captain, a distinction that made her the highest-ranking cadet in their cadet leadership chain of command. The Trump Administration and Secretary Mattis should be applauded for nominating Lorna Mahlock for promotion to BG General on April 10, 2018. She became the first black woman in the history of the Marine Corps to become a general on August 3, 2018.

Although these achievements are long overdue, we celebrate them because they are triumphs over the remaining inequity. These triumphs do not represent equality, but they do signify that the machinery perpetuating inequality is not absolute. Black Americans must prioritize education now more than ever in order for this nation to move forward on this accord. White Americans must not feel guilty for the sins of their forefathers, but should instead help to disassemble the systems that safeguard inequality. Joining ranks to close disparities in policing and school funding will provide the greatest return on our investment. Once that promissory note is made good, America can declare itself post-racial, and fully focus its energy on larger challenges that lie ahead.

Change doesn't always come eventually, and it certainly doesn't come without prodding. Has America stopped prodding? Many American schools are more segregated today than they were forty years ago. Author and Georgetown Law Professor Sheryll Cashin cites in her book, *Loving Interracial Intimacy in America and the Threat to White Supremacy*, that American public schools hit the high-water mark of integration in 1988 when forty percent of black students went to integrated schools. Today, that number is estimated to be roughly equivalent to that of 1968. The definition of a segregated school has expanded from what it was in 1954 with geography, race, and poverty as confluent variables, but the numbers are roughly the same given these new co-variables.[52] This regression reflects of the ebb and flow of diversity and inclusion that comes and goes like a tide in the US. As the racial attitudes of all Americans advance, the military's task of building a cohesive, diverse, and decisive global force is made easier. As the military advances its strategic objectives for diversity and inclusion, it provides an irrefutable example of the effectiveness and dynamism of strong, diverse units.

Just as the Army has yet to fully denounce racial hierarchies in all forms, America has yet to fully denounce them. The 13th, 14th, and 15th amendments are known as the Civil War Amendments, passed between 1865 and 1870. The 13th (proposed and ratified in 1865) abolished slavery. The 14th (proposed in 1866 and ratified in 1868) provided a broad definition of national citizenship, overturning the Dred Scott case that provided a legal footing for discrimination. This amendment requires states to provide equal protection under the law to all persons (not only citizens) within their jurisdictions. The 15th (ratified in 1870) grants voting rights regardless of "race, color, or previous condition of servitude." For all their eloquence, these amendments do not apologize for the institution of slavery. America must formally acknowledge the atrocities of slavery and begin to atone for the egregious and heinous crimes committed against people of African ancestry, just as America has apologized for the internment of Japanese Americans during World War II, and the centuries of abuse perpetrated against Native Americans. Such acknowledgement would allow the nation to begin healing and uplifting the descendants of African slaves who endured decades more suffering under Jim Crow Laws, and still suffer injustices related to the legacy of slavery.

America also needs to adopt a national common core curriculum that recognizes slavery as the principal cause of the Civil War. This curriculum must be taught to put an end to romanticized notions of chattel slavery and white supremacist ideology. In May of 2018, famed rapper Kanye West infamously stated that 400 years of slavery sounded like a choice.[53] While West was roundly criticized for his uninformed comments, his cavalier characterization reflects a significant knowledge chasm regarding what schools teach students about slavery and Jim Crow Era policies.

In January 2018, the Southern Poverty Law Center released a fifty-two page report entitled, Teaching Hard History: American Slavery. The report details how schools are inadequately teaching the history of American slavery; consequently, students lack a basic knowledge of the important role slavery played in shaping the US, and the impact it continues to have on race relations in America.[54] The report detailed that only eight percent of 1,000 high school seniors surveyed identified slavery as the main reason the South seceded from the Union. The report captures anecdotes from teachers that express why it is so difficult to teach slavery, primarily dealing with feelings of guilt, and how teaching slavery poorly makes it difficult to teach the Civil Rights Movement. Ohio State University History Professor, Hasan Kwame Jeffries, who wrote the report's preface, stated "Slavery is hard history . . . it is hard to comprehend the inhumanity that defined it, the violence that sustained it, and the complacency that abided it."[55] The report examined history texts and standards in fifteen states. They developed a thirty-point scoring rubric to evaluate each; no book scored above 70 percent and five scored below 25 percent.

CLOSING

In spite of the remaining work, I am encouraged by signs that America is beginning to push again for freedom and equality for all. The promotion of Brigadier General Mahlock is one, and the election of Doug Jones as Alabama's first Democratic Senator since 1993 is another. Jones, a moderate Democrat, sat in the courtroom as a second-year law student in 1977 when KKK member Robert "Dynamite Bob" Chambliss stood trial for the murder of four black girls in the Birmingham, Alabama, 16th Street Baptist Church bombing. These innocent girls were eleven-year-old Denise McNair, and fourteen-year-olds Carole Robertson, Addie Mae Collins, and Cynthia Wesley. Chambliss openly bragged about the bombing for decades until finally the State Attorney of Alabama, Bill Baxley, brought him to trial and won a conviction. Jones remembered thinking to himself during that trial that Chambliss couldn't have acted alone. He brought Chambliss' accomplices to trial more than twenty years later while serving as State Attorney of Alabama, securing the convictions of Thomas Edwin Blanton Jr. and Bobby Frank Cherry, two more KKK members.

The black women of Alabama came to Jones' aid in his election more than any other segment, just as he came to theirs forty years after one of the worst hate crimes in American history.

Jones' election reminds us that when Americans unite behind the principals that make our nation great, we can push tyranny into the recesses. The responsibility to lead is inherent in the responsibilities of elected officials. But it is also incumbent upon citizens to participate responsibly in the election process. When elected officials abandon their implied trust to lead and instead appeal to our darkest emotions, the people must push back at the ballot box, and our institutions must be a fail-safe against such tyranny. American institutions are emblematic of the core values that make America exceptional: freedom and equality. The American military has a sacred trust to reflect these values in its rank and file, as well as throughout its policies.

Americans, regardless of race, religion, gender, nationality, and sexual orientation must not only be free to defend this country and the constitution, but they must also be made to feel that their contributions to this mission are valued. If America is to once and for all overcome the ills of racism, sexism, and homophobia, its institutions, policies, and elected officials must denounce injustice unequivocally and at every opportunity. Looking back, we can all see the immorality of divisive ideologies. Hindsight is 20/20 because it is unencumbered by the rose-colored lenses of agenda. Americans must challenge themselves to keep the spectacles of agenda off when looking at present and future challenges. Doing so will require great courage and faith in our institutions, our system of governance, and our citizenry. It is this faith that gives us the courage to take principled stances; "If we do not stand for something, we will fall for anything." As the premier leadership institution in the world, the United States military must promulgate the values of freedom and equality of opportunity for all, and continue to lead through the examples of a storied and diverse history of inclusion and excellence.

NOTES

1. Ian Simpson, "U.S. Hate Groups Proliferate in Trump's First Year, Watchdog Says," *Reuters*, February 21, 2018, http://www.reuters.com/article/us-usa-trump-hate-groups/u-s-hate-groups-proliferate-in-trumps-first-year-watchdog-says-idUSKCN1G5286.

2. US Department of Defense, Military Leadership and Diversity Commission, *From Representation to Inclusion: Diversity Leadership for the 21st Century Military, Final Report*, Washington, DC: DoD, 2011, pdf, https://diversity.defense.gov/Portals/51/Documents/Special%20Feature/MLDC_Final_Report.pdf (2015), xiii.

3. These findings are statistically significant except where indicated otherwise, even after controlling for factors known to affect promotions, such as: prior enlisted service, specific military occupations, commissioning source (e.g. Service Academy, Scholarship Reserve Officer Training Corps (ROTC), Regular ROTC, Officer Candidate School/Officer Training School, Direct Commission).

4. Susan D. Hosek, Peter Tiemeyer, M. Rebecca Kilburn, Debra A. Strong, Selika Ducksworth, and Reginald Rayl, *Minority and Gender Differences in Officer Career Progression* (Santa Monica, CA: RAND Corporation, 2001) https://www.rand.org/pubs/monograph_reports/MR1184.html.

5. For the purposes of this study, MLDC grouped black Hispanics with the black category.

6. US Department of Defense, Military Leadership and Diversity Commission, *From Representation to Inclusion: Diversity Leadership for the 21st Century Military, Final Report*, 2–5.

7. Gillian B. White, "There are Currently 4 Black CEOs in the Fortune 500," *The Atlantic*, Oct 26, 2017, https://www.theatlantic.com/business/archive/2017/10/black-ceos-fortune-500/543960/.

8. Richard L. Zweigenhaft and William Domhoff. *The New CEOs: Women, African American, Latino, and Asian Leaders of Fortune 500 Companies*. (Lanham, MD: Rowman & Littlefield, 2014), 99–104.

9. White, "There are Currently 4 Black CEOs in the Fortune 500."

10. Ibid.

11. Joel Neel, "You, Me and Them: Experiencing Discrimination in America. Poll: Most Americans Think Their Own Group Faces Discrimination," *NPR*, October 24, 2017, https://www.npr.org/sections/health-shots/2017/10/24/559116373/poll-most-americans-think-their-own-group-faces-discrimination.

12. Don Christensen and Yelena Tsilker, *Racial Disparities in the Military, Findings of Substantial and Persistent Racial Disparities within the United States Military Justice System* (Alexandria, VA: Protect Our Defenders, May 20, 2017) http://www.protectourdefenders.com/wp-content/uploads/2017/05/Report_20.pdf (accessed July 17, 2018).

13. Contempt Toward Individuals, 10 U.S.C. § 888-88 (2011), https://www.govinfo.gov/app/details/USCODE-2011-title10/USCODE-2011-title10-subtitleA-partII-chap47-subchapX-sec888.

14. Theodore Schleifer, "Petraeus Sentenced: Two Years Probation; $100,000 Fine," *CNN*, April 23, 2015, http://www.cnncom/2015/04/23/politics/david-petraeus-sentencing/index.html.

15. Howard Altman, "Nearly Five Years After Petraeus Scandal, Bad Decisions Still Resonate," *Tampa Bay Tribune*, January 31, 2016, http://www.tbo.com/apps/pbcs.dll/article?avis=TB&date=20160131&category=article (accessed March 6, 2016).

16. Ibid.

17. Schleifer, "Petraeus Sentenced: Two Years Probation; $100,000 Fine."

18. Altman, "Nearly Five Years After Petraeus Scandal, Bad Decisions Still Resonate."

19. Jessica Bennett, "Paula Broadwell, David Petraeus and the Afterlife of a Scandal," *New York Times*, May 28, 2016, https://www.nytimes.com/2016/05/29/fashion/david-petraeus-paula-broadwell-scandal-affair.html.

20. Craig Whitlock, "Jill Kelley E-mails Depict a Striving Tampa Socialite and a Smitten Military Brass," *Washington Post*, February 3, 2015, https://www.washingtonpost.com/world/national-security/jill-kelley-e-mails-depict-a-striving-tampa-socialite-and-a-smitten-military-brass/2015/02/03/ef8cb06c-a800-11e4-a06b-9df2002b86a0_story.html.

21. Hannah Furness, "Gen John Allen Investigated for 'inappropriate communications' to Jill Kelley," *Telegraph*, November 13, 2012, https://www.telegraph.co.uk/news/worldnews/northamerica/usa/9674163/Gen-John-Allen-investigated-for-inappropriate-communications-to-Jill-Kelley.html.

22. Rajiv Chandrasekaran, "Gen. John Allen Cleared in Misconduct Inquiry," *Washington Post*, January 22, 2013, https://www.washingtonpost.com/world/national-security/gen-john-allen-cleared-in-misconduct-inquiry/2013/01/22/479c776a-64dd-11e2-9e1b-07db1d2ccd5b_story.html.

23. Larry McShane, "U.S. General Demoted Over 'extravagant trips,'" *New York Daily News*, November 13, 2012, https://www.nydailynews.com/news/national/general-demoted-extravagant-trips-article-1.1201284.

24. Tamar Lewin, "Black Students Face More Discipline, Data Suggests," *New York Times*, March 6, 2012, http://www.nytimes.com/2012/03/06/education/black-students-face-more-harsh-discipline-data-shows.html?_r=0Lyfe. Ise Lyfe, "Kicking Black Boys out of Class, Teaching Black Girls a Lesson," September 19, 2012, HuffPost, https://www.huffpost.com/entry/kicking-black-boys-out-of_b_1894719.

25. US Government Accountability Office, *K–12 Education: Discipline Disparities for Black Students, Boys, and Students with Disabilities*, Report to Congressional Requesters, Washington, DC: GAO, March 22, 2018, https://www.gao.gov/assets/700/690828.pdf.

26. Scott Simon, "Research Finds Racial Disparities in Prison Sentences," *NPR*, November 25, 2017, https://www.npr.org/2017/11/25/566438860/research-finds-racial-disparities-in-prison-sentences.

27. US Department of Defense, Military Leadership and Diversity Commission, *From Representation to Inclusion: Diversity Leadership for the 21st Century Military, Final Report*, xix.

28. Ibid., 5.

29. Ibid., 6.

30. US Department of Defense, *Diversity and Inclusion Strategic Plan: 2012–2017*, Washington, DC: DoD, 2012, pdf, https://diversity.defense.gov/Portals/51/Documents/DoD_Diversity_Strategic_Plan_%20final_as%20of%2019%20Apr%2012%5B1%5D.pdf, 7–9.

31. White House, *National Security Strategy*, Washington, DC: White House, February 2015, pdf, https://obamawhitehouse.archives.gov/sites/default/files/docs/2015_national_security_strategy_2.pdf, 4.

32. US Department of Defense, *Diversity and Inclusion Strategic Plan: 2012–2017*, 4.

33. US Department of Defense, *Diversity and Inclusion Strategic Plan: 2012–2017*, 7.

34. Jena McGregor, "Maternity Leave is not Getting Longer, and Number of Women Taking it has Barely Budged," *Washington Post*, March 14, 2017, https://www.washingtonpost.com/news/on-leadership/wp/2017/03/14/the-length-of-maternity-leave-has-barely-budged-and-neither-has-the-number-of-women-taking-it/.

35. Peter Schirmer, Harry J. Thie, Margaret C. Harrell, and Michael S. Tseng, *Challenging Time in DOPMA: Flexible and Contemporary Military Officer Management* (Santa Monica, CA: RAND Corporation, 2006) https://www.rand.org/pubs/monographs/MG451.html.

36. Linda Greenhouse, "Supreme Court Upholds Law on College Military Recruiting," *New York Times*, March 6, 2006, https://www.nytimes.com/2006/03/06/politics/supreme-court-upholds-law-on-college-military-recruiting.html. (accessed August 13, 2016).

37. Jim Michaels, "ROTC Welcomed Back at Ivy League Schools," *USA Today*, May 23, 2016, https://www.usatoday.com/story/news/2016/05/23/rotc-welcomed-back-ivy-league-schools/32622771/ (accessed May 12, 2018).

38. Ibid.

39. She compared data sets from the Integrated Public Use Microdata Series for 1980, 1990, and 2000 against military data sets for 1981, 1999, and 2000.

40. Amy Lutz, "Who joins the military? A look at Race, Class, and Immigration Status," *Journal of Political and Military Sociology* 36, no. 2 (2008): 167–188.

41. Kalhan Rosenblatt and Corky Siemaszko, "Confederate Flag Raised at South Carolina Statehouse in Protest by Secessionist Party," *NBC News*, July 10, 2017, https://www.nbcnews.com/news/us-news/confederate-flag-rises-south-carolina-statehouse-protest-secessionist-party-n781331 (accessed July 12, 2017).

42. Frances Robles, Richard Fausset, and Michael Barbaro, "Nikki Haley, South Carolina Governor, Calls for Removal of Confederate Battle Flag," *New York Times*, June 22, 2015, https://www.nytimes.com/2015/06/23/us/south-carolina-confederate-flag-dylann-roof.html.

43. Aimee Ortiz, "Nikki Haley's Confederate Flag Comments Spark Backlash," *New York Times*, December 7, 2019, https://www.nytimes.com/2019/12/07/us/Nikki-Haley-confederate-flag.html.

44. "Post Locations," US Army, November 28, 2016, https://www.goarmy.com/about/post-locations.html (accessed June 21, 2018).

45. Barbara Starr and Daniella Diaz, "Pentagon: Confederate Base Names Won't be Changed, *CNN*, July 9, 2015, https://www.cnn.com/2015/06/24/politics/confederate-army-bases-names/index.html (accessed July 10, 2015).

46. Jim Mattis, "Military Service by Transgender Individuals," Memorandum for the President (Washington, DC: DoD, February 22, 2018).

47. Jim Garamone, "Biden Administration Overturns Transgender Exclusion Policy," *DoD News*, January 25, 2021, https://www.defense.gov/Explore/News/Article/Article/2482048/biden-administration-overturns-transgender-exclusion-policy/ (accessed July 27, 2021).

48. US Department of Defense, *Summary of the 2018 National Defense Strategy of the United States of America: Sharpening the American Military's Competitive Edge* (Washington, DC: DoD, 2018), pdf, https://dod.defense.gov/Portals/1/Documents/pubs/2018-National-Defense-Strategy-Summary.pdf (accessed January 22, 2018).

49. Post-racial: a society where race is not used as a means to discriminate against individuals.

50. Phillip Kennicott, "Revisiting King's Metaphor About a Nation's Debt," *Washington Post*, August 24, 2011, https://www.washingtonpost.com/lifestyle/style/revisiting-kings-metaphor-about-a-nations-debt/2011/07/26/gIQArshBaJ_story.html (accessed February 1, 2018).

51. Ibid.

52. Sheryll Cashin, *Loving: Interracial Intimacy in America and the Threat to White Supremacy* (Boston: Beacon Press, 2017), 4.

53. Harmeet Kaur, "Kanye West Just Said 400 Years of Slavery was a Choice," *CNN*, May 4, 2018, https://www.cnn.com/2018/05/01/entertainment/kanye-west-slavery-choice-trnd/index.html (accessed May 5, 2018).

54. Kate Shuster, *Teaching Hard History: American Slavery*, Montgomery, AL: Southern Poverty Law Center, January 31, 2018, https://www.splcenter.org/20180131/teaching-hard-history (accessed May 12, 2018).

55. Ibid.

Bibliography

"2000 Democratic Party Platform." *The American Presidency Project*. August 14, 2000. http://www. presidency.ucsb.edu/ws/index.php?pid=29612 (accessed October 9, 2017).

"2000 Republican Party Platform." *The American Presidency Project*. July 31, 2000. https://www.presidency.ucsb.edu/documents/2000-republican-party-platform (accessed October 9, 2017).

"The 1960s-70s, The American Feminist Movement: Breaking Down Barriers for Women." *Tavaana*. June 21, 2018. https://tavaana.org/en/case-studies/1960s-70s-american-feminist-movement-breaking-down-barriers-women.

Adam, Barry D. "Anatomy of a Panic: State Voyeurism, Gender, Politics, and the Cult of Americanism." In *Gays and Lesbians in the Military: Issues, Concerns, and Contrasts*, edited by Wilbur Scott and Sandra Carson Stanley, 103–118. New York: Aldine De Gruyter, 1994.

"Africans in America: The Revolutionary War." *PBS*. April 9, 2015. http://www.pbs.org/wgbh/aia/part2/2narr4.html.

Allison, Marene. "At the Gates of West Point." The Women's Memorial. Oct. 21, 2006. https://www.womensmemorial.org/oral-history/detail/?s=at-the-gates-of-west-point (accessed April 22, 2018).

Altman, Howard. "Nearly Five Years After Petraeus Scandal, Bad Decisions Still Resonate." *Tampa Bay Tribune*. January 31, 2016. http://www.tbo.com/apps/pbcs.dll/article?avis=TB&date=20160131&category=article (accessed March 6, 2016).

"American Women and World War II." *Khan Academy*. Accessed December 27, 2017. https://www.khanacademy.org/humanities/us-history/rise-to-world-power/us-wwii/a/american-women-and-world-war-ii.

Associated Press. "Black Crew of World War II Navy Ship Recognized for Heroism." *The New York Times*. February 19, 1995. https://www.nytimes.com/1995/02/19/us/black-crew-of-world-war-ii-navy-ship-recognized-for-heroism.html (accessed April 17, 2016).

Associated Press. "Don't Ask Don't Tell Costs $363M." *USA Today*. February 14, 2006. https://usatoday30.usatoday.com/news/washington/2006-02-14-dont-ask-report_x.htm (accessed July 19, 2017).

Associated Press. "Goldwater Backs Gay Troops." *New York Times*. June 11, 1993. https://www.nytimes.com/1993/06/11/us/goldwater-backs-gay-troops.html (accessed October 15, 2017).

Associated Press. "Pentagon Delays Decision on Transgender Enlistments by 6 Months." *LA Times*. June 30, 2017. https://www.latimes.com/nation/la-na-transgender-enlistment-delay-20170630-story.html.

Barrett, Frank, Coit D. Blacker, Ralph Carney, Donald Campbell, Kathleen Campbell, Mark Eitelberg, John D. Hutson, et al.. "Financial analysis of Don't ask don't tell: How much does the gay ban cost?" *Palm Center: Blueprints for Sound Public Policy*. February 2006. https://www.palmcenter.org/wp-content/uploads/2018/11/Blue-Ribbon-Report.pdf (accessed March 22, 2007).

Bates, Karen Grigsby. "Remembering Tuskegee Airman Roscoe Brown, Educator and Civil Rights Trailblazer." *NPR*. July 6,2016. https://www.npr.org/sections/codeswitch/2016/07/06/484792854/honoring-tuskegee-airman-roscoe-brown (accessed July 6, 2016).

Bellafaire, Judith. "The Women's Army Corps: A Commemoration of WWII Service." *U.S. Army Center for Military History.* February 17, 2005. https://history.army.mil/brochures/WAC/WAC.HTM (accessed June 21, 2018).

Bennett, Jessica. "Paula Broadwell, David Petraeus and the Afterlife of a Scandal." *New York Times.* May 28, 2016. https://www.nytimes.com/2016/05/29/fashion/david-petraeus-paula-broadwell-scandal-affair.html.

Berube, Allan. *Coming Out Under Fire: The History of Gay Men and Women in World War Two.* New York: The Free Press, 1990.

Bianco, Robert. "20-year flashback: Ellen DeGeneres came out, and paved the way for more gay TV roles." *USA Today.* April 26, 2017. https://www.usatoday.com/story/life/tv/2017/04/26/ellen-degeneres-gay-coming-out-tv-20-year-anniversary/100888584/.

Binning, William C., Larry E. Esterly, and Paul A. Sracic. *Encyclopedia of American Parties, Campaigns, and Elections.* Westport, CT: Greenwood Press, 1999.

"Black Soldiers in the U.S. Military During the Civil War." *U.S. National Archives and Records Administration,* September 1, 2017. https://www.archives.gov/education/lessons/blacks-civil-war.

Blair, Clay. *The Forgotten War: America in Korea 1950-1953.* New York: Times Books, 1987.

Blakemore, Erin. "Jim Crow Laws Created 'Slavery by Another Name.'" National Geographic. National Geographic Partners, February 5, 2020. https://www.nationalgeographic.com/history/reference/united-states-history/jim-crow-laws-created-slavery-another-name/#close.

Bowling, Kirby L., Juanita M. Firestone, and Richard J. Harris. "Analyzing Questions That Cannot Be Asked of Respondents Who Cannot Respond." *Armed Forces & Society* 31, no. 3 (April 2005): 411–37. https://journals.sagepub.com/doi/10.1177/0095327X0503100305.

Branch, Taylor. *Parting the Waters: America in the King Years 1954-63.* New York: Simon & Schuster, 1988. 61.

Branum, Don (October 28, 2011) "Academy Experts Discuss Effects of DADT Repeal." US Air Force Academy. October 28, 2011. https://www.usafa.af.mil/News/News-Display/Article/428632/academy-experts-discuss-effects-of-dadt-repeal/ (accessed November 9, 2015).

Brook, Tom V. "Defense Secretary Jim Mattis' New Policy on Transgender Troops Expected by Wednesday." *USA Today.* February 19, 2018. https://www.usatoday.com/story/news/politics/2018/02/19/defense-secretary-jim-mattis-new-policy-transgender-troops-expected-wednesday/352918002/ (accessed November 5, 2016).

Brooks, Rebecca. "British and American Strategies in the Revolutionary War." *History of Massachusetts Blog.* July 28, 2017. https://historyofmassachusetts.org/revolutionary-war-strategies/.

Buckley, Gail. *American Patriots: The Story of Blacks in the Military from the Revolution to Desert Storm.* New York: Random House, 2001.

"Buffalo Soldiers and the Spanish-American War." *National Park Service: Presido of San Francisco.* February 28, 2015. https://www.nps.gov/prsf/learn/historyculture/buffalo-soldiers-and-the-spanish-american-war.htm

Burchard, Hank. "Omar N. Bradley, 'GIs' General,' Is Dead at 88," *The Washington Post.* April 9, 1981. https://www.washingtonpost.com/archive/local/1981/04/09/omar-n-bradley-gis-general-is-dead-at-88/7f187d1a-9867-4cf5-ba93-246f3cd45ad5/.

Butterfield, Roger. *The American Past.* New York: Simon and Schuster, 1957.

Cannon, Carl M. *On This Date: From the Pilgrims to Today, Discovering America One Day at a Time.* New York: Twelve Hatchett Book Group, 2017.

Cashin, Sheryll. *Loving: Interracial Intimacy in America and the Threat to White Supremacy.* Boston: Beacon Press, 2017.

Chandrasekaran, Rajiv. "Gen. John Allen Cleared in Misconduct Inquiry." *Washington Post.* January 22, 2013. https://www.washingtonpost.com/world/national-security/

gen-john-allen-cleared-in-misconduct-inquiry/2013/01/22/479c776a-64dd-11e2-9e1b-07db1d2ccd5b_story.html.
Christensen, Don, and Yelena Tsilker. *Racial Disparities in the Military, Findings of Substantial and Persistent Racial Disparities within the United States Military Justice System* . Alexandria, VA: Protect Our Defenders, May 20, 2017. http://www.protectourdefenders.com/wp-content/uploads/2017/05/Report_20. pdf (accessed July 17, 2018).
Chuck, Elizabeth. "Kristen Griest and Shaye Haver, First Female Army Rangers, Graduate Grueling School." NBC News.com. NBC Universal News Group, August 21, 2015. https://www.nbcnews.com/news/military/history-making-first-female-army-rangers-graduate-n413766 (accessed August 22, 2015).
Chuck, Elizabeth. "Lone Juror Says He Can't Convict Ex-Cop in Walter Scott Killing." *NBC News*. December 5, 2016. https://www.nbcnews.com/news/crime-courts/jury-says-it-s-deadlocked-trial-officer-who-shot-walter-n691291.
Clifford, Clark, M. "The Politics of 1948." Official memorandum to Harry S. Truman. Washington, DC: White House, November 19, 1947. https://www.trumanlibrary.gov/library/research-files/memo-clark-clifford-harry-s-truman (accessed April 9, 2016).
"Col. Charles Young, Leader and Builder." *National Park Service: Sequoia and Kings Canyon*. October 30, 2019. http://www.nps.gov/seki/learn/historyculture/young.htm.
Collins, Gail. *When Everything Changed: The Amazing Journey of American Women from 1960 to the Present*. New York: Little, Brown & Company, 2009.
Collins, Shannon. "WASPs Were Pioneers for Female Pilots of Today, Tomorrow." *U.S. DoD News*. March 2, 2016. https://www.defense.gov/Explore/News/Article/Article/684700/wasps-were-pioneers-for-female-pilots-of-today-tomorrow/ (accessed December 5, 2017).
Condon-Rall, Mary Ellen. *Attack on the Pentagon: The Medical Response to 9/11*. Fort Detrick, MD: Borden Institute, 2011.
"Contagion: Historical Views of Diseases and Epidemics." *Harvard Library*. Accessed April 19, 2015. https://library.harvard.edu/collections/contagion-historical-views-diseases-and-epidemics.
Contempt Toward Individuals. 10 U.S.C. § 888-88 (2011), https://www.govinfo.gov/app/details/USCODE-2011-title10/USCODE-2011-title10-subtitleA-partII-chap47-subchapX-sec888.
Cook, Bernard A. *Women and War: A Historical Encyclopedia from Antiquity to the Present*. Vol. 1. Santa Barbara, CA: ABC-CLIO, 2006. 242.
Cornelsen, Kathleen. "Women Airforce Service Pilots of World War II: Exploring Military Aviation, Encountering Discrimination, and Exchanging Traditional Roles in Service to America." Journal of Women's History 17 (2005): 111-119. https://www.semanticscholar.org/paper/Women-Airforce-Service-Pilots-of-World-War-II%3A-and-Cornelsen/4b9fd1b4cf051b127c3dfff7c51f6d74928eefb9.
Crandell, Carla. "The Effects of Repealing Don't Ask, Don't Tell: Is the Combat Exclusion the Next Casualty in the March Toward Integration?" *Georgetown Journal of Law and Public Policy* 10, no. 1 (2012) http://www.law.georgetown.edu/academics/law-journals/gjlpp/upload/zs800112000015.pdf (accessed March 23, 2018).
"Crispus Attucks." *Biography.com*. January 19, 2018. https://www.biography.com/people/crispus-attucks-9191864.
Cronk, Terry. "Transgender Service Members Can Now Serve Openly, Carter Announces." *U.S. DoD News*. June 30, 2016. https://www.defense.gov/Explore/News/Article/Article/822235/transgender-service-members-can-now-serve-openly-carter-announces/ (accessed February 1, 2016).
Cruikshank, Margaret. "Gay and Lesbian Liberation: An Overview." In *Gays and Lesbians in the Military: Issues, Concerns, and Contrasts*, edited by Wilbur Scott and Sandra Carson Stanley, 3–16. New York: Aldine De Gruyter, 1994.

Cuningham, Henry. "Obama Nominates E.E. Smith Grad for Army Surgeon General." *Fayetteville Observer.* May 5, 2011. http://www./#2/a477ecb2-6a43-5de7-97c3-9e87b8e9afee.html (accessed March 10, 2017).

Dalfiume, Richard M. "The Fahy Committee and Desegregation of the Armed Forces." *The Historian* 31, no. 1 (1968): 1–20. www.jstor.org/stable/24440952.

Davis, Benjamin O. Jr. *Benjamin O. Davis, Jr., American: An Autobi ography.* Washington, D.C.: Smithsonian Books, 1991.

Davis, Mark H., and Stephen L. Franzoi. "Adolescent Loneliness, Self-disclosure, and Private Self-consciousness: A Longitudinal Investigation." Journal of Personality and Social Psychology 51, no. 3 (1986): 595–608. https://doi.org/10.1037/0022-3514.51.3.595.

"Desegregation of the Armed Forces." *Harry S. Truman Library and Museum.* Accessed July 7, 2014. https://www.trumanlibrary.gov/library/online-collections/desegregation-of-armed-forces.

Dickinson, Tim. "It Got Better: Lesbian Couple Share Navy's 'First Kiss.'" *Rolling Stone.* December 22, 2011. https://www.rollingstone.com/politics/politics-news/it-got-better-lesbian-couple-share-navys-first-kiss-244688/ (accessed January 2, 2018).

"Don't Stand Silent When Soldier is Booed." October 1, 2011. MSNBC. http://www.msnbc.msn.com/id/4474458/ns/politics-white_house/t/obama-dont-stand-silent-when-soldier-booed/.

Drescher, Jack. "Out of DSM: Depathologizing Homosexuality." *Behavioral Sciences* 5, no. 4 (December 2005): 565-75. https://www.ncbi.nlm.nih.gov/pmc/articles/PMC4695779/.

DuBois, Ellen Carol and Lynn Dumenil. *Through Women's Eyes: An American History with Documents.* Boston: Bedford St. Martins, 2015.

Ebert, Jean and Marie-Beth Hall. *Crossed Currents: Navy Women from WWI to Tailhook.* Brassey's: Washington, D.C., 1993.

"Edith Nourse Rogers: 1881–1960." *History, Art & Archives: United States House of Representatives.* Office of Art & Archives, June 21, 2018. https://history.house.gov/People/Listing/R/ROGERS,-Edith-Nourse-(R000392)/.

"FDR Signs Public Law 18 that Mandates the Army Air Corps to Train Blacks." *Smithsonian National Air and Space Museum.* 2017. https://pioneersofflight.si.edu/content/fdr-signs-public-law-18-mandates-army-air-corps-train-blacks (accessed June 19, 2018).

"Female POW in Gulf War was Sexually Assaulted." *Washington Post.* June 11, 1992. https://www.washingtonpost.com/archive/politics/1992/06/11/female-pow-in-gulf-war-was-sexually-assaulted/2bacbed7-5279-4126-a772-f1918c6598c2/ (accessed April 12, 2017).

Ferdinando, Lisa. "Carter Announces 12 Weeks Paid Military Maternity Leave, Other Benefits." *U.S. DoD News.* January 28, 2016. https://www.defense.gov/Explore/News/Article/Article/645958/carter-announces-12-weeks-paid-military-maternity-leave-other-benefits/ (accessed January 18, 2018).

Fitzpatrick, Mary Anne. "Marriage and Verbal Intimacy." In *Self-disclosure: Theory, Research, and Therapy,* edited by Valerian J. Derlega and John H. Berg, 131-154. New York: Springer Science and Business Media, 1987.

Fleischman, John. *Black and White Airmen: Their True History.* New York: Houghton Mifflin, 2007.

Fletcher, Marvin. *The Black Soldier and Officer in the United States Army: 1891 –1917.* Columbia, MO: University of Missouri Press, 1974. 178.

Flipper, Henry Ossian. *The Colored Cadet at West Point.* New York: Start Publishing, 2012.

Flipper, Henry Ossian. "The Colored Cadet at West Point. Autobiography of Lieut. Henry Ossian Flipper, U.S.A., First Graduate of Color from the U.S. Military Academy." *The Multiracial Activist.* January 1, 2001. https://multiracial.com/index.php/2001/01/01/the-colored-cadet-at-west-point-autobiography-of-lieut-henry-ossian-flipper/

Francis, Thomas. "On Base, Don't Ask, Don't Tell' Demise is Cause for Celebration." *NBC News*. September 21, 2011. http://www.nbcnews.com/id/44607673/ns/us_news-life/t/base-dont-ask-dont-tell-demise-cause-celebration/#.Xry6MBNKjOQ (accessed Oct 9, 2016).

"Frank Knox." *Naval History and Heritage Command*. June 9, 2015. https://www.history.navy.mil/our-collections/photography/us-people/k/knox-frank.html.

Fuller, Jaime. "Four Presidents are converging on Texas to celebrate the 50th anniversary of the Civil Rights Act." *Washington Post*, April 8, 2014, https://www.washingtonpost.com/news/the-fix/wp/2014/04/08/four-presidents-are-converging-on-texas-to-celebrate-the-50th-anniversary-of-the-civil-rights-act-heres-what-you-need-to-know/.

Furness, Hannah. "Gen John Allen Investigated for 'inappropriate communications' to Jill Kelley." *Telegraph*. November 13, 2012. https://www.telegraph.co.uk/news/worldnews/northamerica/usa/9674163/Gen-John-Allen-Investigated-for-inappropriate-communications-to-Jill-Kelley.html.

Gabrielson, Ryan, Eric Sagara, Ryann Grochoski Jones. "Deadly Force in Black and White." *ProPublica*, October 10, 2014, http://www.propublica.org/article/deadly-force-in-Black-and-white).

Gade, Paul A. "Repealing Don't Ask, Don't Tell: A Brief History." *The Military Psychologist* 27, no. 2 (2012): 21–25. https://www.militarypsych.org/uploads/8/5/4/5/85456500/military_psychologist_27-2.pdf.

Garamone, Jim. "Biden Administration Overturns Transgender Exclusion Policy." *DoD News*. January 25, 2021. https://www.defense.gov/Explore/News/Article/Article/2482048/biden-administration-overturns-transgender-exclusion-policy/ (accessed July 27, 2021).

Gardner, Michael. *Harry Truman and Civil Rights: Moral Courage and Political Risks*. Carbondale, IL: Southern Illinois University Press, 2002, 11–13.

Gates Jr., Henry L. *100 Amazing Facts About the Negro*. New York: Pantheon Books, 2017.

Gatewood, Willard B. "John Hanks Alexander (1864-1894)." *Encyclopedia of Arkansas*, September 18, 2009. https://encyclopediaofarkansas.net/entries/john-hanks-alexander-46/.

"General Janet C. Wolfenbarger." U.S. Air Force. July 1, 2015. https://www.af.mil/About-Us/Biographies/Display/Article/107934/general-janet-c-/ (accessed March 9, 2017).

George, Denise and Robert Child. *The Lost Eleven: The Forgotten Story of Black America Soldiers Brutally Massacred in World War II*. New York: Random House, 2017.

Gero, Anthony. *Black Soldiers of New York State, A Proud Legacy*. Albany, NY: State University of New York Press, 2009.

Geselbracht, Raymond. *The Civil Rights Legacy of Truman*. Kirksville, MO: Truman State University Press, 2007. 156-158.

Glaude, Eddie S. *Democracy in Black: How Race Still Enslaves the American Soul*. New York: Crown, 2017.

Goldstein, Richard. "Charity Adams Earley, Black Pioneer in Wacs, Dies at 83." *NY Times*. January 22, 2002. https://www.nytimes.com/2002/01/22/us/charity-adams-earley-black-pioneer-in-wacs-dies-at-83.html (accessed March 9, 2018).

Goodson, Susan H. *Serving Proudly*. Annapolis, MD: Naval Institute Press, 2001.

Gordon, Lewis R. "A Short History of the 'Critical' in Critical Race Theory." *American Philosophy Association Newsletter* 98, no. 2. https://web.archive.org/web/20030502193950/http://www.apa.udel.edu/apa/archive/newsletters/v98n2/lawblack/gordon.asp (accessed July 27, 2021).

"The Great War: A Nation Comes of Age." *PBS*. Aired July 3, 2018. https://www.pbs.org/wgbh/americanexperience/films/great-war/.

Greenhouse, Linda. "Supreme Court Upholds Law on College Military Recruiting." *New York Times*. March 6, 2006. https://www.nytimes.com/2006/03/06/politics/

supreme-court-upholds-law-on-college-military-recruiting.html (accessed August 13, 2016).

Gumbel, Andrew. "The Great Undoing?" *The Advocate*. June 20, 2009. https://www.advocate.com/news/2009/06/20/great-undoing (accessed July 9, 2012).

Hackett, Thomas. "The Execution of Private Barry Winchell: The Real Story Behind the 'Don't Ask, Don't Tell' Murder." *Rolling Stone*. March 2, 2000. http://www.davidclemens.com/gaymilitary/rolstobarry.htm (accessed February 13, 2016).

Halley, Janet E. *Don't: A Reader's Guide to the Military's Anti-gay Policy*. London: Duke University Press, 1999.

Hammons, Megan. "Is There a Gender Gap in the U.S. Military?" *Veteran Aid*. January 25, 2017. https://www.veteranaid.org/blog/2017/01/25/gender-gap-u-s-military/ (accessed Jan 27, 2018).

Hancock, Joy Bright. *Lady in the Navy*. Annapolis, MD: Naval Institute Press, 1972.

Hawkins, Walter L. *Black American Military Leaders: A Biographical Dictionary*. Jefferson, NC: McFarland and Company, 2007.

Hechler, Kenneth. *Working with Truman: A Personal Memoir of the White House Years*. Columbia, MO: University of Missouri Press, 1996.

Hechler, Kenneth. "Military and Federal Services Integration 60th Anniversary." Speech, August 6, 2008. *C-Span*. National Cable Satellite Corporation, 2016. https://www.c-span.org/video/?280333-1/military-federal-services-integration-60th-anniversary.

Herek, Gregory and Aaron Belkin. "Sexual Orientation and Military Service: Prospects for Organizational and Individual Change in the United States." *Palm Center: Blueprints for Sound Public Policy*. December 1, 2005. https://www.palmcenter.org/publication/sexual-orientation-military-service-prospects-organizational-individual-change-united-states/ (accessed May 11, 2007).

Herek, Gregory M.. "Oral Statement to the House Armed Services Committee." Washington, DC, May 5, 1993. *Sexual Orientation: Science, Education, and Policy*. http://www.lgbpsychology.org/html/miltest2.html (accessed November 11, 2017).

"A History of Women in the U.S. Military." *Infoplease*. February 28, 2017. http://www.infoplease. com/us/military/women-history.html (accessed October 7, 2015).

Historical Section Bureau of Naval Personnel. "The Negro in the Navy: United States Naval Administration History of World War II #84." *Naval History and Heritage Command*. April 24, 2020. https://www.history.navy.mil/research/library/online-reading-room/title-list-alphabetically/n/negro-navy-1947-adminhist84.html.

History.com Editors. "Japanese Internment Camps." *History.com*. October 29, 2009. https://www.history.com/topics/world-war-ii/japanese-american-relocation (accessed March 3, 2016).

History.com Editors. "Reconstruction." *History.com*. October 29, 2009. https://www.history.com/topics/american-civil-war/reconstruction.

History.com Editors. "Sharecropping." *History.com*. June 24, 2010. htt ps://www.history.co m/topics/black-history/sharecropping.

"History of the WAC and Army Women." *Women's Army Corps Veterans'-Army Women United (WACVA-AWU)*. March 19, 2016. https://www.armywomen.org/wacHistory.shtml.

Holland, Frederic M. *Frederick Douglass: The Colored Orator*. New York: Funk and Wagnalls, 1891. 301.

Horsely, Scott. "A Churchill 'Quote' That U.S. Politicians will Never Surrender." NPR. NPR, October 28, 2013. https://www.npr.org/sections/itsallpoliti cs/2013/10/28/241295755/a-churchill-quote-that-u-s-politicians-will-never-surrender.

Hosek, Susan D., Peter Tiemeyer, M. Rebecca Kilburn, Debra A. Strong, Selika Ducksworth, and Reginald Ray. *Minority and Gender Differences in Officer Career Progression*. Santa Monica, CA: RAND Corporation, 2001. https://www.rand.org/pubs/monograph_reports/MR1184.html.

Hulse, Carl. "Senate Repeals Ban Against Openly Gay Military Personnel." *NY Times*. December 18, 2010. https://www.nytimes.com/2010/12/19/us/politics/19cong.html (accessed January 11, 2018).

Iskra, Darlene M. *Women in the United States Armed Forces: A Guide to the Issues*. Santa Barbara, CA: Praeger, 2010.

Jabar, Karem, and Anthony Walton. *Brothers in Arms: The Epic Story of the 761st Tank Battalion, WWII's Forgotten Heroes*. New York: Broadway Books, 2004. 52.

Jackman, Tom. "U.S. Police Chiefs Group Apologizes for 'Historical Mistreatment' of Minorities." *The Washington Post*. October 17, 2016. https://www.washingtonpost.com/news/true-crime/wp/2016/10/17/head-of-u-s-police-chiefs-apologizes-for-historic-mistreatment-of-minorities/.

James, Rawn Jr. *The Double V: How Wars, Protest, and Harry Truman Desegregated America's Military*. New York: Bloomsbury, 2013.

Johnson, Chris. "New Report Undermines Officers' Letter Supporting Don't Ask." *Washington Blade*. March 3 2010. https://www.washingtonblade.com/2010/03/03/new-report-undermines-officers%E2%80%99-letter-supporting-%E2%80%98don%E2%80%99t-ask%E2%80%99/ (accessed March 23, 2018).

Johnson, Jeremy. "'Don't Pursue, Don't Harass' the Other Half of 'Don't Ask, Don't Tell.'" *Palm Center: Blueprints for Sound Public Policy*. May 8, 2010. http://archive.palmcenter.org/press/dadt/in_print/dont_pursue_dont_harass_the_other_half_of_dont_ask_dont_tell (accessed March 28, 2018).

Johnson, Kevin. "Michael Slager, Former South Carolina Cop Who Killed Walter Scott, Pleads Guilty on Civil Rights Charges." USA Today. Gannett Satellite Information Network, May 2, 2017. https://www.usatoday.com/story/news/2017/05/02/ex-sc-cop-plead-guilty-civil-rights-charges/101194668/.

Jordan, William G.. *Black Newspapers and America's War for Democracy: 1914–1920*. Chapel Hill, NC: Chapel Hill Press, 2001.

Kashima, Tetsuden. "Internment Camps." *Encyclopedia of American Studies*, edited by Simon J. Bronner. Baltimore, MD: Johns Hopkins University Press, 2016. https://eas-ref.press.jhu.edu/view?aid=390 (accessed March 29, 2017).

Katz, Friedrich. *The Life and Times of Pancho Villa*. Stanford, CA: Stanford University Press, 1998.

Katz, Johnathan. "Alexander Hamilton and John Laurens: 1777–1783." *Out History*. http://outhistory.org/exhibits/show/hamilton-laurens/hamilton-laurens-letters (accessed January 29, 2018).

Kaur, Harmeet. "Kanye West Just Said 400 Years of Slavery was a Choice." *CNN*. May 4, 2018. https://www.cnn.com/2018/05/01/entertainment/kanye-west-slavery-choice-trnd/index.html (accessed May 5, 2018).

Kazin, Michael. *War Against War: The American Fight for Peace, 1914–1918*. New York: Simon & Schuster, 2017. 95–97.

Kelly, S.H. "Seven WWII vets to receive Medals of Honor." *Army News Service*. January 13,1997. https://history.army.mil/moh/7(AfrAm)WWIIVetsMOH.pdf (accessed January 11, 2016).

Kennicott, Phillip. "Revisiting King's Metaphor About a Nation's Debt." *Washington Post*. August 24, 2011. https://www.washingtonpost.com/lifestyle/style/revisiting-kings-metaphor-about-a-nations-debt/2011/07/26/gIQArshBaJ_story.html (accessed February 1, 2018).

Kettler, Sara. "Harriet Tubman's Service as a Union Spy." *Biography.com*, February 12, 2017. https://www.biography.com/news/harriet-tubman-biography-facts.

King Jr., Martin L. *Where do We Go from Here: Chaos or Community?* Boston: Beacon Press, 2010.

Kitchen, Martin. " The Ending of World War One, and the Legacy of Peace." *BBC*. February 17, 2011. http://www.bbc.co.uk/history/worldwars/wwone/war_end_01.shtml (accessed April 12, 2016).

Korb, Lawrence J., Sean Duggan, and Laura Conley. "Implementing the Repeal of Don't Ask, Don't Tell in the U. S. Armed Forces." *Center for American Progress*. March 23, 2010. https://www.americanprogress.org/issues/security/reports/2010/03/23/7502/implementing-the-repeal-of-dont-ask-dont-tell-in-the-u-s-armed-forces/ (accessed March 23, 2018).

Lamura, Linda. *Nisei Soldiers Break Their Silence: Coming Home to Hood River*. Seattle: University of Washington Press, 2012.

Lang, John. "Albuquerque Woman to Command Navy Fighting Ship." *Albuquerque Times* (Albuquerque, NM), March 25, 1998.

Lee, Ulysses. *The United States Army in World War II: The Employment of Negro Troops*. United States Center of Military History. Washington, DC: Government Printing Office, 1963.

Lentz-Smith, Adreane D. *Freedom Struggles African Americans and World War I*. Cambridge, MA: Harvard University Press, 2009.

Lewin, Tamar. "Black Students Face More Discipline, Data Suggests." *New York Times*. March 6, 2012. http://www.nytimes.com/2012/03/06/education/black-students-face-more-harsh-discipline-data-shows.html?_r=0Lyfe, L. (2012).

Lieker, James N. *Racial Borders Black Soldiers Along the Rio Grande*. College Station, TX: Texas A&M University Press, 2002, 91.

"Lieutenant Henry O. Flipper." *Mobeetie Jail Museum*. Accessed September 5, 2015. http://www.mobeetie.com/pages/flipper.htm.

Loft, Sarah and Dunbar, Brian. 2017. "Katherine Johnson Biography." *NASA*. Accessed October 2017. https://www.nasa.gov/content/katherine-johnson-biography.

Lopez, Todd. "First Female Four-star General Retires from Army." *U.S. Army*. August 16, 2012. https://www.army.mil/article/85606/First_female_four_star_general_retires_from_Army/ (accessed March 9, 2017).

Lowry, Brian. "The Strange History of Don't Ask, Don't Tell." *Variety*, September 18, 2011. http://www.variety.com/review/VE1117946143 (accessed January 3, 2016).

Lutz, Amy. "Who joins the military? A look at Race, Class, and Immigration Status." Journal of Political and Military Sociology 36, no. 2 (2008): 167–188.

Lyfe, Ise. "Kicking Black Boys out of Class, Teaching Black Girls a Lesson." September 19, 2012. HuffPost. https://www.huffpost.com/entry/kicking-black-boys-out-of_b_1894719.

MacGregor, Morris J. *Integration of the Armed Forces, 1940-1965*. Washington, DC: Government Printing Office, 1981.

Maksel, Rebecca. "The Roald Dahl Aviation Story that Disney Refused to Film." *Air & Space Magazine*, May 22, 2014. https://www.airspacemag.com/daily-planet/fifinella-mischievous-gremlin-180951401/.

Mann, Judy. "The Woman Who Said 'No' to the Navy." *Washington Post*. February 5, 1993. https://www.washingtonpost.com/archive/local/1993/02/05/the-woman-who-said-no-to-the-navy/7a2f5549-ea8d-41e9-8862-be98ef660bbb/ (accessed April 29, 2017).

Marinucci, Carla. "Romney defends general, don't ask, don't tell policy." *SF Gate*. March 17, 2007. https://www.sfgate.com/politics/article/CAMPAIGN-TRAIL-Romney-defends-general-don-t-2569666.php.

Marszalek, John. *Assault at West Point, The Court Martial of Johnson Whitaker*. New York: Atheneum Books for Young Readers, 1984.

"Mary Edwards Walker: The Only Woman to Receive the Medal of Honor." *NBC News*. May 21, 2014. https://www.nbcnews.com/news/military/mary-edwards-walker-only-woman-receive-medal-honor-n111596 (accessed March 5, 2018).

Mattis, Jim. "Accession of Transgender Individuals into the Military Services." Memorandum for Secretaries of the Military Departments Chairman of the Joint Chiefs of Staff. Washington, DC: DoD, June 30, 2017. http://lc.org/070517TGDODmemo30JUNE2017.pdf, (accessed Jun 19, 2016).

Mattis, Jim. "Military Service by Transgender Individuals." Memorandum for the President. Washington, DC: DoD, February 22, 2018. https://media.defense.gov/

2018/Mar/23/2001894037/-1/-1/0/MILITARY-SERVICE-BY-TRANSGENDER-INDIVIDUALS.PDF.

McGregor, Jena. "Maternity Leave is not Getting Longer, and Number of Women Taking it has Barely Budged." *Washington Post*. March 14, 2017. https://www.washingtonpost.com/news/on-leadership/wp/2017/03/14/the-length-of-maternity-leave-has-barely-budged-and-neither-has-the-number-of-women-taking-it/.

McGuire, Phillip. *He, Too, Spoke for Democracy: Judge Hastie, World War II, and the Black Soldier*. Westport, CT: Greenwood Press, 1988, 10.

McKissack, Pat, and Frederick McKissack. *Red-tail Angels: The Story of the Tuskegee Airmen of World War II*. London: Walker Childrens, 1995, 34–35.

McShane, Larry. "U.S. General Demoted Over 'extravagant trips.'" *New York Daily News*. November 13, 2012. https://www.nydailynews.com/news/national/general-demoted-extravagant-trips-article-1.1201284.

Memmott, Mark. "Boos Heard at GOP Debate After Gay Soldier Asks About 'Don't Ask.'" *NPR*. September 23, 2011. https://www.npr.org/sections/thetwo-way/2011/09/23/140732553/boos-heard-at-gop-debate-after-gay-soldier-asks-about-dont-ask.

Meyer, Leisa D. *Creating G.I. Jane: Sexuality and Power in the Women's Army Corps During World War II*. New York: Columbia University Press, 1998.

Michaels, Jim. "Emerging from history: Massacre of 11 Black Soldiers." *USA Today*. November 8, 2013. https://www.usatoday.com/story/news/nation/2013/11/07/wereth-black-soldiers-battle-of-bulge-army-world-war-ii-history/3465059/ (accessed March 18, 2016).

Michaels, Jim. "ROTC Welcomed Back at Ivy League Schools." *USA Today*. May 23, 2016. https://www.usatoday.com/story/news/2016/05/23/rotc-welcomed-back-ivy-league-schools/32622771/ (accessed May 12, 2018).

Mieder, Wolfgang. *"Making a Way Out of No Way": Martin Luther King's Sermonic Proverbial Rhetoric*. New York: Peter Lang Publishing, 2010.

Miller, Zeke J., "President Trump has Taken a Key Step to Implement his Transgender Military Ban." *Time*. August 25, 2017. https://time.com/4916871/donald-trump-transgender-military-ban/ (accessed May 2, 2018).

"Milestones: Understanding the History of Women's Representation Helps to Inform our Work for Gender Parity." *Represent Women: Parity for Women in Politics*. March 17, 2017. https://www.representwomen.org/women_history.

Mintz, S., and S. McNeil. "The Espionage and Sedition Acts." *Digital History*. Accessed June 7, 2016. http://www.digitalhistory.uh.edu/disp_textbook.cfm?smtID=2&psid=3479.

Muldoon, Caitlin V.. "Honor, Courage, Commitment: Understanding Sexual Assault in the United States Navy." PhD diss., Old Dominion University, 2015.

Myers, Steven Lee. "Officers Riled by Policy on Gays Proposed in Gore-Bradley Debate." *New York Times*. January 7, 2000. https://www.nytimes.com/2000/01/07/us/officers-riled-by-policy-on-gays-proposed-in-gore-bradley-debate.html.

Nalty, Bernard C. *Strength for the Fight*. New York: Free Press, 1986.

Nalty, Bernard C. *The Right to Fight: African American Marines in World War II*. Marines. 2002. https://www.marines.mil/Portals/1/Publications/The%20Right%20to%20Fight%20African-American%20Marines%20in%20World%20War%20II%20PCN%2019000313200_1.pdf.

Neel, Joel. "You, Me and Them: Experiencing Discrimination in America. Poll: Most Americans Think Their Own Group Faces Discrimination." *NPR*. October 24, 2017. https://www.npr.org/sections/health-shots/2017/10/24/559116373/poll-most-americans-think-their-own-group-faces-discrimination.

"Negro Revealed as 'Messman Hero' at Pearl Harbor." *Pittsburgh Courier*. March 12, 1942. https://www.newspapers.com/clip/7598595/oakland_tribune/ (accessed February 8, 2016).

Nesbit, Jeff. "America, Racial Bias Does Exist." *U.S. News and World Report*, January 13, 2015, https://www.usnews.com/news/blogs/at-the-edge/2015/01/13/america-racial-bias-does-exist.

Noble, Andrea. "Federal Judge Defies Trump Admin, Removes Pentagon Block on Funds for Gender Reassignment." *Washington Times*. November 21, 2017. https://www.washingtontimes.com/news/2017/nov/21/judge-removes-block-funds-gender-reassignment/ (accessed December 1, 2017).

Obama, Barack. "State of the Union Address." Speech, January 27, 2010. *New York Times*, 2010. https://www.nytimes.com/2010/01/28/us/politics/28obama.text.html.

Ortiz, Aimee. "Nikki Haley's Confederate Flag Comments Spark Backlash." *New York Times*. December 7, 2019. https://www.nytimes.com/2019/12/07/us/Nikki-Haley-confederate-flag.html.

Pearson, Patricia, A. "John Hanks Alexander 1864-1894." *Encyclopedia.com*. April 20, 2020. https://www.encyclopedia.com/african-american-focus/news-wires-white-papers-and-books/alexander-john-hanks.

Plante, Trevor K. "Ending the Bloodshed: The Last Surrenders of the Civil War." *Prologue Magazine*. 47, no. 1 (Spring 2015), https://www.archives.gov/publications/prologue/2015/spring/cw-surrenders.html (accessed June 13, 2018).

Policy Concerning Homosexuality in the Armed Forces. 10 U.S.C. § 654 (2011), https://www.govinfo.gov/app/details/USCODE-2010-title10/USCODE-2010-title10-subtitleA-partII-chap37-sec654/summary.

"Post Locations." US Army. November 28, 2016. https://www.goarmy.com/about/post-locations.html (accessed June 21, 2018).

President's Committee on Civil Rights. *To Secure These Rights: The Report of the President's Committee on Civil Rights*. Internet Archive. New York: Simon and Schuster: 1947. https://archive.org/details/tosecuretheserig00unit.

"Public Law 111–40—July 1, 2009: Women Airforce Service Pilots Congressional Gold Medal." *Congress.gov*. Accessed January 25, 2018. https://www.congress.gov/111/plaws/publ40/PLAW-111publ40.pdf.

Queen, Howard and Mary Penick-Motley. *The Invisible Soldier: The Experience of the Black Soldier, World War II*. Detroit: Wayne State University Press, 1987.

"Randy Philips, Gay Airman, Comes Out to Mom on YouTube." *The Huffington Post*. September 29, 2011. https://www.huffpost.com/entry/airman-comes-out-to-mother_n_988047 (accessed Feb 7, 2017).

Rasmussen, Frederick. "Lt. Cmdr. Wesley A. Brown, Broke Color Barrier at Naval Academy." *Baltimore Sun*. May 24, 2012. http://www.baltimoresun.com/news/obituaries/bs-md-ob-wesley-brown-20120524-story.html (accessed June 11, 2016).

Red Tails: The Real Story of the Tuskegee Airmen. 2012; Pittsburgh, PA: WQED, 2012. DVD.

Richard Slotkin, *Lost Battalions: The Great War and the Crisis of American Nationality*, New York: Holt, 2005.

Robles, Frances, Richard Fausset, and Michael Barbaro. "Nicky Haley, South Carolina Governor, Calls for Removal of Confederate Battle Flag." *New York Times*. June 22, 2015. https://www.nytimes.com/2015/06/23/us/south-carolina-confederate-flag-dylann-roof.html.

Rosenblatt, Kalhan and Corky Siemaszko. "Confederate Flag Raised at South Carolina Statehouse in Protest by Secessionist Party." *NBC News*. July 10, 2017. https://www.nbcnews.com/news/us-news/confederate-flag-rises-south-carolina-statehouse-protest-secessionist-party-n781331 (accessed July 12, 2017).

Rostker, Bernard D., Scott A. Harris, James P. Kahan, Erik J. Frinking, C. Neil Fulcher, Lawrence M. Hanser, Paul Koegel, et al.. *Sexual Orientation and U.S. Military Personnel Policy: Options and Assessment*. Santa Monica, CA: RAND Corporation, 1993. https://www.rand.org/pubs/monograph_reports/MR323.html.

Roulo, Claudette. "Defense Department Expands Women's Combat Role." *U.S. DoD News*. January 24, 2013. https://archive.defense.gov/news/newsarticle.aspx?id=119098 (accessed February 01, 2016).

"Rutherford B. Hayes." n.d. *The White House.* Accessed April 7, 2017. https://www.whitehouse.gov/about-the-white-house/presidents/rutherford-b-hayes/.

Scarborough, Rowan. "Obama to Delay Repeal of Don't Ask Don't Tell." *Washington Times.* November 21, 2008. https://www.washingtontimes.com/news/2008/nov/21/obama-to-delay-repeal-of-dont-ask-dont-tell/ (accessed March 28, 2017).

Schaefer, Agnes Gereben, Radha Iyengar Plumb, Srikanth Kadiyala, Jennifer Kavanagh, Charles C. Engel, Kayla M. Williams, and Amii M. Kress. *Assessing the Implications of Allowing Transgender Personnel to Serve Openly.* Santa Monica, CA: RAND Corporation, 2016. https://www.rand.org/pubs/research_reports/RR1530.html.

Schirmer, Peter, Harry J. Thie, Margaret C. Harrell, and Michael S. Tseng. *Challenging Time in DOPMA: Flexible and Contemporary Military Officer Management.* Santa Monica, CA: RAND Corporation, 2006. https://www.rand.org/pubs/monographs/MG451.html.

Schleifer, Theodore. "Petraeus Sentenced: Two Years Probation; $100,000 Fine." CNN. April 23, 2015. http://www.cnncom/2015/04/23/politics/david-petraeus-sentencing/index.html.

Schneller, Robert J. Jr. *Breaking the Color Barrier: The U.S. Navy Academy's First Black Midshipmen and the Struggle for Racial Equality.* New York: NYU Press, 2005.

Schudel, Matt. "Anthony Acevedo, U.S. Army Medic who Endured Prison-Camp Horrors During WWII, dies at 93." *The Washington Post.* March 11, 2018. https://www.washingtonpost.com/local/obituaries/anthony-acevedo-us-army-medic-who-endured-prison-camp-horrors-in-wwii-dies-at-93/2018/03/10/ac2273f0-23e2-11e8-86f6-54bfff693d2b_story.html.

Scott, Emmett. *Scott's Official History of the American Negro in the World War.* Chicago: Homewood Press, 1919.

Shalikashvili, John M.. "Second Thoughts on Gays in the Military." *New York Times.* January 2, 2007. https://www.nytimes.com/2007/01/02/opinion/02shalikashvili.html

Shanker, Tom and Patrick Healy. "A New Push to Roll Back Don't Ask, Don't Tell." *New York Times.* November 30, 2007. https://www.nytimes.com/2007/11/30/us/30military.html.

Shaw, Henry. *Blacks in the Marine Corps.* Collegeville, MN: St. Johns Press, 2018.

Shellum, Brian G. *Black Cadet in a White Bastion: Charles Young at West Point.* Lincoln, NE: University of Nebraska Press, 2006.

Shellum, Brian G. *Black Officer in a Buffalo Soldier Regiment: The Military Career of Charles Young.* Lincoln, NE: University of Nebraska Press, 2010.

Shenon, Philip. "Sailor Victorious in Gay Case of On-Line Privacy." *New York Times.* June 12, 1998. https://www.nytimes.com/1998/06/12/us/sailor-victorious-in-gay-case-of-on-line-privacy.html (accessed October 5, 2017).

Shilts, Randy. *Conduct Unbecoming: Lesbians and Gays in the Military.* New York: St. Martin's Press, 1993.

Shuster, Kate. *Teaching Hard History: American Slavery.* Montgomery, AL: Southern Poverty Law Center, January 31, 2018. https://www.splcenter.org/20180131/teaching-hard-history (accessed May 12, 2018).

Simon, Scott. "Research Finds Racial Disparities in Prison Sentences." *NPR.* November 25, 2017. https://www.npr.org/2017/11/25/566438860/research-finds-racial-disparities-in-prison-sentences.

Simpson, Ian. "U.S. Hate Groups Proliferate in Trump's First Year, Watchdog Says." *Reuters.* February 21, 2018. https://www.reuters.com/article/us-usa-trump-hate-groups/u-s-hate-groups-proliferate-in-trumps-first-year-watchdog-says-idUSKCN1G5286.

Sinclair, G. Dean. "Homosexuality and the Military: A Review of the Literature." *Journal of Homosexuality* 56, no. 6 (2009): 701–718. https://www.tandfonline.com/doi/full/10.1080/00918360903054137.

Southerland, Jonathon. *African Americans at War: An Encyclopedia.* Vol. 1. Santa Barbra, CA: ABC-CLIO Press, 2004.

Sporkin, Stanley. "McVeigh v. Cohen, 983 F. Supp. 215 (D.D.C. 1998)." Memorandum Opinion. Justia US Law. January 26, 1998. https://law.justia.com/cases/federal/district-courts/FSupp/983/215/1989052/ (accessed October 13, 2017).

Stanley, Clifford. "Repeal of Don't Ask Don't Tell and Future Impact on Policy." Memorandum for Secretaries of the Military Departments. Washington, DC: DoD, January 28, 2011. https://archive.defense.gov/home/features/2010/0610_dadt/USD-PR-DADT_28Jan11.pdf

Starr, Barbara and Daniella Diaz. "Pentagon: Confederate Base Names Won't be Changed. *CNN*. July 9, 2015. https://www.cnn.com/2015/06/24/politics/confederate-army-bases-names/index.html (accessed July 10, 2015).

Stentiford, Barry M. *Landmarks of the American Mosaic: Tuskegee Airmen*. Santa Barbara, CA: Greenwood, 2012.

Sterner, Douglas C. *Go for Broke: The Nisei Warriors of World War II Who Conquered Germany*. Clearfield, UT: American Legacy Historical Press, 2007.

Stewart, Richard W., ed.. "Peace Becomes Cold War," in *American Military History*. 2nd ed., Vol. 2, *The United States Army in a Global Era, 1917–2008*, 203–220. Washington, D.C.: Government Printing Office, 2010.

Stillwell, Paul. *The Golden Thirteen: Recollections of the First Black Naval Officers*. Annapolis, MD: Naval Institute Press, 1993.

Stone, Geoffrey R.. *Perilous Times: Free Speech in Wartime from the Sedition Act of 1798 to the War on Terrorism*. New York: Norton, 2004. 541.

"A Story of Honor and Continuous Innovation." U.S. Air Force Academy. Accessed June 21, 2018. https://www.usafa.edu/about/history/.

Taylor, Jon E.. *Freedom to Serve: Truman, Civil Rights, and Executive Order 9981*. New York: Routledge, 2012.

Taylor, William A.. *Every Citizen a Soldier,* College Station, TX : Texas A&M University Press, 2014.

Terman, Sharon. *The Practical and Conceptual Problems with Regulating Harassment in a Discriminatory Institution*. Santa Barbara, CA: UC Santa Barbara Center for the Study of Sexual Minorities in the Military, May 2004. https://escholarship.org/uc/item/5n9649fm#main.

Thomas, Rachel, Marianne Cooper, Ellen Konar, Magan Rooney, Ashley Finch, Lareina Yee, Alexis Krivkovich, et al.. *Women in the Work Place Study 2017*. New York: McKinsey & Company, 2017.

Tiepe, Emily J.. "Will the Real Molly Pitcher Please Stand Up?" *Prologue Magazine* 31, no. 2 (Summer 1999). Accessed June 21, 2018. https://www.archives.gov/publications/prologue/1999/summer/pitcher.html.

"Time Line: Women in the U.S. Military." *Colonial Williamsburg Foundation*. 2008. http://www.history.org/History/teaching/enewsletter/volume7/images/nov/women_military_timeline.pdf (accessed January 30, 2017).

"Timeline: A history of don't ask, don't tell." *Washington Post*. November 30, 2010. https://www.washingtonpost.com/wp-srv/special/politics/dont-ask-dont-tell-timeline/ (accessed Jan 26, 2018).

Tolleson, Maria. "Maj. Gen. Nadja West Confirmed as 44th Army Surgeon General." *U.S. Army*. December 11, 2015. https://www.army.mil/article/159884/maj_gen_nadja_west_confirmed_as_44th_army_surgeon_general (accessed March 29, 2017).

Treadwell, Mattie E.. *United States Army in World War II: Special Studies, The Women's Army Corps*. United States Army Center of Military History. Washington, DC: Government Printing Office, 1991. https://history.army.mil/books/wwii/Wac/index.htm

Trickey, Erick. "World War I: 100 Years Later: One Hundred Years Ago, the Harlem Hellfighters Bravely Led the U.S. into WWI." *Smithsonian Magazine*. May 14, 2018. https://www.smithsonianmag.com/history/one-hundred-years-ago-harlem-hellfighters-bravely-led-us-wwi-180968977/ (accessed May 27, 2016).

Truman, Harry S.. "On the State of the Union." Speech, Washington, DC, January 6, 1947. History, Art & Archives: United States House of Representatives. National Archives. https://history.house.gov/Media?mediaID=15032450453

Trump, Donald. "Military Service by Transgender Individuals." Memorandum for the Secretary of Defense and the Secretary of Homeland Security. Washington, DC: White House, March 23, 2018. https://www.whitehouse.gov/presidential-actions/presidential-memorandum-secretary-defense-secretary-homeland-security-regarding-military-service-transgender-individuals/.

Trump, Donald. "Military Service by Transgender Individuals." Memorandum for the Secretary of Defense and the Secretary of Homeland Defense. Washington, DC: White House, August 25, 2017. https://www.whitehouse.gov/presidential-actions/presidential-memorandum-secretary-defense-secretary-homeland-security/ (accessed May 23, 2017).

Turner, Natasha. "10 Things that American Women Could not do Before the 1970s." *Ms. Magazine*. May 28, 2018. https://msmagazine.com/2013/05/28/10-things-that-american-women-could-not-do-before-the-1970s/ (accessed February 9, 2016).

"Tweets on Transgender Military Servicemembers." *Harvard Law Review* 131, no. 3 (2018): 934-943. https://harvardlawreview.org/2018/01/tweets-on-transgender-military-servicemembers/.

US Department of Defense, Military Leadership and Diversity Commission. *From Representation to Inclusion: Diversity Leadership for the 21st Century Military, Final Report*. Washington, DC: DoD, 2011. Pdf, https://diversity.defense.gov/Portals/51/Documents/Special%20Feature/MLDC_Final_Report.pdf (2015).

US Department of Defense, Office of the Deputy Assistant Secretary of Defense for Military Community and Family Policy. *2015 Demographics: Profile of the Military Community*. Washington, DC: DoD, 2015. Pdf, https://download.militaryonesource.mil/12038/MOS/Reports/2015-Demographics-Report.pdf (2016).

US Department of Defense, Office of the Deputy Assistant Secretary of Defense for Equal Opportunity and Safety Policy. *Black Americans in Defense of Our Nation*. Washington, DC: DoD, 1985. 25.

US Department of Defense. "Department of Defense Press Briefing by Secretary Carter." Transcript, Pentagon Briefing Room, Washington, DC, December 3, 2015. https://www.defense.gov/Newsroom/Transcripts/Transcript/Article/632578/department-of-defense-press-briefing-by-secretary-carter-in-the-pentagon-briefing/ (accessed July 7, 2016).

US Department of Defense. "Mission and History." *Sexual Assault Prevention and Response*. Accessed April 11, 2017. https://www.sapr.mil/mission-history.

US Department of Defense. *Annual Report on Sexual Assault in the Military: Fiscal Year 2017*. Washington, DC: DoD, May 4, 2018. https://sapr.mil/public/docs/reports/FY17_Annual/DoD_FY17_Annual_Report_on_Sexual_Assault_in_the_Military.pdf.

US Department of Defense. *Department of Defense Instruction 1332.14: Enlisted Administrative Separations*. Washington, DC: DoD, 1993. Pdf, https://archive.defense.gov/news/DoDI%201332%2014%20-%20REVISIONS%20032510.pdf.

US Department of Defense. *Diversity and Inclusion Strategic Plan: 2012-2017*. Washington, DC: DoD, 2012. Pdf, https://diversity.defense.gov/Portals/51/Documents/DoD_Diversity_Strategic_Plan_%20final_as%20of%2019%20Apr%2012%5B1%5D.pdf.

US Department of Defense. *Summary of the 2018 National Defense Strategy of the United States of America: Sharpening the American Military's Competitive Edge*. Washington, DC: DoD, 2018. Pdf, https://dod.defense.gov/Portals/1/Documents/pubs/2018-National-Defense-Strategy-Summary.pdf (accessed January 22, 2018).

US General Accounting Office. *Homosexuality in the Military: Policies and Practices of Foreign Countries*. Washington, DC: GAO, June 1993. Pdf, http://archive.gao.gov/t2pbat5/149440.pdf.

US Government Accountability Office. *K-12 Education: Discipline Disparities for Black Students, Boys, and Students with Disabilities*. Report to Congressional Requesters.

Washington, DC: GAO, March 22, 2018. https://www.gao.gov/assets/700/690828.pdf.

"U.S. Navy Biography: Admiral Michelle Howard." *America's Navy: Forged by the Sea.* U.S. Navy, December 1, 2017. http://www.navy.mil/navydata/bios/navybio_ret.asp?bioID=394, (accessed March 9, 2017).

Vander Schaaf, Derek J.. "Report of Investigation: Tailhook 91-Part 2, Events of the 35th Annual Tailhook Symposium." Official memorandum for Secretary of Defense. Arlington, VA: Department of Defense, April 12, 1993. https://apps.dtic.mil/dtic/tr/fulltext/u2/a269008.pdf (accessed April 9, 2018).

Waller, Nikki. "How Men and Women See the Workplace Differently." *The Wallstreet Journal.* September 27, 2016. http://graphics/wsj.com/how-men-and-women-see-the-workplace-differently/ (accessed December 20, 2017).

Warren, C.J. Earl. Brown v. Board of Education of Topeka, 347 U.S. 483 (1954).

Webb, James. "Women Can't Fight." *The Washingtonian.* November 1, 1979. https://www.washingtonian.com/1979/11/01/jim-webb-women-cant-fight/ (accessed January 12, 2018).

White House. *National Security Strategy.* Washington, DC: White House, February 2015. Pdf, https://obamawhitehouse.archives.gov/sites/default/files/docs/2015_national_security_strategy_2.pdf.

White, Gillian B. "There are Currently 4 Black CEOs in the Fortune 500." *The Atlantic.* Oct 26, 2017. https://www.theatlantic.com/business/archive/2017/10/black-ceos-fortune-500/543960/.

Whitlock, Craig. "Jill Kelley E-mails Depict a Striving Tampa Socialite and a Smitten Military Brass." *Washington Post.* February 3, 2015. https://www.washingtonpost.com/world/national-security/jill-kelley-e-mails-depict-a-striving-tampa-socialite-and-a-smitten-military-brass/2015/02/03/ef8cb06c-a800-11e4-a06b-9df2002b86a0_story.html.

Wiedman, Budge. " Black Soldiers in the Civil War: Preserving the Legacy of the United States Colored Troops." *U.S. National Archives and Records Administration,* March 19, 2019. https://www.archives.gov/education/lessons/blacks-civil-war/article.html.

Wilford, Melissa K. "Army Celebrates Service of Women Soldiers." U.S. Army. October 20, 2008. https://www.army.mil/article/13428/army_celebrates_service_of_women_soldiers (accessed June 21, 2018).

Williams, Yohuru. "Great Migration." History.com. A&E Television Networks, retrieved May 5, 2016. https://www.history.com/topics/black-history/great-migration-video.

Willon, Phil. "Judge Declares U.S. Military's Don't Ask, Don't Tell Police Openly Banning Gay Service Members Unconstitutional." *LA Times.* September 10, 2010. https://latimesblogs.latimes.com/lanow/2010/09/federal-judge-declares-us-military-ban-on-openly-gay-service-members-unconstitutional-.html (accessed March 3, 2018).

Wilson, Woodrow. "Third Annual Message to Congress." Speech, Washington, DC, December 7, 1915. *The American Presidency Project.* UC Santa Barbara. Accessed April 17, 2016. https://www.presidency.ucsb.edu/documents/third-annual-message-19.

Winerip, Michael. "Revisiting the Military's Tailhook Scandal." *New York Times.* May 13, 2013. https://www.nytimes.com/2013/05/13/booming/revisiting-the-militarys-tailhook-scandal-video.html (accessed March 30, 2018).

"Women in the Army." *U.S. Army Heritage and Education Center.* U.S. Army, September 8, 2017. https://www.army. mil/women/history/.

Wroughton, Lesley and Sandra Maler. "Time to Review Policy on Gays in the U.S. Military: Powell." *Reuters.* July 5, 2009. https://www.reuters.com/article/us-usa-miltary-gays/time-to-review-policy-on-gays-in-u-s-military-powell-idUSTRE5641A920090705.

"The Woman Suffrage Timeline." Library of Congress. Accessed January 8, 2014. http://www.thlizbrary.org/suffrage/.
Yarrison, James L. "The U.S. Army in the Root Reform Era, 1899–1917." *U.S. Army Center of Military History*. May 3, 2001. https://history.army.mil/documents/1901/Root-Ovr.htm.
Zarya, Valentina. "The 2017 Fortune 500 Includes a Record Number of Women CEOs." *Fortune Magazine*. June 7, 2017. https://fortune.com/2017/06/07/fortune-women-ceos.
Zogby, John, John Bruce, Rebecca Wittman, Sam Rodgers, Zogby International. "Opinions of Military Personnel on Sexual Minorities in the Military." *Palm Center: Blueprints for Sound Public Policy*. December 1, 2006. https://www.palmcenter.org/publication/opinions-military-personnel-sexual-minorities-military/.
Zweigenhaft, Richard L. and William Domhoff. *The New CEOs: Women, African American, Latino, and Asian Leaders of Fortune 500 Companies*. Lanham, MD: Rowman & Littlefield, 2014.

Index

Acevedo, Anthony, 125–127
achievement gap, 207
Adams, Charity, 136
Adkins, Bill, 74
AEF. *See* Army Expeditionary Force
AGCT. *See* Army General Classification Test
Air Force Academy, U.S., 171; sexual abuse in, 153; women in, 144, 144–146, 147
Alexander, John Hanks, 53; 9th Cavalry command, 53–54; as university professor, 54; at West Point, 50, 52–53
Alexander, Sadie Tanner, 26
Allen, John, 192, 194–195
Allison, Marene, 145–146
Almond, Edward, 93, 125; 92nd Infantry led by, 92, 122, 124; racist views of, 122–123, 124
American exceptionalism, 197
American Revolution, 4; blacks in, 46–47, 48; Boston Massacre, 21; homosexuals in, 159–160; women in, 133–134
The American Negro in World War I (Scott, E. J.), 77
Arbor, Jesse W., 111
Army, U.S.: confederate names for bases, 12–13, 38; court martial rates, 191; integration plans, 36–37; Officer's Advanced Course, 1; promotion rates, 185; racial policy examination, 121; renaming Confederate bases, 203–205; segregation as management policy, 36; slow to integrate, 60. *See also specific Army regiments*
Army Air Corps, 36, 87, 100, 102, 104, 105. *See also* Tuskegee Airmen

Army Air Force, 103, 104, 112, 113, 120, 139; court martial rates, 191
Army Expeditionary Force (AEF), 66, 71
Army General Classification Test (AGCT), 90–91, 92, 119
Arnold, Hap, 139–140
Asian Americans, 185
Askew, Simone, 207
Attucks, Crispus, 21, 46
Austin, Lloyd, 198
awakening moment, 13–14, 16, 17

Back to Africa Movement, 79
Baker, Edward L., Jr., 58
Baker, Henry Edwin, 110–111
Baker, Newton D., 66–67
Baker, Vernon, 93
Baltimore, Charles, 68
Barnes, Phillip G., 111
Barnes, Samuel E., 111
Bates, Paul L., 96
Battle of Séchault, 73, 74
Baugh, Dalton L., 111
Berger, David, 12
Bethune, Mary McLeod, 136
Bible Belt, 162
Biden, Joe, 192
Biemiller Plank, 32
Bilbo, Theodore G., 23
black codes, 12, 64
black freedmen, 47
Black Lives Matter (BLM), 25, 79, 82; founding of, 4
blackness, 16
Black Panthers. *See* 761st Tank Battalion; Tuskegee Airmen
Black Power Movement, 79
blacks: achievement gap among, 207; in American Revolution, 46–47, 48;

231

CEOs, 185–186; in Civil War, 48; current link to slavery, 207; marginalization of, 140; military training of, 63; at Panama Canal, 58; in Spanish-American War, 56–58; student suspension and expulsion rates, 195; at West Point, 50–56; in World War I, 64–70
Blair, Clay, 122, 123
BLM. *See* Black Lives Matter
Blue Helmet Division. *See* 93rd Infantry
Boston Massacre, 21, 46
Bouldin, G. W., 69
Bradley, Bill, 166
Bradley, Omar, 118, 121–122; on desegregation, 35; Joint Chiefs of Staff chairman, 35
brass ceiling, 147
Brito, Gary, 207
Broadwell, Paula, 193–194, 195
Brown, Charles Q., 182
Brown, Roscoe C., 106
Brown, Wesley A., 111
Brown vs. Board of Education of Topeka, 3, 18
Buffalo Soldiers (Rough and Ready Regulars), 50, 57–58, 83n35; in Indian Campaigns, 49–50; Pershing with, 66
Bullard, Eugene, 104
Bush, George H. W., 151
Bush, George W., 166

call and response, 26–27
Cammermeyer, Grethe, 164
Campbell, William, 106
Carr, Robert K., 29
Carroll, Henry, 49–50
Carter, Ashton, 151, 172, 172–173
Carter, Jimmy, 94, 121, 201
Cashin, Sheryll, 208
Chamberlain, Edwin W., 91–92
Charlottesville, Virginia, 18, 181
Chenault, Kenneth, 185
Chung, Margaret (Mom Chung), 137–138
Civilian Pilot Training Program (CPTP), 103

Civil Liberties Act (1988), 95
civil rights: American Civil Rights Movement, 6, 7; choosing sides in, 188; Civil Rights Committee, 26–29, 31; FDR as advocate, 29; as human rights, 3; legislation for, 189–190; Truman platform, 6, 7–8; Truman proposal, 31–35
Civil Rights Act (1964), 3; challenges to, 14; defiance of, 38; passage of, 18; Republican Party and, 38; stage set for, 34
Civil Rights Act (1968), 41
Civil War, U.S., 4, 66; black codes enacted after, 12; blacks in, 48; Civil War Amendments, 208; end of, 5; women in, 134
Clark, Tom, 25
Clinton, Bill, 52, 93; awards from, 96–97, 113; lifting ban on gays, 161–162; One America Initiative, 95; open service proposal, 163; promotions by, 106
Clinton, Hillary, 19
Coast Guard: promotion rates, 184, 189; training black recruits, 109; transgender members and, 173; women's auxiliary, 135, 140
Cochran, Jacqueline ("Jackie"), 139, 140
Cold War, 123; Truman and, 29, 35
Coleman, Melissa, 152
Collins, Addie Mae, 209
Collins, Richard W., III, 181
combat exclusion policy, xi, 152, 196, 199
Commission on Wartime Relocation and Internment of Civilians (CWRIC), 94
Comprehensive Review Working Group (CRWG), 169, 170
Compromise of 1877, 5
Confederacy: black codes enacted post Civil War, 12; commemorative statues of leaders, 11; current views of flag, 81; map of, 40; memorabilia prohibited on Marine bases, 12; names for Army bases, 12–13, 38; parole to soldiers, 5; renaming Army bases, 203–205

Connally, Tom, 89
Constitution, U.S.: defense of, 210; opposition to values, 38; rights protected in, 88. *See also specific Constitutional Amendments*
Cooper, George C., 112
Cornum, Rhonda, 152
Coughlin, Paula, 153
CPTP. *See* Civilian Pilot Training Program
The Crisis, 27, 104, 146
Critical Race Theory (CRT), 2–3
Cronkite, Walter, 188
CRT. *See* Critical Race Theory
Cruikshank, Margaret, 164
CRWG. *See* Comprehensive Review Working Group
Cullors, Patrisse, 4
Cunningham, Terrance, 4
Curtis, Lemuel, 104
CWRIC. *See* Commission on Wartime Relocation and Internment of Civilians

DADT. *See* Don't ask, don't tell
Dahlquist, John E., 94
Davis, Benjamin O., Jr., 101, 104, 105; as four-star general, 106; at West Point, 88
Davis, Benjamin O., Sr., 87–88, 102, 119
Davis, Manvel, 31
DeBow, Charles, 104
Defense Race Relations Institute (DRRI), 196, 196–197
Democratic Party, 4, 31–33, 63, 121, 162, 166, 209
Denison, Franklin, 48
Department of Defense (DoD): anti-gay sentiments in, 165; diversity as imperative, 196–198; embracing diversity, 40; equitable sentencing of violations by, 206; MLDC assessments of, 199; remaining work of, 199–200; silent agreement in, 45; on women in combat, 151
desegregation: Bradley, O., on, 35; of military, xi, 41; opponents of, 3; Truman platform and, 7
Dewey, Thomas, 33, 121

Dickey, John S., 29
discrimination, xi; DuBois resisting, 67; legislation against, 27; significance of EO 9980, 34
diversity, xii; commitment to, 40; in corporate America, 186–187; DoD embracing, 40; Obama and, 205; in ROTC, 182; socioeconomic, 201–203; as strategic imperative, 196–198; Trump and, 205
diversity, history in military: African American draftees, 63; blacks at Panama Canal, 58; blacks at West Point, 50–56; blacks in American Revolution, 46–47, 48; blacks in Civil War, 48; blacks in Spanish-American War, 56–58; blacks in World War I, 64–70; Buffalo Soldiers in Indian Campaigns, 49–50; Houston Mutiny and, 68–70; Jim Crow as caste system, 45; in Mexican border war, 59; 92nd Infantry in World War I, 76–77; 93rd Infantry in World War I, 69, 70–71, 71, 72–73; reintegration post World War I, 77–79; 370th Infantry in World War I, 72; 371st Infantry in World War I, 72; 372nd Infantry in World War I, 72–76; 369th Infantry in World War I, 71–72; training for World War I entry, 61–63
Diversity Fatigue, 186–187
Dixiecrats, 32, 121
DoD. *See* Department of Defense
domestic terrorism, 12
Don't ask, don't tell (DADT), 196; cost of, 167; evolution of, 161–166; Marine Corps and, 171; Obama and, 168, 169, 172; Powell and, 168; as public law, 168–172; public opinion shift, 166–168, 178n68; in World War II, 160
Dorsey, George, 23–24, 26
Dorsey, Mae, 23–24, 26
DRRI. *See* Defense Race Relations Institute
DuBois, W. E. B., 27, 66, 68; discrimination resisted by, 67; Young and, 55

Dunwoody, Ann, 147, 149, 181–182, 198, 199
Dwyer, Mollie, 51, 52

education gap, 88
18th Depot Company, 117–118, 120
Eisenhower, D. D., 97, 121–122
Electoral College, 41
Elliot, Robert Brown, 110
Emancipation Proclamation, 48
enlightened society, 16
EO 9980. *See* Executive Order 9980
EO 9981. *See* Executive Order 9981
Equal Credit Opportunity Act (1974), 143
equal rights. *See* civil rights
Espionage Act (1917), 61, 69
Ethiopian Regiment, 47
Evers, Medgar, 93
Executive Order 9980 (EO 9980): significance for discrimination, 34; Truman commission for, 26–27; Truman signing, 6, 33; violations of, 34
Executive Order 9981 (EO 9981), 65; aftermath of, 37–42; anniversary of, xi, 8, 30; execution of, 35–37; lack of timetable for, 121–122; provisions in, 100; Truman signing, xi, 3, 12, 28–29, 33

Fahy, Charles, 36
Fahy Committee, 36, 37, 196–197
Fair Employment Officer, 34
FDR. *See* Roosevelt, Franklin, D.
The Feminine Mystique (Friedan), 148
feminism, 148–149
Fifteenth Amendment, 5, 206, 208
Fifth Amendment, 170, 174
54th Massachusetts Infantry, 48
First Amendment, 170, 174
Fish, Hamilton, 89
Flipper, Henry Ossian, 51; court martial of, 52; posthumous pardon of, 52; transfer of, 51; at West Point, 50
flipping the script, 31–35
Ford, Gerald, 144
The Forgotten War (Blair), 122

Forrestal, James V., 114–115
442nd Infantry (Go For Broke): Japanese Americans in, 94; as Purple Heart Battalion, 94; veterans of, 95; in World War II, 93–94
Fourteenth Amendment, 5, 206, 208
Fox, John R., 93
Franklin, John Hope, 95
Friedan, Betty, 148–149

Gaeta, Marissa, 171
Gardner, Michael, 22
Garza, Alicia, 4
gay rights, 161, 162, 163–164, 165–166, 166, 168–169
Gesssell Committee, 196, 197
Gibson, Truman, 120
Gildersleeve, Virginia C., 138
glass ceiling, 41
Glaude, Eddie S., Jr., 80
Glover, Calvin, 164–165
Goethals, George, 54, 58
Go for Broke. *See* 442nd Infantry
Golden 13, 111–112
Goldwater, Barry, 163
Goodwin, Reginald, 111
Gore, Al, 166
Graham, Frank P., 91
Granger, Elder, 74
Grant, Ulysses, 5
Gray, Gordon, 36–37
Great Migration: for job opportunities, 64; lynching and, 64, 79; for relief from racial oppression, 79
Griest, Kristen, 151–152
Gulf War, 151, 152, 182

Hair, James E., 111
Haley, Nikki, 203–204
Hamilton, Alexander, 159–160
Harlem Hellfighters. *See* 369th Infantry
Hastie, William, 89, 91, 102, 103, 105
Haver, Shayne, 151–152
Hayes, Rutherford B., 5
Hays, Anna Mae, 143
Hayward, William, 71
Hechler, Ken, 30, 35
Herek, Gregory M., 162
Hester, Leigh Ann, 150

Hobby, Oveta Culp, 136
Hoisington, Elizabeth P., 143
Holcomb, Thomas, 115–116
homophobia, xi, xii, 21
homosexuality: acceptance of, 159; in American Revolution, 159–160; concealment and, 160; mainstreaming of, 165; mental disorder classification, 162
Horoho, Patricia, 148
Houston, Charles Hamilton, 89
Houston Mutiny, 68–70
Howard, Michelle, 147, 149
Huff, Edgar R., 117
human rights: civil rights as, 3; Human Rights Campaign, 172; Obama on, 169; Truman on, 29, 169; violations of, 26
Humphrey, Hubert, 32

IACP. *See* International Association Chiefs of Police
"I Have a Dream" (King, M. L.), 206
Implicit Association Test, 38
inclusion, xi; in Army Air Corps, 104; protection for transgender of individuals, 205; removing barriers to, 4; in ROTC, 182; struggle for, 13; unwritten truce for thwarting, 11; women pioneers of, 147–148
income gap, 149
Inouye, Daniel, 93, 95
integration, 196; in Air Force, 36; of armed services, 23–26; Army plans, 36–37; during Korean War, 123–125; legacy of early integrators, 125–127; in Marine Corps, 116; in Navy, 36, 119–120
International Association Chiefs of Police (IACP), 4
intolerance, xi
Israel, 35

James, Chappie, 181
Japanese Americans: in detainment camps, 94–95; in 442nd Infantry, 94
Jeffries, Kwame, 209
Jim Crow, xi; as caste system, 45; as immoral, 8; oppression of, 81; rebellion against, 68; ripple effects of, 26; suffering under, 208; voting and, 31
Johnson, Andrew, 5
Johnson, Campbell C., 102
Johnson, Gilbert, 117
Johnson, Henry, 73
Johnson, Louis, 36, 37, 122
Johnson, Lyndon B., 6, 143
Jones, Doug, 209–210

Kelley, Jill, 193, 194
Kennedy, John F., 196
Kester, Howard, 91
key terrain, 30
King, Martin Luther, Jr., 79–80, 206
King, Rodney, 80
KKK. *See* Ku Klux Klan
Knox, Frank, 101, 114, 116, 137; FDR appointing, 109
Kollar-Kotelly, Colleen, 174
Korean War, 18, 35; integration during, 123–125; 24th Infantry in, 124–125
Ku Klux Klan (KKK), 5, 22, 22–23, 31, 209

Langer, Mathias, 99
Laurens, John, 159–160
Lear, Charles B., 112
LGBTQ: armed services open to, 4; challenges in 1970's and 1980's, 161; Clinton, B, lifting ban, 161–162; gay rights, 161, 162, 163–164, 165–166, 166, 168–169; inclusion, 8; inequality, xii. *See also* Don't ask, don't tell; homosexuality; transgender
Logan, Rayford W., 89
Log Cabin Republicans, 170
Loving Interracial Intimacy in America and the Threat to the White Supremacy (Cashin), 208
Lutz, Amy, 202
lynching, 22, 31, 62; Great Migration and, 64, 79

MacArthur, Douglas, 22, 123–124, 141
Mahlock, Lorna, 206, 207
Malcolm, Dorothy, 23, 26

Malcolm, Roger, 23, 26
Malmedy Massacres, 100
Mao Tse-tung, 123
Marine Corps, U.S.: black Marines in World War II, 117–118; confederate memorabilia prohibited, 12; court martial rates, 191; DADT and, 171; defense of segregation, 36; exclusion and, 69; exclusion policies, 87, 115; integration of, 116; promotion rates, 184, 186, 188; racism in, 115; sexual assault in, 153; slow to integrate, 60; training black recruits, 109; warrior ethos in, 120; women in, 207
Marshall, George C., 91, 92, 105, 135
Marshall, Napoleon Bonaparte, 71
Marshall Plan, 35–36
Martin, Graham E., 111
Mason, USS, 113
McAuliffe, Anthony C., 18
McChrystal, Stanley, 192–193, 193, 195
McClennon, Alonzo Clifton, 110
McConnell, E. G., 97
McGrath, Kathleen, 150
McNair, Denise, 209
McTague, Linda, 150
McVeigh, Timothy R., 165
Melton, Lawson, 110
Messerschmitt Me 262, 106, 108
Me Too movement, 153
Middies, 110–111
military: advances of women, 148–150; America's problems reflected in, 181–182; desegregation of, xi, 41; diversity objectives, 208; former slaves and, 21; lessons learned from segregation in World War II, 118–123; milestones for women, 150–151; social change and, 18, 40, 122, 145; transgender issues and, 8; unwritten truce and, 87; value gap and, 103–104; white privilege and, 202–203. *See also* diversity, history in military
Military Leadership Diversity Commission (MLDC), 184, 185, 186, 188, 189; assessments of DoD, 199; data restratification, 201; founding of, 196; recommendations, 182; tasks and responsibilities, 197, 198
Military Occupational Skill (MOS), 109, 112, 119
military style campaign, 31, 32, 34; for gay and lesbian service members, 171; slander against women, 140–141
The Military Morale of Nations and Races (Young), 56
Militia Act (1792), 48
Miller, Doris J., 89–90
Mitchell, Jesse, 36
MLDC. *See* Military Leadership Diversity Commission
Mom Chung. *See* Chung, Margaret
Momyer, William, 105
Montford Point Marines, 115, 116, 117
MOS. *See* Military Occupational Skill
Mosey, Troy, 74
Mother Emanuel African Methodist Episcopal Church, 81, 203, 204
Murray, Florence K., 136
Murray, John, 47

NAACP. *See* National Association of Colored People
National Advisory Committee for Aeronautics (NACA), 6
National Anthem protests, 80
National Association of Colored People (NAACP), 26, 27; appealing to Navy, 65; founders of, 55; lobbying of, 89; ranks and influence of, 90
National Defense Authorization Act (NDAA), 163–164, 170, 182, 203
National Guard, 22, 63, 69; expansion of, 63; in New York State, 70, 71; 141st Infantry, 94; Wallace and, 38; women in, 143
NATO. *See* North Atlantic Treaty Organization
Naval Academy, U.S.: Brown, W. A., in, 111; first black Middies in, 110–111; Golden 13 and, 111–112; McClennon in, 110
Navy, U.S.: black sailors in World War II, 107–109; Career Intermission Pilot Program, 150–151; cooks in, 87;

court martial rates, 191; integration in, 36, 119–120; menial labor in, 69; NAACP appealing to, 65; promotion rates, 186; racial tension in, 113–116; slow to integrate, 60; Stewards Branch, 107–108; Tailhook scandal, 152–155; training black recruits, 109
Nazi Germany, 7; racial theories, 91; racism and, 7
NDAA. *See* National Defense Authorization Act
Nelson, Dennis D., 112
Newsome, Bree, 203
Newton, Isaac, 3
New Women Auxiliary Commissionees, 142
Nimitz, Chester, 22
19th Depot Company, 118, 120
Nineteenth Amendment, 134, 149
94th Engineer Battalion, 37
99th Fighter Squadron, 102, 105–106, 106
92nd Infantry, 94, 101; Almond leading, 92, 122, 124; formation of, 67, 68, 69; officers, 72; training and education in, 76–77; in World War I, 76–77; in World War II, 92–93, 116
93rd Infantry (Blue Helmet Division): formation of, 67; in World War I, 69, 70–71, 72–73; in World War II, 92, 124
9th Cavalry, 49–50, 56, 57; Alexander, J. H., command, 53–54; in World War I, 66; Young in, 54–56
Nixon, Richard, 143
Nolan, Nicholas M., 50–51
North Atlantic Treaty Organization (NATO), 35

Obama, Barack, 19, 192; DADT and, 168, 169, 172; diversity and, 205; election of, 133; gender equality and, 150; on human rights, 169; N-word and, 39; on transgender individuals, 174–175; vote breakdown of, 39
Officer's Advanced Course, US Army, 1

One America Initiative, 95
100th Pursuit Squadron, 105, 106
141st Infantry, 94

P-51 Mustang, 107
Packard, Gary, 171
Panama Canal, 58
Panetta, Leon, 151, 171, 192, 193
Parental Leave, Support for New Parents Program, 150
Patterson, Robert P., 91, 101
Patton, George S., 96, 118
pay equity, 196
Pershing, John, 58, 59, 63, 69; with Buffalo Soldiers, 66; Johnson, H., recognition, 73
Petraeus, David, 192, 193–194, 195
Philips, Randy, 171
Pickens, Harriet Ida, 139
Pitcher, Molly, 133–134
Plessy vs. Ferguson, 76
police brutality, 27, 28, 80
poll taxes, 27, 31
post-racial society, 38, 39, 206, 207
Powell, Colin, 67, 163, 181, 198; DADT and, 168
Preparedness Movement, 63
promotion rates: Air Force, 186; Clinton, B., and, 106; Coast Guard, 184, 189; Marine Corps, 182, 184; Navy, 186; noncommissioned officers, 183–184; one-star generals, 183–184; studies, 183–184
Purple Heart Battalion, 94

Quadrennial Defense Review (QDR), 197
Queen, Howard Donovan, 93

race, 3; micro-aggressions and, 17; race riots, 25; racial supremacy, xi
racism, xi; anguish due to, 18; denial of, 38–39; domestic terrorism and, 12; ebb and flow of, 16–19; institutionalized, 3; in Marine Corps, 115; Nazi Germany and, 7; racial terrorism, 14; state-sanctioned, 3; views of Almond, 122–123, 124; in wartime, 21

Randolph, A. Phillip, 67, 101
Reagan, John W., 111
Reagan, Ronald, 95
Reconstruction, 88; Hayes halting, 5; incomplete, 6; Reconstruction Amendment, 22
Red Summer, 22–23, 25, 79
Reed, Walter, 58
reintegration, 77–79
Republican Party, 38, 162
Reynard, Elizabeth, 138
Ridgeway, Matthew, 18, 37
Rivers, Ruben, 96–97
Roberts, Cokie, 150
Roberts, George, 104
Roberts, Needham, 73
Robertson, Benjamin, 71
Robertson, Carole, 209
Robinson, Jackie, 96
Rogers, Edith Nourse, 133, 137, 141
Romney, Mitt, 167–168, 172
Roof, Dylann, 203–204
Roosevelt, Eleanor, 88–89, 101, 113, 138, 141
Roosevelt, Franklin, D. (FDR), 33; on black sailors, 112, 114, 115; as civil rights advocate, 29; Knox appointment, 109; New Deal of, 22, 88; on segregated armed forces, 100–145
Roosevelt, Theodore, 57, 58, 63, 67
Root, Elihu, 58, 63
Ross, Mac, 104
ROTC, 1; access to, 202; diversity and inclusion in, 182; removal of, 201
Rough and Ready Regulars. *See* Buffalo Soldiers
Rowan, Carl, 93
Royall, Kenneth, 36
rush to judge, 1–2
Russell, Richard, 32

same-sex marriage, 196
Sanchez, Ricardo, 182, 198
Santana, Feidin, 25
SAPRO. *See* Sexual Assault Prevention and Response Office
school segregation, 3, 208
Schwartz, Harry H., 103
Scott, Emmett J., 66, 76, 77, 89
Scott, Walter, 25–26
2nd South Carolina Volunteers, 48
"Secure These Rights" report, 22, 31
Sedition Act (1918), 61
Seefried, Josh, 171
segregation: arguments against, 11; as Army management policy, 36; defense, in Marine Corps, 36; de jure segregation, 3; education gap and, 88; fight to preserve, 4; as immoral, 6, 8; lessons learned from World War II, 118–123; school, 3, 208; Truman understanding, 30–31; Wilson, W., and, 59
Selective Service Act (1917), 63, 66
Selective Service Act (1940), 95, 100
Semper Paratus/Always Ready (SPARs), 135
Separate but Equal, 88, 103; as law of land, 104
761st Tank Battalion (Black Panthers), 120; in concentration camp liberation, 97; documentary on, 97; in World War II, 95–97
sexism, xi; in wartime, 21
sexual assault, 152; in Air Force Academy, 153; in Marine Corps, 153; paternalism, power and, 154–155; SAPRO, 153, 154. *See also* Tailhook scandal
Sexual Assault Prevention and Response Office (SAPRO), 153, 154
Sexual Orientation and U.S. Military Personnel Policy (National Defense Research Institute), 163
Shafter, William Rufus, 51, 56
Shalikashvili, John, 163, 167, 182
sharecropping, 64, 79
Shaw, Marie, 74, 99
Shinseki, Eric, 95, 182, 198
Shull, Lynwood L., 23, 24–25, 25, 26
Simpson, O. J., 1–2
16th Street Baptist Church (Birmingham, Alabama), 209
Slager, Michael, 25–26
slavery, xi, 3; as American original sin, 12; black people today and, 207; end of, 4–5, 5; as hard history, 209; slave

quarters, 78. *See also* awakening moment
Smalls, Robert, 109
Small Standing Army Supporters, 63
Smith, James W., 50
Snipes, Macio, 23
social change, 140, 189; advance of positive, 26; ebb and flow of, 16–19; history of, 186; military and, 18, 40, 122, 145; private organizations and, 26; resistance to, 16
socioeconomic diversity, 201–203
Southern social caste system, 5
Southern States Rights Party, 32. *See also* Dixiecrats
Spanish-American War, 55, 66, 72, 76; blacks in, 56–58
Sparks, Lee, 68
SPARs. *See* Semper Paratus/Always Ready
Spingarn, Joel, 76
Stance, Emmanuel, 49–50
Stark, Lloyd, C., 31
Steinman, Alan, 171
Stimson, Henry, 63, 89
Sublett, Frank E., 111
Sullivan, John L., 36
Swann, Edward, 116
Swarzkopf, Norman, Jr., 182
Symington, Stuart, 36, 120

Tailhook scandal, 152–155
10th Cavalry, 49–50, 50, 56, 57–58; transfers from, 59; in World War I, 66
things get real, 21
3rd Marine Ammunition Company, 117–118, 120
Thirteenth Amendment, 5, 206, 208
Threadgill-Dennis, Sara, 69
370th Infantry, 69, 71, 93; in World War I, 72
371st Infantry, 69, 71, 73; in World War I, 72
372nd Infantry, 69, 71; in World War I, 72–76
369th Infantry (Harlem Hellfighters), 69, 70, 71; in World War I, 71–72

333rd Field Artillery Regiment: experimental black combat unit, 98; Wereth 11 in, 99–100; in World War II, 98–100
Thurmond, Strom, 29, 32
Tillman, Benjamin, 63
Toeti, Opal, 4
transgender: Coast Guard and, 173; military and, 8; protection for inclusion of individuals, 205; struggle of individuals, 172–175; Trump on, 173–175
Travers, Sarah, 68
Treaty of Paris, 4
Truman, Harry S., 23; on Army integration plan, 37; atomic bomb and, 22; as civil rights advocate, 29–31; Civil Rights Committee and, 26–29; civil rights platform, 6, 7–8; civil rights proposal of, 31–35; civil rights timeline, 24; Cold War and, 29, 35; de jure segregation and, 3; EO 9980 commission, 26–27; EO 9980 signed by, 6, 33; EO 9981 signed by, xi, 3, 6, 12, 28–29, 33; on human rights, 29, 169; key terrain and, 30; MacArthur rift, 123; mandates of, 122; returning war veterans and, 22; Senate campaign of, 31; ten-point plan of, 28, 29; timing of armed services integration, 23–26; Turnip Day held by, 33; in World War I, 22
Trump, Donald J., 181; campaign rhetoric of, 18–19; diversity and, 186–187, 205; racial hatred and, 12; reversing policies for transgender military members, xi; stumping for black vote, 77; on transgender individuals, 173–175
Tubman, Harriet, 48
Turnip Day, 33
Tuskegee Airmen (Black Panthers), 116, 120; constitution of, 100; as experiment, 102–103, 104–106; P-51 Mustang flown by, 107; in World War II, 104–106
Tuskegee Institute, 66
20th Depot Company, 117–118, 120

25th Infantry, 49–50, 56, 57; in World War I, 66
24th Infantry, 49–50, 56, 57; in Korean War, 124–125; in World War I, 66

Uniformed Code of Military Justice (UCMJ), 160; disparities in, 190–195; equitable sentencing of violations, 206
unwritten truce, 1, 2, 11; America's promise hijacked by, 206; end of, 26; military and, 87; preservation of, 65; rippling effects of, 17
US Military Academy (USMA), 145

value gap, 52, 79, 80; military and, 103–104
Vardaman, James K., 63
Veterans of Foreign Wars (VFW), 16–17
Vietnam War, 106, 143, 201
Villa, Pancho, 59
voting rights, 6
Voting Rights Act, 12

WAAC. *See* Women's Army Auxiliary Corps
WAC. *See* Women's Army Corps
Waddy, Harriet West, 136
WAFS. *See* Women's Auxiliary Ferrying Squadron
Wagner, Robert F., 89
Walker, Mary, 134
Wallace, George, 38
Ward, William, 99, 192, 195
War of 1812, 48
Washington, Booker T., 66
Washington, George, 4
Washington Post, 22, 35
WASP. *See* Women Air Force Service Pilots
WAVES. *See* Women Accepted for Volunteer Emergency Service
We Are Our Mother's Daughters (Roberts, C.), 150
Webb, Jim, 144
Wereth 11, 99–100
Wesley, Cynthia, 209
West, Nadja, 148, 182, 198

West Point: Alexander, J. H., at, 50, 52–53; Baker, H. E., in, 110–111; blacks at, 50–56; Davis, B. O., Jr., at, 88; Flipper at, 50; West Point follies, 50; women in, 144, 207; Young at, 50, 54
WFTD. *See* Women's Flying Training Detachment
Where Do We Go from Here (King, M. L.), 79–80
Whitaker, Jonathon C., 50
White, Walter, 89, 91, 101
White, William S., 112
white privilege, 4, 189–190; military and, 202–203
white supremacy, 5; belief in, 11; opposing military training of blacks, 63; Southern rule and, 5; in Southern states, 12
Wiesel, Elie, 97
Wilkie, Wendell, 102, 114
Williams, Serena, 13
Wills, Frances, 139
Wilson, Charles, 26
Wilson, Woodrow, 59, 67; Espionage and Sedition Acts of, 61; on German sympathizers, 60–61; segregation and, 59
Winchell, Barry, 164–165
woke, 13–16, 17
Wolfenbarger, Janet, 147, 149
women: achievements, challenges, opportunities of, 151–152; advances in military, 148–150; advances in society, 148–150; in Air Force Academy, 144, 144–146, 147; in American Revolution, 133–134; in Civil War, 134; in combat roles, 40, 151; in Gulf War, 151, 152; in Marine Corps, 207; milestones in military, 150–151; in military academies, 144–146; in National Guard, 143; pioneers of inclusion, 147–148; slander against, 140–141; struggle for equality, 133; WAC creation, 135–136; WASP creation, 135, 139–140; WASP ethnic diversity, 140; WAVES creation, 135, 137–139; in West Point, 144–145, 207; in

World War I, 134; in World War II, 134–135, 140–141
Women Accepted for Volunteer Emergency Service (WAVES), 135, 137–139
Women Air Force Service Pilots (WASP), 135, 139–140
Women's Armed Services Integration Act (1948), 139, 141–142
Women's Army Auxiliary Corps (WAAC), 133, 135
Women's Army Corps (WAC): creation of, 135–136; expansion of, 143
Women's Auxiliary Ferrying Squadron (WAFS), 139, 140
Women's Flying Training Detachment (WFTD), 139, 140
women's rights, 133; advances in, 144; corporate America and, 143
Woodward, Isaac, 24–25, 25, 25–26
World War I: black sailors in, 107–109; blacks in, 64–70; 92nd Infantry in, 76–77; 93rd Infantry in, 69, 70–71, 72–73; 9th Cavalry in, 66; reintegration post World War I, 77–79; returning black veterans, 22; 10th Cavalry in, 66; 370th Infantry in, 72; 371st Infantry in, 72; 372nd Infantry in, 72–76; 369th Infantry in, 71–72; training for entry, 61–63; Truman in, 22; 25th Infantry in, 66; 24th Infantry in, 66; women in, 134
World War II: black and minority experience in, 92–93; black Marines in, 117–118; black veterans of, 23; DADT in, 160; end of, 22; 442nd Infantry in, 93–94; lessons learned from segregated military, 118–123; 92nd Infantry in, 92–93, 116; 93rd Infantry in, 92, 124; returning war veterans, 22; 761st Tank Battalion in, 95–97; 3rd Marine Ammunition Company in, 117–118; 333rd Field Artillery Regiment in, 98–100; women in, 134–135, 140–141
Wright, Bruce M., 119

Young, Charles, 55, 66, 67, 76, 83n35; death of, 67; DuBois and, 55; forced from active duty, 102; in Mexican border war, 59; military intelligence and, 56; at National Parks, 56; in 9th Cavalry, 54–56; publications and awards, 56; as university professor, 55, 67; at West Point, 50, 54

About the Author

Troy Mosley is a retired Army Lieutenant Colonel and 20-year veteran. He grew up in Jacksonville Beach, Florida, and graduated from Duncan U. Fletcher High School in 1985. He attended Florida State University for two years before transferring to Florida A&M University (FAMU), where he graduated with a BS in Psychology and earned his commission through FAMU's ROTC Program. Troy held various military assignments in his 20-year career. Troy taught medical support and evacuation at the United States Infantry Center and School, Fort Benning, Georgia, before being selected to attend Baylor University through the Army's Advanced Civil Schooling Program.

Troy completed his administrative residency at Landstuhl Regional Medical Center where he was the lead project officer for the first-ever Fisher House dedicated outside the continental United States. The event was so successful that the Fisher House committed to donating a second house within 6 months. Troy served as the Executive Officer for the 212th Mobile Army Surgical Hospital. He helped redeploy the hospital from Operation Iraqi Freedom in 2003, and led the hospital's $3.1 million recovery and refit in 60 days. Troy served as the Administrative Director, Department of Surgery, Walter Reed Army Community Hospital for two years before being selected to be the Army Surgeon General's Assistant Executive Officer. Troy served as COO for Weed Army Community Hospital (WACH) in 2009 where he led the Hospital to the best Joint Commission (TJC) Accreditation score in the Army that year. His efforts were instrumental in securing funds for a $300 million new hospital at Fort Irwin, California, the DoD's first solar-powered hospital.

www.ingramcontent.com/pod-product-compliance
Lightning Source LLC
Chambersburg PA
CBHW052058300426
44117CB00013B/2189